FELLINI'S ROAD

Fellini's Road

Donald P. Costello

UNIVERSITY OF NOTRE DAME PRESS
NOTRE DAME & LONDON

Library of Congress Cataloging in Publication Data

Costello, Donald P.
    Fellini's road.

    1. Fellini, Federico.   I. Title.
PN1998.A3F335 1983   791.43′0233′0924   82–50286
ISBN 0–268–00958–9
ISBN 0–268–00961–9 (pbk.)

Manufactured in the United States of America

FOR

John
Matthew
Paul
Monica
Maria
Christopher

Contents

Acknowledgments

FELLINI'S ROAD HAS FOUND its direction over many years. Many people have guided me along it. I first saw great films with my wife Christine, and through our good talk came to know that some films could bear analysis. My teacher, Dalma Hunyadi Brunauer, first taught me to look deeply, and Professor Elder Olson taught me to find form in what I saw. My students at Notre Dame have taught me more—not only those who now have their books, their Emmies, and their Oscars—but also the likes of Gregory Solman and Donald Bohlinger, who are starting out along that road. Perhaps most of all I have learned from the hundreds of students in between, who taught me more than I can remember, who taught me to sharpen my eye as I tried to teach them to discipline theirs. The six young people to whom this book is dedicated have—all their lives long—been my students and teachers.

In recent months I have tried out portions of the manuscript, in varying forms, at conferences and symposia at Notre Dame and elsewhere. I have received insights through presenting Fellini papers at the Conference of the Southern Comparative Literature Association, the first and second International Conference on the Fantastic, the Conference on Quest and Discovery in 20th-Century Literature, two Annual Fellows' Meetings of the Society for Values in Higher Education, the 86th Annual Meeting of the Michigan Academy of Science, Arts, and Letters, and Purdue University's 6th Annual Conference on Film.

Portions of Chapter Three of this book have appeared, in different form, in "Layers of Reality: 8 1/2 as Spiritual Autobiography" in *Notre Dame English Journal* 13 (Spring 1981), pp. 1–12. Portions of Chapter Four have been rewritten into an essay entitled "Fellini and His Giulietta: From Neorealism to Surrealism" to appear in volume VI of

Film Studies, and other portions of that chapter will appear in different form in "Fellini, Juliet, and the Feminists, or: What *Does* Fellini Think About Women?" in volume XV of *Michigan Academician.*

I remember a great lecture on *La Dolce Vita* by Father Patrick Sullivan of the National Catholic Film Office. And the books cited in the notes probably have given me more than I can specifically acknowledge.

I do want to thank the College of Arts and Letters of the University of Notre Dame for the leave which supported the writing of this manuscript and for the honor of the Frank O'Malley Publication Series Award. And special thanks to my Notre Dame colleague William Krier for editorial help.

Mary Corliss, curator of the fine Film Stills Archive of the Museum of Modern Art, has been helpful beyond the mere call of duty. Picture credits: Museum of Modern Art/Film Stills Archive, Janus Films, American International Pictures, Macmillan Audio Brandon, Avco Embassy Pictures, Cinemation Industries, Ivy Films, Corinth Films.

I can't really sort out all of my memories, nor accurately apportion thanks. I wish I could. Instead: on behalf of all of those whom I should thank, I'll end this acknowledgment page by thanking the one to whom we all owe thanks—Il Maestro himself, and his lady Giulietta.

Introduction

FEDERICO FELLINI OUGHT TO BE the hero of the "me generation." Pop psychology has taken up his obsessive theme—the search for self. It has become a generation's obsession, not just the obsession of a celebrated Italian filmmaker. "The only thing I want to know," Fellini has said, is *"Why am I here? What is my life?"*[1] To seek answers to such questions is the purpose of his film art: "Making a film is something quite other for me than a simple professional fact. It's a way of realizing myself, and giving my life a meaning."[2] His search for self through his films began in his neo-realistic days with Roberto Rossellini. This is what Fellini then learned: "I understood that to be a director and to make films could fill my life; I couldn't ask for anything more; it could become so rich, so fascinating, so moving—a thing that justifies you and helps you find a meaning."[3]

But in his own subjective search to find meaning Fellini is very different from the self-seeking cultists of today. Perhaps, after all, he should not be their hero. Passively, they look only inward. He knows that he must look outward in order to look inward. He does not wait for the world to do something for the *me*, to the *me*, or with the *me*. Instead, Fellini's search has been active. Perhaps he belongs with an "I generation." His search for self has gone beyond self, as a longer journey, a quest, an aspiration, as the *I* seeks completion. Seeking context, Fellini has searched in art for a self intermixed between his characters and himself; and he has sought it along roads crossing the land and he has surveyed the sea and the sky. Fellini has searched among the humble and the sophisticated, in the provinces and in the city, amidst the happy/sad contrasts of life and of the circus.

From the circus, Fellini learned to revel in the spontaneous and in the contradictory, in the three-ring nature of life, to work toward the

1

integration of all that spirit into a happy acceptance. The circus taught Fellini to search more with his heart than with his head. To understand the art of the Fellini search—the road travelled over the years—is to understand that Federico Fellini can belong to all generations.

The metaphor of a search along a road comes as easily to Fellini's tongue and pen as it does to his camera. We don't have to accept as gospel every word of Fellini's frequent joking interviews; but we should attend to the revealing metaphor which underlies his language and his art. That metaphor will be found again and again, with variations, throughout the following pages. One of his fullest statements of the search metaphor was spoken by Fellini in an interview with Pierre Kast: "At bottom, I am always making the same film, to the extent that what arouses my curiosity, what interests me definitively, what unlatches my inspiration, is that, each time, I am telling the story of characters in quest of themselves, in search of a more authentic source of life, of conduct, of behavior, that will more closely relate to the true roots of their individuality."[4] Federico Fellini said that about the nature of his art while filming *Juliet of the Spirits*, the last of the four Fellini films dealt with in this book. And he was right. Fellini is not always right when he talks about his own work. No artist ever is. This book tries to prove that Fellini is right when he says that his films deal with a quest for self. This book traces that theme through Fellini's major phase: *La Strada*, *La Dolce Vita*, *8½*, and *Juliet of the Spirits*. It is just because Fellini was always making the same film that this close study of the four central Fellini films can tell the reader much about all Fellini films, even those made before *La Strada*, even those made after *Juliet of the Spirits*, even those not yet made.

Each Fellini film is recognizably Fellini. That is a major sign of a great artist. It is the reason that André Bazin can canonize Fellini as one of his "auteurs." Bazin acknowledges that Fellini's message has been noticeably the same throughout his career, and Bazin adds: "This is not to be taken as a sign of sterility. On the contrary, while variety is the mark of a 'director,' it is unity of inspiration that connotes the true 'author.' "[5]

Fellini acknowledged that all of his films have one father. But each is born at a different time: "Thus, all are the same, and all are different."[6] All are the same because his search for the true roots of the individuality of his characters and of himself is the genesis and metaphor base of all of his films. All are different because each develops a new manner of dealing with its developing matter. In each new film, Fellini finds a form to express that which now, in each new stage of his awareness, must be expressed. And in doing so he opens up new roads for himself and others. That is what Fellini himself admires: "I believe in artists who, if they are great, will open new roads."[7]

Because Federico Fellini makes films as an expression of his own search for self, it is necessarily his own experience with which he must begin. And it is that personal experience which he embroiders, as his own imagination plays upon myths and experiences known and felt by all of us. Thus, his films are personal, but never private. So, too, from all of this does his method follow, which is necessarily intuitional, working toward harmony and order. And his intention, often expressed, informs all his films: "I want to suggest to modern man a road of inner liberation, to accept and love life. . . ."[8]

La Strada

THE TITLE OF FEDERICO FELLINI'S 1954 film, *La Strada*, The Road, proclaims the great Fellini theme and form. Throughout all his films, Fellini is concerned with the road of life. His intention when he begins a new film, he tells us, is always the same: "To try, first of all, to tell something about myself; and in doing so, to try to find a salvation, to try to find a road toward some meaning."[1] The journey along that road toward meaning is, in other Fellini words, "a quest for the essential self, my own and others, along all the paths of life."[2] Both thematically and formally, a Fellini film is a journey toward discovery of the essential self.

The journey in *La Strada* begins by Fellini placing his Gelsomina in her context. We first see her in the place she must leave: the seashore. Her journey begins dynamically, with Gelsomina walking diagonally —the most dynamic of compositional designs—across the screen, toward the sea, with sea reeds tied, in an opposing diagonal pattern, across her back. The dynamism of both movement and composition is immediately reinforced by the opening words of the film: "Gelsomina, you should come home right away!" The context expands, from sea to home. The voice continues, "A man is over there with a great big motorcycle!" Gelsomina runs to see it. And what a motorcycle it is! "Only the cinema," wrote André Bazin, "could endow the extraordinary motorcycle caravan of Zampano with the force of concrete myth which this object, both unusual and banal, attains."[3] The motorcycle is

5

the new "home"—always moving—that Gelsomina will find with Zampano. It is the motorcycle of Zampano that will take these two travellers on a spiritual odyssey along the road, away from her old home by the sea, and then back again.

The structure of the journey is, in *La Strada*, exceedingly simple. It is even elemental, or as Bazin and Fellini and others suggest, mythical. *La Strada* has the simplicity, perhaps even the naiveté, perhaps even the sentimentality, of a folk tale, a parable, a myth. Its center is mythic triads. The film is the story of sea, of roads traversing the land, and of sky. The characters are three isolates: simpleton, brute, and holy fool. "Sometimes a film," says Fellini about *La Strada*, "can incarnate in mythic figures."[4] Gelsomina is taken away from her sea, inland, along the road of Zampano. Then the messenger from the sky, the Fool, leads both Gelsomina and Zampano to self-discovery, back to the sea. Fellini has told us that the film is also a revelation of *his* essential self, not just of Gelsomina's and Zampano's: "*La Strada* is really the complete catalogue of my entire mythical world, a dangerous representation of my identity, undertaken without precautions."[5]

Gelsomina

As Gelsomina is introduced to Zampano, she is visually outlined against the sea. The basic mythic image of the sea is employed by Fellini throughout this film and all his films. "In Italy we have water all around us," Fellini has explained, as if in apology for his frequent use of the symbol.[6] Born near the sea in Rimini, Fellini will continue to associate the sea with the security and naturalness of youth, and with pure and innocent women. He himself acknowledges that, in his films, "water is a feminine thing."[7] And related to its femininity, the sea is, of course, a natural symbol for the beginning of life. When Gelsomina realizes that she will now travel away from this seaside home to take up a new life, she walks a few feet toward the sea, then kneels down facing it. "Gelsomina kneels before the sea as if in a last moment of confidence, perhaps in a final giving-up of herself," writes Genevieve Agel. "She seems to receive a sort of consecration from it."[8]

The life to which Gelsomina was born is ending, but a new one is beginning. In the mythology of the film, Gelsomina is about to start the process of coming of age. "You're a big girl now," her mother assures her. Gelsomina's first smile comes from the thought of learning: "You'll promise to teach her, won't you Zampano?" After Gelsomina's brief farewell to the sea, the place of birth, it is with a resolve in her step that she walks toward Zampano's motorcycle, her new home, and her education. And it is with the exaltation of a beginning adventure: "I am going to work . . . I will dance and sing!" Gelsomina sees her new role as the bringer of music, of dance, of life. We understand that she will become the Felliniesque clown-artist.

Fellini is careful to let us know that, whatever her age, Gelsomina is still childlike, a novice, an innocent. His wife Giulietta Masina, who plays the role of Gelsomina, has always meant that to Fellini: "With her clownlike gift for mimicry, she embodies in our relationship my nostalgia for innocence."[9] It is with innocent children that Giulietta/Gelsomina will continually be closely identified. In this first scene children interrupt Gelsomina's determined march toward Zampano. She stops to hug the little members of her family; obviously, behind her bravado she is fearful of the prospect of no longer being one of them, of leaving her sea and its simple family community. "Gelsomina, don't go away," the children plead. But her resolve to find the new holds out. "I'm going now," she announces. Her mother begins to share the reluctance of the children, and calls out, "Gelsomina, Gelsomina, my little Bambina!" In the final shot of this opening sequence, the growing distance between Gelsomina and the young children, as she and Zampano drive along the road, is the cause of Giulietta Masina's first magically sad face. And then Gelsomina pulls down the canvas to hide herself, in fearful anticipation of her true initiation.

We don't yet know Zampano as well as we know Gelsomina. In our first view of him, he was leaning sullenly against a thick pillar, cigarette dangling from his mouth. Behind him was not the sea but the land. We learn something more through Fellini's method of visual contrast: Gelsomina is small, light, humble, and gentle; Zampano is big, dark, arrogant, and brutal.

The next scene, our first view of Zampano's profession, further reveals his character. Contrasted with Gelsomina's dynamic line, Zampano is associated with the figure of the circle. In this journey film, Zampano moves without getting anywhere. As Zampano introduces himself and his act, he walks around and around, the camera almost dizzy as it keeps circling with him. The audience who watches Zampano's never–changing act forms an enclosing circle around him.

The animal imagery that helps characterize Zampano is also developed in this scene. We have already noticed that Zampano's motorized contraption is decorated with images of mythic animals, the owl and the mermaid. We see now that his arm is tattooed with the equally mythic image of a snake. And now Fellini reinforces the visual with the verbal. "That stuff's for pigs!" Zampano mutters about his soup. Yet Zampano eats all of *his* soup. Gelsomina stealthily throws hers away. Zampano's circus act itself tells us about him. We see him as a chained animal bound by his own brutishness. His task is to break his chains, to find a human self within. Yet the climax of his act never brings a sense of escape or freedom; he has destroyed a link, but not freed himself.[10] That becomes Gelsomina's job.

In the lesson sequence, in which Zampano inducts Gelsomina into travelling circus life, Gelsomina is revealed further by very personal Fellini imagery. She tries on a funny hat, and dances with delight behind Zampano's back when for the first time she enters the world of costume. In subsequent films, Fellini will again and again show hats as costume, as Pirandello-like attempts to try on new selves. He will picture circus clowns, disguised and trying out roles, just as Gelsomina now does. Nino Rota's lively circus music carries us in spirit to new worlds of fantasy, away from the reality of this barren field.

A short while after her first lesson, that same field is the site of a Gelsomina ritual dance before a fire. Fire, warmth, sunshine—all life-sustaining imagery and all part of Fellini's mythic catalogue—will follow her throughout the film. And, indeed, her fire dance is associated immediately with her other life-giving element: water. Gelsomina chants: " . . . fire glows bright; sparks fly up and vanish from sight . . . " "What are you doing?" Zampano interrupts. "It will rain the day after tomorrow," is her confident answer. So it is thus very early in the film that Fellini begins to use the liturgical elements of fire and water to help raise into the mythic a film that might have remained merely simple.

The next scene is a different kind of lesson: Gelsomina's sexual initiation. Some time after Zampano has forced Gelsomina into the trailer with him, the lesson sequence ends as we see Gelsomina looking at the sleeping Zampano, and smiling, through her tears, that affirmative and incomparable Giulietta Masina smile. She has now seen Zampano's entire repertory: food, drink, work, sex, sleep. Her smile suggests that that is perhaps somehow enough for her to work with.

We next see what Gelsomina has added to Zampano's circus act. She brings to it her natural gifts of laughter and life. Not until the arrival of Gelsomina does Zampano add comedy—such as it is—to his static and solemn performance. And, dressed and made up as a clown, with her spontaneous funny faces, she *does* get laughs, and sighs of sadness, and applause. Giulietta Masina's spiritual kinship with Charlie Chaplin begins to show itself, aided mightily by Nino Rota's music, which sounds much like the music that Chaplin himself wrote for his own

i. 1. The face of Giulietta Masina. Gelsomina as the Fellini clown-artist.

films. All of this is no accident. Fellini has said that he has been profoundly "moved to tears" by the films of Chaplin.[11]

As Gelsomina performs, we see by her face that once more mere reality is left behind. As she becomes a part of the world of pretense and performance, of spontaneity and joy, of masks, she becomes one of those Fellini clowns who live up beyond reality, who by their painted faces and by their very nature ask questions about the location and even the relevance of reality. (i. 1)The circus seems to be the natural place for the mystical Gelsomina, surely more natural for her than it is for the plodding, unchanging, and earthbound Zampano.

Fellini has told us that he sees the circus as "a way of travelling through one's own life." The reason, he tells us, that "the circus is congenial to me" is that as he travels the circus road, he encounters the clown, the Gelsomina character, the "fantastic creature who expresses the irrational aspect of man," the person who lives in the world of "miracle, fantasy, jest, nonsense, fable." That is the Fellini world. And so Fellini can create and love Gelsomina and his other clowns because he too can admit: "I am a clown, a big clown."

Fellini describes his own first circus: "As soon as I saw the first show, I was mesmerized. I didn't eat or sleep for days. I didn't even want to get up. Afterwards, I didn't miss one performance, and even today when the notes of the opening parade are played, I feel a kind of electric shock, which sends shivers up my spine." And so, "it was inevitable," Fellini has written, "that when I finally ran away from home the first time, it was to follow a circus." Fellini's love for the circus has infused his own filmmaking, and is especially clear in *La Strada*. Of course he understands the connection: "The cinema is very much like the circus . . . that way of creating and living at one and the same time." Fellini is obviously living *La Strada* as he is creating it. When he inducts Gelsomina into the circus, it is clear that he is introducing her to his own world.[12]

Throughout several subsequent episodes, until the structure changes by the introduction of the Fool, the film remains focussed on only Gelsomina and Zampano. Other characters met along the way serve their purposes and then are seen no more. The film continues with a double linear structure, two destinies moving along side by side, each contrasting with the other in various ways. As the episodes continue, one after another, Gelsomina continues to learn and hence to grow. Zampano remains unchanged. Fellini simply reinforces what he has already established. To keep the mythic simplicity, he builds without complicating. Early on, Fellini developed the sea/land contrast between Gelsomina and Zampano, and he gradually broadens that

single contrast into soul/body, love/sex, innocence/cynicism, sweet-
ness/ brutality, humanity/animality, magic/realism, just as the style of
telling is a contrast between the fablelike quality of his new lyricism
and the reportorial quality of his past neo-realism.

The child of the sea, the collector of reeds, remains close to nature. In
the first scenario for *La Strada*, written by Fellini and Tullio Pinelli in
1951, Gelsomina actually talked to the rocks and trees.[13] The final film
does not retreat that far into the primal, but it does show a Gelsomina
in close touch with the elements of life. She can do more than predict
rain through fire. She imitates a tree, as a watching little girl laughs
delightedly. She puts one ear, and then the other, against a post as if to
listen to nature's secrets throbbing through the wood. She looks precisely as amazed at the sound in the wood as she had looked when she
pressed her ear to the chest of the sleeping Zampano, listening to his
sounds. In the words of Suzanne Budgen, Gelsomina "seems to be
aware of something continuous under the surface of things."[14] A little
boy tells Gelsomina, "my dog died in there," and she joins him in
sorrow and mystery, recognizing easily that death is a natural part of
life. In the entire sequence at the tomato field, the camera is free and
natural, sweeping, mobile, spontaneous. Gelsomina shouts proudly
from the field: "I planted some tomatoes!" But to Gelsomina, alert to
nature's continuity, merely to plant and not to nurture is not enough.
"Are we leaving?" she asks, as if making a sad discovery about her new
mobility. "Well, what do you want to do?" Zampano replies, "Stay
here until your tomatoes come up?" Of course she does. But once again
Gelsomina leaves her own spot and sets off down Zampano's road.

On that road, Gelsomina remains the simple child, drawing other
children to her. Even when Gelsomina had bungled her first circus
lesson, three children had applauded her awkward thumping on
Zampano's drum. Children always appreciate Gelsomina and recognize a connection between themselves and her. The child in her finds
immediate access to their world and immediate pleasure in simple
childlike things, in natural things. For example, in Gelsomina's first
public appearance in Zampano's act, it is the children who are particularly delighted with her clown costume and with her laughter-creating
performance. And after Zampano leaves her on the side of the road for
his night with the redhead, Gelsomina's only companions—except for
a mysterious and unnaturally riderless horse that comes walking by
alone—are four children who shyly watch her, until one of them gives
her an offering and sits down beside her on the curb. Later, a little girl
watches Gelsomina as she paces off her tomato field. In a beautiful
composition, with a rhythmic camera, Fellini shows both the little girl

and Gelsomina walking slowly across the frame, one gently reflecting the movement of the other, child and child/woman in perfect harmony.

After the nature sequence is the wedding sequence, and here, too, Gelsomina is surrounded with children. Although the adults in the crowd scarcely notice her, several children stare wonderingly at Gelsomina, even before she announces, "Now watch me do my act!" And as she does her act, they imitate her motions and rhythms. Once more we see children moving in harmony with Gelsomina.

It is in the scene with Oswaldo that the connection between children and Gelsomina reaches its climax, both in meaning and in emotion. Like many of the most memorable Fellini scenes, the Oswaldo scene is taken directly from life:

> It is a remembrance of my childhood just as it happened, when I lived at Gambettola . . . at my grandmother's. Once I went with some wild peasant boys to a farm beyond the hill. The farm had once been a convent. Going around this large, romantic building, full of magical spots, of corridors, vaults, in a garret, among the apples that had been put there to ripen and the sacks of maize, there was something like a dog's bed—it could not even be called a bed—a kind of pallet, where an idiot child was lying. . . . It caused me a grievous shock. . . .[15]

Gelsomina, too, will be shocked by Oswaldo. It is children who bring Gelsomina to Oswaldo: "Come on, I want to show you something. . . . This way. . . . This way. . . . Shh. . . . Be quiet. . . . Come see Oswaldo!" The children usher Gelsomina into a dark room. She stares at a strange little boy with a big head. He is described in the scenario as "of no definite age, but pale as a white mushroom."[16] Above his head are small mobiles, swirling like universes out of order. Almost as if the children can recognize the laughter-bringing function of Gelsomina, they ask her to make Oswaldo laugh. As the meaning of Oswaldo overcomes Gelsomina, she stops, awestruck, takes off her hat and approaches him reverently. She smiles her tender smile of connection as he stares uncomprehendingly at her.

Oswaldo is alone like Gelsomina. Fellini explains: "Uniting him in a close-up with Gelsomina, who comes right next to him and who looks at him with curiosity, underlines with rather great suggestive power Gelsomina's own solitude."[17] Oswaldo, who will always be a child, meets the childlike Gelsomina. They are lonely innocents, set apart along the road. Her smile is recognition. We remember her mother's attempt at consolation in the first scene: "It's not your fault that you're different from the others." "I recognize something in you," Gelsomina seems to say to Oswaldo, "and yet I also need to give you something." Oswaldo is a fact in Gelsomina's education. But until the Fool, her need to give remains inarticulate and stillborn.

Although Gelsomina will always remain apart, a child in her innocence and simplicity, she is growing, developing, learning, unlike the static Oswaldo and the static Zampano. She *wants* to learn. She constantly strives to express herself: "Why don't you teach me to play the trumpet, Zampano?" It is so that she can play the Fool's Theme that Gelsomina wants to learn to play the trumpet. Even before the Fool appears, he is working his magic on Gelsomina: "That song! Do you remember it, Zampano? . . . Remember how nice it was?" They had first heard the Fool's Theme in the rain. Gelsomina hums the tune. We hear it for the first time, the haunting melody by Nino Rota that contributes so much to the feel—and to our memory—of this lovely little film. Later, the Fool *will* teach her. Zampano will not. It is at that crucial point, just as Zampano refuses to teach her, when Gelsomina declares, "I want to go back to my mother." She makes clear the reason: "Not because of the work. Because I like the work. I like being an artist. It's you I don't like."

For much of the film, Gelsomina has been seeking some closer relationship with Zampano. (i. 2) Having given up something of her

i. 2. Food and security. Gelsomina's acceptance of the physical.

own self when she left sea and family, she tries to find some identity in the self of Zampano. In the delightful trattoria scene, she imitatively picks her teeth with a toothpick, trying to take on Zampano's gestures. Fellini has described her as "a little creature who wants to give love."[18] But Zampano steadfastly remains separate, using Gelsomina but always isolating and rejecting her. Fellini shows, in wonderfully cinematic ways, that Zampano will not meet Gelsomina. The road without a meeting place, without even a destination, is Zampano's medium. Gelsomina is lost upon it. She is left alone and framed in the middle of the road when Zampano drives off with the redhead. We see her there, "scruffy as a stray cat," as she is described in the original scenario.[19] In a later scene, the camera becomes subjective, assuming Gelsomina's viewpoint, as we look down the road toward the receding garden where Gelsomina had hoped to see something take root. Zampano drives along the road, separated. He doesn't even hear the comments and questions which Gelsomina shouts at him.

An important sign of Zampano's separation from Gelsomina is his unwillingness to communicate. He will not answer her questions: "Say, from where do you come?" "From my mother." "Where were you born?" "In my father's house." He understands only one kind of human contact. In amazement, Gelsomina asks, "Do you do *it* with all the women you know?" Zampano summarizes for Gelsomina his attitude toward any other kind of contact: "Look, if you're gonna stay around me, there's only one thing: Keep your eyes open, and your mouth shut." Talk is not his thing. But if Zampano refuses to talk, he also refuses to listen, and he refuses to look. Zampano's negations are, in the world of this film, refusals to establish human contact. He is asleep when Gelsomina asks him such crucial questions as, "Zampano, do you like me a little?" As Gelsomina is soon to point out, he even refuses to think.

Zampano defines himself by brute power. He breaks things— furniture, doors, people. Power is even his profession. He is a Strong Man. "The strength of four bulls" is his boast. And that is all that he has to offer others. "Come here, feel that," he says to the redhead in the trattoria as he flexes his bicep. "What a man!" is her reply. That is all he knows a man to be. Throughout the film, his response to other men whom he cannot understand, and who thus always seem to get the better of him, is the sarcastic dismissal, the ironic comparison with himself: "Big man!" The only relationship that he will tolerate with Gelsomina is the only one he knows: dominance, to be the "big man." When he does not ignore her, he switches her legs, slaps her, beats her, pushes her into the back of his cart for sex.

In the barn after the wedding, Fellini summarizes the Zampano-Gelsomina relationship in a particularly visual way. After Zampano dismisses a whole series of Gelsomina questions with a mere grunt, she weeps, and, in a characteristic gesture, she huddles against a wall, as though she were trying to disappear. As an angry Zampano comes closer, his looming shadow blocks her from our view. Then, just after she disappears in the darkness of his shadow, she breaks free for a moment, runs off left, and tumbles down a hole. She has disappeared entirely. Zampano stands dominantly above; the camera shoots down to her, small at the bottom of a hay chute.

At the end of the wedding sequence, Gelsomina determines that she must leave Zampano. The entire scene is one of wonderful contrasts, all of which point out to Gelsomina that with Zampano she apparently can have no role. A cool objective camera surveys the whole wedding picture: the dinner, the gaiety, the horseplay, the musicians, the children. The long tracking shot effectively separates Gelsomina, the single observer, from all the communal festivities. The lonely Gelsomina looks longingly at the cuddling and kissing wedding couple; and Zampano goes off with another woman. She sees that the bride is dressed in white; the widow is dressed in black. She is nondescript. At the end of all this, the widow gets Zampano; Zampano gets the dead husband's clothes; and Gelsomina falls down a hole. "He never pays any attention to me," she mutters to herself. Gelsomina has learned enough to know that she will never discover herself within this kind of relationship with Zampano. So she shouts at him the crucial line: "I am leaving!" She takes off her costume, exchanging her new clothes for her old ones. Gelsomina takes on again the trappings of her old self. She sets off alone—on foot. The side-by-side linear Gelsomina-Zampano structure that has held the film together up to this point is broken. Gelsomina's education has progressed as far as it can with only Zampano. A new structural and thematic element is needed. It is time for the Fool.

The Fool

Just before Fellini introduces the outside messenger who will change the Gelsomina-Zampano relationship, he creates a sequence that predicts much of what will come in later Fellini films. After Gelsomina walks out on Zampano, she is totally alone, away from family and the sea and away from Zampano and his journey down the road. For the first time since she left the sea, we see her walking down a road, under her own power, not being driven by Zampano. She is free. And she is in nature; the sun is shining brightly, and children are close by, working in the fields. But, although she is free, she is directionless. She stops; looking puzzled, she turns a complete circle in the middle of the road, momentarily adopting Zampano's figure, momentarily as directionless as he. But she is not *enclosed* in the circle, for she moves to the side of the road and sits down in the long, lovely grass. As she sits in the sun by the side of the road, with intense interest and purpose she puts a weed into an insect hole, lifts out a creature, and places it on the back of her hand. It falls off, but she gets another one, puts it on her hand, blows it away, and smiles as it flies upward to freedom. Gelsomina, just freed in life, exults as she frees another little creature. But the insect goes straight up toward the sky. Where will Gelsomina go? Her face changes from exultation to sorrow. She remains still, as if frozen in that position by the side of the road.

Suddenly a wonderful little Felliniesque circus parade mysteriously enters the frame. Fellini provides no rational explanation. It just comes along, as if expressly for the purpose of cheering up Gelsomina, of showing her—and us—that the joy and music of life are unquenchable. "My films," Fellini admits, "are born not from logic but from love."[20]

The procession is another item in Fellini's mythological catalog. A procession is itself a quest. It is liturgical. It is a primordial celebration. And such celebrations—out of time—destroy isolation as they create community. Three musicians march along the meadow, with flute, clarinet, and horn, playing a happy tune. Gelsomina is not surprised. All life is equally wondrous to her. She gets up and skips along, rhythmically following the musicians, as she spins around in a complete circle once more, but this time not in a lost and directionless way, but as one part of a patterned happy dance.

This procession of pure natural joy blends visually and musically into a religious procession which combines joy with sorrow, happiness with fear. We move from magic back to reality. The new procession feels personal; its mood seems to be Fellini's own. And it is: "I remember the Collina delle Grazie, a place of pilgrimage with a Way of the Cross, to which can be traced the terrifying, miraculous, apocalyptic effect of religion which I later evoked in some sequences of my films."[21]

The music of the secular procession was light and gay; the same melody in the religious procession is heavy and ominous. The unbroken light of the fields fades into flickering candles and menacing shadows. The people processing are universalized: young children and old priests; they carry a picture of the virgin, promising divine birth, and a crucifix, predicting death. Just as Gelsomina was carried along by the joyous natural procession, so is she carried along by the mixed mood of the religious procession. Both are aspects of life. The one procession has led her to the other. Gelsomina genuflects, crosses herself, runs happily and excitedly along with the procession; but she stops in front of a butcher shop that has a pig carcass hanging obtrusively in the window. Gelsomina's direction of movement is not completely free. She tries to go down one street; a policeman stops her. She is carried along by the crowd, is almost trampled by people rushing out of a side alley. She is filled with loving awe at a beautiful icon of the Madonna, set in the center of a golden sunburst; but the camera lingers on the picture long enough to reveal the ugly and makeshift structure supporting the lovely image. Obtrusively, once more purposely calling attention to his camera's gesture, Fellini pulls his camera back and up in a long shot, revealing a garish neon "BAR" sign overwhelming the little procession far below. Gelsomina's procession has been spotted with negative reminders of Zampano.

The procession sequence shows what religious manifestations always are in Fellini films: beautiful, but frightening. Enlivening, but deadening. Impressive, but staged. Partaking both of heaven and of earth. In Catholic Italy, this is all part of the scene along the road. But Fellini has said still more in this sequence. He has shown Gelsomina reacting positively to order, to form, to art. She watched people formed into lines; she listened to sounds ordered into music. Cinematically, Fellini also created form and pattern. His moving camera and his timed editing formed a dance, swooping, gliding, guiding our reactions alternately into exaltation and depression, into highs and lows, into feeling and thought.

Toward the end of this extraordinary sequence, Fellini becomes so self-consciously symbolic that he ignores his characters. Gelsomina disappears from our view. What *we* are seeing becomes the important fact. The camera, and thus the viewer, follows the procession inside a cathedral. Our eyes move upward toward the Gothic ceiling. If we are praying, we look up for an answer. We see not a cathedral ceiling but the Fool, flying free, perhaps like Gelsomina's insect, but surely more like an angel, this one with glowing wings. We see the Fool's flying shadow on the illuminated buildings surrounding a large, people-filled square. Under him burns a flame on a monument, very like an altar. We now know that both processions—the secular and the religious—have led us away from Zampano and to the Fool. Fellini has broken with the natural to get us ready for a supernatural character. (i. 3)

i. 3. One-third of the mythic triad: the spirit of the sky.

The Fool's act is as airborne as Zampano's is earthbound. We first see the Fool, his assistant boasts, "two-hundred feet in the air." As we watch him, the Fool appears to be flying as he twirls, with the aid of his balancing stick, round and round on his tightrope. It is only then that Fellini returns his camera to Gelsomina, to show us how *she* is affected by this apparition from the sky. She stares up adoringly. Later, back down on earth, on Gelsomina's level now, the Fool encounters her reverent stare, and grins widely back at her. Eye to eye, with a tear painted on his cheek and a smile on his face, a connection is made between the Fool and Gelsomina. A connection had also been made with Oswaldo. Gelsomina will learn from the Fool, too.

Still later, roaming the windswept and almost deserted piazza, Gelsomina imitates the Fool as she had recently imitated Zampano. In the middle of the square, she walks carefully on an imaginary tightrope, using her cloak as wings. Zampano suddenly invades the almost sacred space with his roaring motorcycle. He beats Gelsomina, menaces her once more with his looming shadow, and shouts his continued dominance over her: "To me you don't say 'No'!" After Zampano forces Gelsomina back into the trailer, Fellini re-establishes Zampano's figure of the circle. The camera pulls back and watches Zampano drive all around the fountain. The camera lingers on another favorite item of Fellini mythology: the deserted town square, the central spot of communal life, become dark, empty and lifeless. In response to a question from Gideon Bachmann, Fellini explained the role of the lonely piazza in the structure of his films: "All my films to date are concerned with people looking for themselves. Night and the loneliness of empty streets, as shown in the shots of piazzas you mention, is perhaps the best atmosphere in which I see these people."[22] The piazza scene operates in both sight and sound: as the scene ends, Nino Rota brings up Zampano's road music, and Zampano and Gelsomina again drive off together down the deserted road.

Although Zampano and Gelsomina are together again, their relationship cannot ever be the same. Something new has intervened. Some message connected with art, some message connected with religion, has entered their lives. Fellini expands the religious imagery that had introduced the Fool. Even his name has suggested the holy fool of folklore and religion. Fellini utilizes specifically Christian mythology to clarify and enrich the function of the Fool, and in so doing quite consciously continues to break the style of naturalism with which the film began. Angel imagery is repeated when we see the Fool's act in the Giraffa Circus, located, not accidentally, in the Holy City of Rome. The dialog makes an obvious point of locating us: "This is Rome. That's St. Paul's over there." We peer up at the Fool, again wearing his angel wings, twirling in the lights, and we watch, at the same time, his soaring shadow. As he jumps off the tightrope, the camera catches his flapping wings. Angel imagery moves into specific Christ imagery. Giraffa, the proprietor of the circus, calls out toward the Fool: "Nazarino! Watch the tent. It is blowing away!" After his act, the Fool exits the arena in triumph, riding on a donkey. This is soon before his death. Later, as the Fool is teaching his new disciple, Gelsomina, as he tries to bring her from Zampano's world into his own, he tells her: "Follow me." When the Fool is killed, three Golgotha-like trees stand stark in the background. As Zampano drags away the Fool's body, the camera lingers on its cruciform position. None of this means that the Fool is to be taken in any literal way as an angel or as Christ. Fellini may well say that the Fool "is also Jesus"; but he means, of course, that Christian mythology is also part of Fellini's catalogue of myths.[23]

The Fool is an instrumental character. We know very little about him. He drops out of the sky into the film, and remains separate: "I come. I go. . . . I like to go my own way. That's how I am. I can't help it. I have no home, no roots." He functions as a messenger from outside the realms of land or sea, a messenger whose function in the film is to deliver to Gelsomina the parable of the stone. He can be the messenger to everyman because he himself is rooted nowhere. It is this messenger who brings into the film the concept of a God who, the Fool tells us, *does* know the purpose served by every object on this earth, as well as by every person. The Fool confronts Gelsomina's elemental, despairing, and yet cosmic, question: "Why was I put here on this earth?" That question is central to Fellini films. It is this messenger who convinces Gelsomina that everything, even a stone—even Gelsomina with her funny little artichoke head—serves some purpose: "Because if that pebble is useless, then . . . then, so are the stars." To this messenger from the sky, the purpose of the stars is self-evident.

The rest of the film shows us that it is through Gelsomina's staying with Zampano that she finds her purpose, and, in that purpose, her self. As the Fool's disciple, Gelsomina will become, in her own simpler way, the messenger who brings Zampano to a discovery of *his* self. It is through listening to a parable, a tale, a message, that Gelsomina receives her destiny. Her education, her initiation, is now completed.

Let us see, first of all, how Gelsomina is affected by the Fool's message. Even before he appears, she is mystically attracted to him and to his art. It was the Fool's song that made her want to learn to play the trumpet. And it is that same song that she hears again as soon as she arrives in Rome. The Fool sits in the tent playing the song on his tiny violin, drawing Gelsomina to him. But she is separated from the Fool by a sturdy rope. She fills the screen with a Gelsomina grimace when Zampano, with a harsh whistle, calls her back to him. It is that same song that Gelsomina hears one night as Zampano gruffly orders her to go to bed. For the first time, she disobeys Zampano. Entranced, she walks over to the Fool, who gestures that he will serenade her. Later, it is that same song that draws her again to the tent, where now the Fool will give her the music lessons that were refused to her by Zampano. (i. 4) As she had earlier begun to imitate the tightrope walking gestures of the Fool, replacing the teeth-picking gestures of Zampano, now she compares the magic art of her new acquaintance with the brutal reality of her old one. As the Fool's song plays just for her, she crawls into bed next to Zampano; and that wondrous smile of hers changes—as she gazes at Zampano—into a sad and disapproving grimace of comparison.

The Fool gives Gelsomina, for the first time, approval and self-respect. We have watched her continual search for a confirmation of her own individuality. The Fool gives her that. He graciously salutes here as "Madame!" (and so unnerves her that she bumps into the tent post). And he—not without irony—plies her with compliments on her

i. 4. The magic of music. Gelsomina learns from the Fool.

musical ability: "It's easy to see that you have talent. . . . Very Good! . . . Wonderful!" So Gelsomina is, psychologically, ready to be receptive to the Fool when he brings to her his message.

The actual delivery of the parable of the stone is accompanied on the sound track by the Fool's Theme, which we had previously heard Gelsomina humming and the Fool playing. This is the first time that the Fool's Theme comes from no visible source, the first time that it becomes background music; the first time, that is, that it pervades the film. Thanks to that "very sad song," as the Fool calls it, the Fool's presence will remain in the film even after his death.

Giulietta Masina lets us know, by her loving fondling of the actual stone used in the parable, just how important is Gelsomina's discovery of her purpose. She begins to act on the message. Her self-possession, after she hears the parable of the stone, is so immediate that she can fly into a fury against Zampano, while she now knows that she will stay with him forever. She threatens to "burn everything," to "put poison in his soup," but this simply shows that she has become independent enough that she can *choose* to stay with him. Her resolve is soon tested, three times.

Her first temptation is to choose the circus, a natural life for Gelsomina. The Fool asks her to choose between staying with Zampano or going away with the other members of the circus. Her reply is merely a resigned smile, and another look at her stone. The second temptation comes from the Fool himself, and it is a harder one to resist: "Would you . . . would you like to come with me?" In reply, she can only bow her head in submission to her new-found purpose. In the touching scene of farewell, the Fool is as brave as Gelsomina: As the distance between them grows, the Fool sings "Gel-so-mi-na, Gel-so-mi-na," waves his "Ciao," and kicks another stone in mock indifference.

During the convent sequence, Gelsomina is tempted for the third time. The young nun praises Gelsomina's playing of the Fool's Theme: "Doesn't she play beautifully?" Since the departure of the Fool, that is the first compliment that Gelsomina has received, a rare instance when she is acknowledged as possessing something important in herself. Gelsomina obviously loves the purity and innocence of the convent. It is in the midst of nature. While nestled in the granary, with rain falling outside, Gelsomina concludes: "It's very nice here." The convent is stable: "Do you know that it is over a thousand years old?" Then comes the explicit test: "Would you like to remain here? Shall I tell the Mother you'll stay?" Both the temptation to stay with the circus and the temptation to stay at the convent present Gelsomina with a chance to find again a piece of her old self. They do not offer her a sea, but they do offer her a family. Yet she refuses.

Gelsomina has learned once more how unworthy Zampano is of her sacrifice. During the storm, he tried to steal the convent's gold relics, while vigil lights threw imprisoning shadows of bars across his body and onto the wall. But Zampano's unworthiness, the isolating selfish enclosure suggested by those shadows, is not the issue, except that it makes Gelsomina's sacrifice all the more needed. The basic issue is the truth of the Fool's message. By now Gelsomina's education has resulted in knowledge. She has already said, "If I don't stay with him, who will stay?" She knows her *role*. And so Gelsomina, once more, chooses to remain with Zampano. "You follow your husband and I follow mine," the little nun reminds Gelsomina. The nun has been another naif, another innocent—like Oswaldo and the Fool, a messenger of grace to one of their number.

Gelsomina's departure from the convent is as moving and memorable a scene as was the Fool's departure from her. As she glances back at the convent, Gelsomina pushes the motorcycle with one hand, wipes her eyes with the other, and then, once more, gives the "Ciao" salute. She crawls into the trailer and, in her characteristic gesture of submission, hides her face. As the distance between Gelsomina and the convent grows, she waves her handkerchief without looking. The road music swells on the sound track once more, telling us again that

i. 5. The child of the sea.

Gelsomina is travelling along Zampano's road. This time we know that it is a decision rather than a compulsion.

In her new relationship with Zampano, Gelsomina has tried to let him know what she has learned, why she waited for him while he was in jail. When he emerged from the shadows of the jail, she called out proudly, as if making a momentous announcement, "Zampano, I'm here!" But he returns her smile with a scowl. "They asked me if I wanted to go along with the circus," she announces. "Why didn't ya?" is his only reply. She looks at the stone, as if to convince herself again of her reasons. She goes back to the routine of serving him: she goes to the trailer, gets his leather jacket, and puts it on him. The shot fades into another road scene, complete with the road music.

The one road scene fades into another road scene, this time along the sea. Here, at a climax in the film, after Gelsomina has discovered her purpose, Fellini gives us another view of the sea. (i. 5) It reminds us of the opening scene, the place from which Gelsomina started, and prepares us for the final scene, the place where Gelsomina will arrive. But between these scenes, Fellini keeps up the connection between Gelsomina and water. He has shown her bathing her face in the fountain in the lonely square after she ran away from Zampano, and he has shown her carrying pails, fetching water, pouring it. Now water enters again, and in the presence of the sea Gelsomina will find the courage to begin to pass on to Zampano the message that she has learned from the Fool. They stop by the sea. She gets out of the trailer, stares wonderingly at her sea, and runs straight to it. Awed, she stops at the shore. Zampano, unawed, wades into the water and spreads his legs to urinate into the sea.

Gelsomina looks down the beach and asks Zampano to show her where her home is. She then passes on to him part of the message: "You know what? I used to dream of going back home. But I don't any more." She smiles at Zampano as she adds, "Now it's like my home is with you." He doesn't react. Later, she goes so far as to say, "At one time I really wanted to die. Rather than stay with you. But now, I'd even marry you." He still doesn't react. Gelsomina tries to humanize Zampano: "Don't you ever *think*?" she asks him at the sea. At another time, she asks him, "Do you know that even a stone is useful? . . . Why, you don't ever think of these things!" His response: "There's nothing to think about." Just before Zampano abandons Gelsomina in the snow, she fully confesses to the role given to her by the Fool: "I wanted to run away, but he said I should stay with you."

Not only Gelsomina, but Zampano as well, is affected by the Fool. Just as Gelsomina from the very first is attracted toward the Fool, so Zampano from the very first is hostile toward the Fool. They had met before, under conditions which we will never know, but conditions that seem to have had something to do with Gelsomina's sister Rosa. Fellini avoids giving us the details. "He knows nothin' about Rosa and me. Nothin'!" Zampano insists, a bit too vehemently for full belief. Fellini obviously wants only to hint as to psychological motivation. Fellini wants us to know no distracting personal details, but rather— and more importantly—to feel the *natural* antipathy between these two rival representatives of different elements. Neither Zampano nor the Fool can explain their mutual antipathy in any rational way. Zampano answers "Who knows?" to Gelsomina's question about the reason for their conflict. All the Fool can do to explain it is to say, "I have nothing against him. It's just that, whenever I see him, I have to tease him. I don't know why. I really don't. I just have to."

A major part of the teasing consists of the Fool's articulation of the animal imagery which Fellini had already built up around Zampano. When the Fool sees Zampano for the first time in the film, he greets him with, "Look who's here! . . . We needed some animals in the circus." "What a beast," he says later. And the Fool tells Gelsomina that the trailer "smells like a pigsty," and asks her how she "teamed up with that big gorilla." The proprietor of the circus picks up the imagery: "He's like an animal!" Even Gelsomina joins in: "You are a beast!" she shouts at Zampano when he persists in misunderstanding the message of the Fool by saying that she stays with him only because with him she eats regularly. Zampano's initial response to the Fool is, characteristically, both a retreat from language and a threat: "Don't talk to me. Don't ever talk to me, or there's gonna be trouble." The Fool knows that Zampano's refusal of language is a sign of his refusal of the human. He explains the situation clearly to Gelsomina: "He looks like a man, but even when he wants to talk, he barks." Gelsomina, also characteristically, has a response of compassion: "That's sad, no?" "Yeah," the Fool admits, "sad."

Zampano feels threatened by the Fool. To Zampano, the Fool represents the magic and hence powerful characteristics of the clown-artist. "You lousy clown," Zampano shouts to the Fool, "I'll kill ya! When I catch you, I'll wipe that smile off your face!" Gelsomina asks Zampano the basic question about the Fool: "Who is he?" Zampano replies, "He's a lousy clown, that's who he is." Zampano seems to intuit some connection between this laughing clown and the laughter-bringing clownlike Gelsomina. He might even have noticed the similarity of their costumes: bright horizontal stripes on Gelsomina's jersey and on the Fool's trousers, gay stripes on both, characteristic of the costume of a clown.

André Bazin, who joins Zampano and Gelsomina in calling the Fool "the Clown," explains the effect that the Fool and Gelsomina have on Zampano: "Gelsomina and the Clown carry with them the aura of the marvelous, which baffles and annoys Zampano." But for those two typical Felliniesque affirmative clown-artists, "this element of wonder appears simply as a quality of nature," one that Zampano cannot understand.[24]

The Fool, the clown with powers of natural wonder so unlike Zampano's powers, threatens to come between Zampano and his possession, Gelsomina. The Fool has weapons—music, gaiety, his message of human worth—that Zampano doesn't know how to fight. How do you fight magic and art? Zampano knows only the weapons of power and dominance, weapons of his own brutality and strength, of his "pectoral muscles, or chest, that is." At the murder scene, Fellini shows us cinematically the only power that Zampano possesses, the only way that he knows how to fight the Fool. As Zampano approaches the Fool, who is repairing his flat tire, Zampano's shadow covers the Fool—the same symbol through which Fellini had indicated Zampano's dominance over Gelsomina. But this time the dominance is, in a physical sense, total. Zampano begins to beat the Fool, all the way to death, as the still-smiling Fool well knows: "You wouldn't be tryin' to kill me, would you?" The wise Fool has always known that his death was coming. He had told Gelsomina that he would die young. As Zampano beats the Fool, Zampano can only repeat inarticulately his standard taunt, "Big man!" But in a more important sense than life and death, it is the Fool who conquers. The Fool dies. The Fool's death is sacramentalized by fire and water. And the Fool remains, still affecting Zampano through Gelsomina.

Zampano

While the Fool was alive, Zampano had understood Gelsomina to be the prize to be awarded to one or to the other. Zampano has only seen women as objects; he purchased Gelsomina to replace the previously purchased Rosa. "She works with nobody but me," Zampano shouts. Zampano reasserts his exclusive dominance over Gelsomina: "Nobody tells her what to do but me!" But Zampano cannot continue to hold that exclusive power with the same comfort that he could before Gelsomina met the Fool. (i. 6) In the convent scene, when Gelsomina plays the Fool's Theme on the trumpet—which the Fool had taught her

i. 6. At the convent. The Fool returns through the music of his disciple.

i. 7. The man of the earth: Zampano alone on his road.

to play—Zampano knits his brow as though he recognizes something disturbing. Ironically, these small signs of jealousy are the first signals of a possible human need in Zampano. Edward Murray sees in Anthony Quinn's face in this scene something of the workings of the Fool's magic: Zampano is "uneasy, humble, softened, bashful, embarrassed; positive forces appear to be stirring inside him."[25]

The Fool's special power increases after his death. Zampano begins to show human characteristics of fear and need, and perhaps of even more. "What am I gonna do?" he almost pleads to Gelsomina after he realizes that the Fool is dead. In anquish, he concludes, "You're no help to me." Visually in subsequent shots, Zampano's road becomes barren. We see, in quick succession, shots of hills, rocks, snow, all cold, bare, lifeless. (i. 7)

Fellini returns to a favorite visual motif: the solitary tree. In the garden scene, we saw a tree that promised fruition, the tree that Gelsomina imitated as she planted tomatoes. But in the wedding scene, we saw a barren tree that an isolated Gelsomina stared at when the party was over. Now we see a series of gnarled trees, stark against the cold sky. The situation seems to have created the setting. Nature seems to imitate Gelsomina's feelings, for we saw her stark and cold before we saw, beyond the trees, the stark black and white contrasts in the landscape, created by spots of cold snow next to patches of dark hard ground. Nature seems to be taking its cue from its child.[26]

Gelsomina whimpers that the clown is dead: "Zampano, he won't laugh any more." "He, who had virtually given her being," in the words of André Bazin, "has suddenly ceased to exist. Little groans like the cries of mice irresistibly escape from her lips: 'The Clown is sick; The Clown is sick.' "[27] In his fear, Zampano begins to consider Gelsomina: "You want me to take you back?" And he even asks her, almost politely, "Mind if I sleep here tonight?" When she screams, "NO! Don't come in here!" he quietly submits: "I'll sleep outside." We are reminded of the distance between his current submission and his early dominance when he virtually threw Gelsomina into the trailer and climbed in after her. He and Gelsomina have now changed positions. And Fellini shows that visually: Now, for the first time, we see Zampano sitting down in Gelsomina's characteristic position, huddled against a wall as if he would like to disappear, to blend into the background.

In the abandonment scene, Zampano shows some clear signs of human kindness. He seems to respond with some emotion to her last words: "The fire's almost out." He puts blankets on Gelsomina, leaves clothes for her, leaves her money, and—in an important afterthought —goes back and lays the trumpet beside her. As Zampano drives away, a subjective camera, taking on his point of view, shows her receding into the distance. It is a shot that surely suggests *his* sadness as well as ours. He sees Gelsomina lying curled up in the sunshine, nestled in the sun that had so recently warmed her. Just a few minutes earlier, circus music had played as Gelsomina caressed the sun shining on her, the sun that she had found so tactile and comforting.

Gelsomina's purpose is not yet complete, as even the environment shows. In a device that is a Fellini favorite, he films her against a structure that mirrors her condition. Behind her is a half-built, half-collapsed wall. It is a sign of incompletion and separation. The music as Zampano abandons Gelsomina is not the road theme: it is the Fool's Theme. Like the trumpet, the Fool is left behind with Gelsomina.

When Zampano next appears on the screen, he is more lifeless than we have ever seen him. And, for the first time, we see him walking down a road. Memories of both the Fool and of Gelsomina re-enter the film through a woman's voice heard humming the Fool's Theme. The song draws Zampano to the woman, just as it had earlier drawn

Gelsomina to the Fool. Zampano calls out: "Hey, where'd you learn that song?" The camera shows Zampano grasping the barbed wire that symbolically separates him from the woman. She is hanging pure white clothes, and is surrounded by singing children. As the woman recounts to Zampano the story of Gelsomina's final days, shots of her playing children, the sound of their laughter, and the Fool's song—images and sounds which have all been so clearly connected with Gelsomina—fill our eyes and ears. The children hold hands and dance in a circle, a suggestion of completion and acceptance that will reappear in a later film at the center of Fellini's art. And the woman's words reintroduce more Gelsomina imagery: "My father found her over there on the beach. . . . When she felt better, she would sit in the sun and play on her trumpet." The woman reveals that Gelsomina had been invited to join their family but, as with the circus performers and the nuns, she had once more rejected community.[28] In a striking visual symbol, the entire screen is filled with the pure white of the clean linen as the woman says, "Then one morning, she just didn't wake up."

In the next scene, Zampano is obviously obsessed with memories of Gelsomina. The sea is plainly visible in the background as a circus trapeze artist performs. The camera holds there for a long time, watching the sea; and then slowly we move down to a close shot of Zampano spiritlessly performing his unchanging circular act.

Zampano's isolation is clear throughout his violent drunkenness in the subsequent tavern scene. Outside again, he shouts defiantly, for a final time, his standard taunt: "You're all big men in a crowd!" He repeats the exact words of the Fool: "I don't need anybody!" Then he adds, "Just me alone!" Visually, the loneliness of Zampano is reinforced by the composition of Fellini's shot: Zampano is imprisoned within a V formed by the branching railroad tracks. The camera shoots toward the closed end of the V, showing Zampano, the man of the road, with nowhere to go.

The scene fades then into a Gelsomina shot: a dynamic picture of the sea breaking diagonally against the shore. Zampano looks back toward the land, but he turns away and walks right into the sea. It is a sharp reminder of the opening of the film, but now it is Zampano, instead of Gelsomina, who walks home to the sea. There is a note of completion here, yet a feeling of beginning as well as ending. The film began when Zampano came to the sea only to take Gelsomina away from it; the film is now ending when Gelsomina, in spirit, brings Zampano back to the sea. In the words of Stuart Rosenthal, "The sea now acts as an agent for Gelsomina (or perhaps, in the broadest poetic sense, it is the other way around), fulfilling her 'purpose.' "[29]

We remember Gelsomina's fetal position when Zampano abandoned her: if the film has moved from her birth through life to death,
the film also suggests, when we see Gelsomina for the last time, that
her life is beginning again at her death. And indeed, it is after her death
that she completes her self by bringing Zampano to his self. All of this
suggests that the linear structure of the film has changed into a cyclical
one. But it is not now Zampano's circle of enclosure, but a circle of
fulfillment, of completion, of beginnings moving on from endings.
Suzanne Budgen summarizes that structure: "The journey in *La Strada*
is both literal and figurative; the literal journey leads from the sea back
to the sea, while the figurative one leads Gelsomina from the state of
childhood and innocence, through womanhood and knowledge, to
death and a kind of apotheosis."[30]

The next image is indeed one of apotheosis, of beginning, of sacramental birth, as Zampano baptismally bathes himself in Gelsomina's
element, the sea. The shot fades into a close-up of Zampano's battered
and swollen face as he sits on the shore. He looks off toward the sea,
then looks up, toward the sky and stars, in a kind of awe. He looks
around as if frightened, as if he had heard or seen or sensed something.
We cannot know exactly what this means. Edward Murray describes the
change that we have witnessed within the circular structure of the film:
"When we first meet Zampano, he is standing tall and strong in the
sunlight, arrogantly watching Gelsomina on her knees facing the water.
When we take leave of Zampano, however, he remains prostrate before
the sea, no longer proud of his strength but humbly enduring his dark
night of the soul."[31] After saying, "I don't need anybody!" does Zampano now, as he looks around, see himself alone in this whole huge
universe? Does he finally "think"? His eye movement stops when he
again faces the sea. The scenario[32] describes what we see: "A sob fills his
chest and shakes him all over. Zampano is weeping." Having learned,
through his association with Gelsomina, to feel jealousy, fear, need,
kindness, sadness, awe, and perhaps even love, does he now feel guilt?
Does a human life begin for Zampano, during his dark night of the soul,
with an awakening of his conscience? Fellini himself thinks that that is
the meaning of his final sequence in *La Strada*: "It is the story of an
enlightenment, of the shaking awake of a conscience, through the
sacrifice of another creature."[33] But Fellini also suggests that the enlightenment perhaps goes beyond these two creatures and their special
setting:

> The great sea and the distant sky which I like to show in my
> films are no longer enough: beyond sea and sky, through terri-
> ble suffering, perhaps, or the relief of tears, God can be

i. 8. The completion.

glimpsed—his love and his grace, not so much as a matter of theological faith, but as a profound need of the spirit.[34]

The final statement of *La Strada* is visual, not verbal. It is what Fellini shows, not what Fellini says. The closing sequence is therefore more suggestive than definitive. Perhaps Zampano's tears move us more as a human than as a supernatural response to the death of Gelsomina. But the imagery of the final scene suggests not despair and death so much as hope and life. At the end the mobile camera pulls back, showing Zampano and the great sea and the distant sky, all framed into a single ordered shot. (i. 8) The camera continues to recede as the Fool's Theme, for one last time, swells on the sound track. That music that started as the Fool's, that became Gelsomina's, has now become Zampano's. His is now the beauty of the sad song. Zampano lies on the beach. We see him for the last time. He is still weeping, that uniquely human activity. Gelsomina's purpose has been completed. The road has given way to the sea, under the sky.

LA DOLCE VITA

AFTER LA STRADA WAS FILMED and edited, and before it was released, Fellini said: "*La Strada* will remain the crucial point in my life. . . . I have already said all that I can weep for, laugh, suffer or hope for in the film. I have exhausted myself."[1] Yet, exhausted or not, Fellini had further to go. He once described his own filmmaking as a "journey progressing along the same road."[2] So he continued. He summoned the energy to complete his "tetrology of tender nostalgia for lost innocence and lost idealism." *I Vitelloni*, *La Strada*, *Il Bidone*, and *Cabiria*: "These four films," says Andrew Sarris, "are based on a tragic-comic lyricism that is intensely personal."[3] After the tetrology, one phase of Fellini's attempt to form life into art was completed: The tenderness was about to harden a bit and the lyricism would take on a more realistic edge, turning almost into social and moral exposé. But the intensely personal nature of the Fellini film journey was not about to end. The road was still clearly recognizable as Fellini's own road.

Fellini's friend Angelo Solmi tells us that, after *Cabiria*, at the end of the tetrology, Fellini planned a film with Sophia Loren and Gregory Peck, to be called "Journey with Anita," a title later changed to "Journey into Love."[4] Those journeys led nowhere. Instead Fellini began to adapt what seemed to be the perfect novel, one "particularly suited to me, for it sums up all the themes that are important to me." He worked on a film script from Mario Tupino's *The Free Women of Magliano*, a novel in which the hero discovers, in Fellini's clear statement, that "it is

33

necessary that he make a choice." Fellini did indeed know his theme: In the new film, "the necessity to choose" would be "exactly the meaning of the film." And Fellini knew his manner: After the choice could come "a transfiguration that I have sometimes sought for." But Fellini discovered that he must write his own films, not adapt the work of others. He finally rejected the Tupino novel.[5] But he kept its inspiration.

The intensely personal search of one of Fellini's own characters now came back to him. Fellini looked back to an earlier Fellini film. At the end of Fellini's *I Vitelloni*, Moraldo Rubini, that film's alter ego for Fellini himself, was seen leaving the provinces for Rome. Fellini was haunted by the possibility of Moraldo's continuing journey once he got to Rome. Perhaps it was time to follow a journey right into the heart of the modern world, right into Rome, that mythic city. "I thought of a film for this character," Fellini explains, "and it should be a continuation of *I Vitelloni*. It should tell Moraldo's adventures in Rome, the adventures of a young man trying to find his own self."[6]

Solmi tells us that Fellini brooded over the script for "Moraldo in Citta":

> During the spring and summer of 1958, Fellini turned the question over in his mind and contrary to his usual habits frequented the cafés of Via Veneto. And it was there, seated at those little tables, that he saw a great panorama passing before him which he had never closely observed before, the clamorous panorama of wealthy society.[7]

The Moraldo idea began to take on a harder tone; it was becoming more sophisticated, and more social, and it was combining with the theme of *The Free Women of Magliano*. Moraldo would search for self, would try to choose a life, within Rome. Moraldo necessarily became older. Fellini explained that the developing film would be about "Moraldo, no longer as he was when he arrived in Rome, but twenty years later, already a little hardened, already on the edge of shipwreck."[8] He would seek a change in his life, a "transfiguration." Eventually "Moraldo in Citta" became *La Dolce Vita*, and Moraldo Rubini turned into Marcello Rubini, a journalist, that quintessentially modern social profession, a profession very like Fellini's own.

The focus of the new film became as much Rome as Moraldo/Marcello. As always for Fellini, people were inseparable from places; all were part of a mythic whole. "The star of my film is Rome, the Babylon of my dreams," said Fellini while the new film was being made. He added that it will show "a Rome that never budges, the accomplice, partner, and judge. . . . I chose it for its permanence."[9]

Fellini's Roma must be an expression of himself, of his own dreams, if he is to move it to the personal yet mythic level where his art resides: "This town is not Rome—it is *my* Rome," he said later.[10]

This was a far journey. From the provinces to Rome; from a simpleton and a brute to a hardened and sophisticated city dweller; from a little tale of sea and land and sky to a big story of a permanent and international Babylon; from plain Italian dialect to a world of languages: the Fellini style was expanding. Genevieve Agel would soon talk about the "animated, chaotic, lavish, bombastic creations of a dynamic imagination."[11] Fellini himself now admitted to "a spirit curious about everything, impetuous, delirious, passionately seeking a way to get beyond excess." Critics would soon dub him "baroque." But to Fellini, "Baroque is a limited weak word to describe it. . . . Generosity is better; let us say that I like that better than restriction and precaution."[12] The new unrestricted and uncautious Fellini would still be Fellini; his film-making would still be a personal vision abstracted into myth. And it would still be a journey toward self: Fellini would describe the completed *La Dolce Vita* as a "private and confidential confession" and he would describe Marcello as a man "trying to clarify."[13]

"The Sweet Life" suggests a universal statement, just as did "The Road." But the new title, *La Dolce Vita*, also suggests a social statement. The road has now lead to the city, and there Fellini wants to look not just at individuals but at society. He will, in fact, still use "the complete catalogue of my entire mythical world," as he had in *La Strada*, but now, he adds, "I wanted to put the thermometer to a sick world."[14] So, in this film, as the protagonist Marcello Rubini searches for a better self, society intrudes into that search with seven distinct episodes, each of which explicates one of the paths available to social modern man, and each of which plunges Marcello further toward loss rather than toward discovery. Thus the structure must change from the simplicities of *La Strada* and the other early films. The structure of *La Dolce Vita* can be neither linear nor cyclical; it becomes a downward spiral. The structure becomes a modern Roman decline and fall.

Marcello is never just a journalist in Rome. He is modern man faced with modern life, and even, behind the modernity, eternal man faced with eternal life—or death. To signal the mythical quality of Marcello's quest, Fellini breaks his naturalistic manner sooner than he did in the simpler *La Strada*. Indeed, he breaks the naturalistic manner immediately. Fellini places Marcello's downward spiral into a symbolic frame: Both the opening and closing scenes of *La Dolce Vita*—the helicopter and the fish—are mythical incidents which have little to do with storytelling, with the specific search of Marcello. Instead, these scenes symbolically surround the Marcello story so as to generalize it and to place in our consciousness the expanded social *and* mythical meaning—and feeling—of the entire film. The number of episodes in the film—seven—suggests mythic extension: the number of the sacraments, the seven nights of destruction of the Apocalypse, or whatever else one's imagination might conjure concerning that mystical number of seven. Fellini also contrives to make sure that the climax of each episode takes place at night, and that each episode ends with the coming of the dawn. Each day is a Day of Judgment. Nino Rota's music, under the credits and throughout the film, mocks the Dies Irae, sometimes solemnly, sometimes playfully.

Fellini deepens, with *La Dolce Vita*, the conscious autobiographical involvement that will mark most of his subsequent films, including, of course, both *8½* and *Juliet of the Spirits*. Although sometimes Fellini tries to fool the critics by denying that his films are basically autobiographical, many of his own statements, and the facts of his films themselves, say the opposite. Working so intensively with art that explores a search for self, Fellini, most appropriately, involves his own art with his own search, even to the point of including his name in the title and often his person in the pictures within several of his subsequent films. In all of his filmmaking, Fellini has admitted, "I love the feeling of peering in on my own life."[15] And he can't help it. "Even if I set out to make a film about filet of sole," he told Eugene Walter, "it would turn out to be about me."[16] So he doesn't really try: "I think it is absolutely impossible not to be autobiographical."[17]

In *La Dolce Vita*, Fellini gives his hero the same kind of journalist job that Fellini himself once held in Rome. Moreover, Marcello's job, like Fellini's even now, is exposure, and dealing in images. And, also like Fellini, Marcello begins the practice of his profession as an observer, with distance and objectivity, and ends as a participant, involved and subjective. Fellini began as a neo-realist, which means to some people, as Fellini puts it, to "show reality through a very cold, objective eye."[18] But Fellini sees his own art to be an examination of "whatever reality is, not just social reality, but spiritual reality, metaphysical reality, all that there is within a man."[19] That means that he can say, "To hell with the objective. I've got to be in the middle of things."[20]

La Dolce Vita shows Marcello in the middle of things, moving from objectivity to subjectivity. In the first episode of the narrative itself, after the symbolic opening, Marcello is passive, the objective reporter, sitting in a car driven by Maddalena, asking her where they are going, asking her, when they arrive where she has driven them, "Do you want to make love here?" She does. By the seventh episode, Marcello is the leader. It is he who says, "Break down the gate!" and it is he who throws a rock through the window to get the final orgy started. It is he who then controls the party: "I could keep you here a whole week without boring you! But you must do what I say." It is he who tries desperately to keep the party going when the ultimate boredom of vice sets in: "This party mustn't end now." In Marcello's valedictory speech, he recognizes that involvement in the sweet life has actually become his "wonderful career."

To get *us* as subjectively involved in the seemingly real events of the film as are Fellini and Marcello, Fellini shoots most of the film in the flat, overexposed manner of the newsreel, or in the harsh black and white of the flash photograph, and with the mobile camera of TV or of the documentary film. Fellini further breaks down the barrier between observer and participant, between art and reality, by shrinking the distance between actor and role. Marcello Mastroianni is called Marcello; Nadia Gray is called Nadia; Giulio Questi is called Giulio; Anita Ekberg is referred to as a Swede who is now an American actress. Reference is made to Lex Barker—before he sagged a little—having played Tarzan. At the orgy scene, the matinee idol is called Sernas, and he is Jacques Sernas, the French actor who became a matinee idol by playing Paris in the Italian film of *Helen of Troy*. The pigtailed girl at the party is introduced as Sondra Lee, an American dancer; and that is Sondra Lee, the American dancer who played Tiger Lilly in the TV version of *Peter Pan*, a good number of steps up the spiral from "The Sweet Life."

The scandals which the film exposes are close to the banal scandals which Romans and everyone else read about every day; and Fellini based several of the episodes on headlines from the Roman newspapers. Marcello and his photographers fill the morning papers with the scandals of the Via Veneto, that street of modern life, that symbol of modern mobility suggested by the surging crowds, by the cruising automobiles, and by the flickering signs for international airlines. In reality, we sip down the newspaper headlines with the morning coffee, insulated from the hustle-bustle, and from the horror and pain. But in his art, Fellini makes us see the headlines as we didn't see them around the breakfast table. He breaks the distance. "I see no dividing line," Fellini has said, "between imagination and reality."[21]

The Heiress

The first narrative episode introduces Maddalena, the beautiful bored heiress, as well as many of the themes and techniques of the

whole movie. Most importantly, it initiates Marcello's halfhearted
attempt to escape the boredom and meaninglessness of the sweet life
and to discover some sense of purpose in himself. The quest is both an
attempt to escape and an aspiration to discover. The thing to escape is
the current setting. No one needs to say "I'm bored" in that extraordinary scene in the nightclub. We see boredom in the faces, and in the
composition and editing. The camera catches an expressionless, smoking Marcello; it languidly moves to an expressionless, smoking
anonymous woman. After Marcello finds Maddalena, the camera
shows the two acquaintances as separate vertical shapes leaning
against the bar, totally unconnected. (i. 9) In the shot that opens the
nightclub scene, the stolid musclemen in the Siamese act are masked;

i. 9. Maddalena and Marcello: boredom and separation.

the quivering effeminate dancer is masked. No emotions are visible from either set of these opposites. Maddalena and the others seem similarly masked in boredom as they watch. In the shot that closes the nightclub scene, an extremely tall, bored, and expressionless woman and an extremely short, bored, and expressionless man dance into the camera. Everyone is the same, even when they are different.

Boredom and separation are everywhere. And Marcello's job is to report on that boredom. He bribes the headwaiter for trivial information about what the Prince is eating and drinking. The first moral objection arises: "There is the right of privacy!" asserts the bodyguard. Marcello's excuse is typical: "I have my public to inform—it's my job." The bored public wants to be informed of boring details about bored people by bored reporters. In the midst of this kind of deadening life, nothing is seen clearly, in spite of all the journalistic attempts at exposure. When Marcello says, "It's my job," he puts on his sunglasses. Fellini will use an eyeglasses motif throughout the film to show the futile attempt to see, and the corresponding refusal to be seen. Sight imagery is not new to Fellini: Even Zampano knew that "Once you lose your eyesight, you are finished."

Within all of the negations of boredom, of separation, of obscurity, a search is beginning—in structure, in dialogue, and in visual patterns. But Marcello's role is still mostly passive, even negative. What Marcello likes best about the city, which is his element, precisely as the sea had been the element of Gelsomina, is that he can hide himself within it. Maddalena, hiding behind dark glasses, responds, "I'd like to hide too." Although they are both bored, there is no companionship in their mutual boredom. As they talk about boredom, the camera shows them, in a two-shot in Maddalena's car, separated by a windshield divider. When the camera shifts, they are separated by the steering wheel. Continually, they are framed into separate sectors of the screen. The published English screenplay is explicit in its description of Maddalena's response to these negations. She wants not only to get away from but to go toward: "She is lost and sad, looking for something important enough to believe in."[22] "What I need," she concludes, "is a whole new life." It is Maddalena's restlessness, her attempts to move toward both escape and aspiration, that give the spark to this entire opening sequence, that give the film forward thrust in the midst of its vision of stasis and separation. We see the restlessness in Anouk Aimée's face, and in her acting. She looks, the published text tells us, "as if her nerves were scraped raw." And Fellini emphasizes her restlessness when Maddalena begins to speed down the road in her Cadillac.

The entire film deals with boredom and meaninglessness and with the restless or even frenzied attempt to escape it. All of the episodes, except the climactic Steiner one, are approached in speeding vehicles: Maddalena's Cadillac convertible, Sylvia's Alitalia airliner, Marcello's Triumph sports car, Paparazzo's Vespa motorscooter, Cerusico's Lambretta, Robert's white Corvette, Fanny's little Fiat, the aristocrats' Jaguar, a white Thunderbird convertible, a black Ferrari. These machines are the pilgrims in the modern Felliniesque ritual processions. The speeding machines cut across the compositional frame at every angle, but mostly diagonally. The editing is sharp, quick, dynamic. Locomotion is the continual concern. The characters are as spiritually mobile as they are physically frenzied. Human meetings, for sex or business, are casual and sporadic. Quick, separate episodes. The episodic structure of *La Dolce Vita* is no accident.

Maddalena's speeding car introduces one visual motif. The headlights of her car introduce another. When Maddalena shines her car's headlights into the eye of the camera, she starts a motif that Fellini will expand—with flashbulbs, torches, bicycle lights, arc lights, searchlights, floodlights, candles, flashlights, spotlights. But how much is revealed by all these shining bursts of light? Are they blinding or illuminating? How much is exposed? What is escaped? What is discovered? The questions concerning light and sight begin to accumulate in this first episode.

Maddalena leads Marcello to a new attempt to escape from boredom—fornication in a whore's bed. Fellini ritualizes the approach to the house of Adriana the whore. He creates a cinematic dance. Circled in the spotlight of the car's headlights, Maddalena floats along a wall, the camera picking up the gliding motion, gliding itself, and then varying the Maddalena and camera rhythms with Marcello's twirling of a rose. This dance introduces to us the central compositional figure of the film: the twirling spiral.

The spiral figure becomes a geometric metaphor for Marcello's metaphysical journey. Zampano's circle merely doubled back upon itself; Marcello's spiral leads him downward. Marcello and Maddalena spiral down the stairs into Adriana's flooded apartment, which is located—and the whore laughs at the irony—in the "Dead Souls district." Every episode of *La Dolce Vita* shows us a stairway. In this first episode, Marcello is still passive; he follows Maddalena as they descend. In the other episodes, although overall Marcello continues to spiral downward, in each episode he aspires upward. A spiral goes both up and down. As he searches, Marcello will ascend literally, but, never discovering, will continually descend figuratively.

The Maddalena episode ends, as do all seven, with negation, with no escape or discovery. Dawn comes without bringing light. The morning after the night at Adriana's looks much like the morning after the wedding celebration in *La Strada*. The morning does not mean refreshment; it means litter and waste and exhaustion. This morning foreshadows all the mornings in the film. "In Fellini's world," Gilbert Salachas has written, "dawn signals the moment of truth. The spell is shattered, and a person finds himself once again alone and shivering, abandoned, pathetic, left with neither energy nor illusion."[23] Maddalena and Marcello drive away, cool, matter-of-fact, disconnected from each other still. They speed off to another attempt to overcome boredom, back into another desperate search for energy and illusion. "Don't go too fast with that nice car," the whore warns, as the pimp comes over to get his money.

The Goddess

Sylvia enters Marcello's life with more frenzy than did Maddalena and her "nice car." And the personal expands into the public and into the mythic. An Alitalia jet cuts across the screen. In the words of Eric Rhode, "The legendary Anita Ekberg descends from the aeroplane like a diva ex machina."[24] And then about a hundred worshipping photographers break loose from restraints and run toward the camera. The sweet life is not only continual motion, but also continual exposure. Cerusico shouts, "I just want one picture, just one!" as he runs up the steps of Sylvia's arriving airliner. (i. 10)

Frenzied worship continues. A modern motorcade zooms along the classic Appian Way: "Suddenly a big car comes in sight, surrounded by swarms of photographers on motor scooters. . . . Cerusico leans way out taking pictures. . . . A motor scooter buzzes up with a photographer hanging off the back." Edward Murray points out that this is a secular procession imitating a sacred one, made up of "a long line of cars, containing devout worhippers of the flesh."[25] The ritual press conference of the sex goddess begins with blinding flashbulbs popping in our eyes. It is a few seconds before we can see where we are. And then: "There are people coming and going constantly. The reporters are firing questions at Sylvia in French, Italian, German—all the languages of Europe." The babble (and the Babel) of languages is recorded and amplified and pictured: we see newsreel photographers, still photographers, TV, radio, telephones, lights, wires, technicians. Even Sylvia's subsequent flight up the steps of St. Peter's becomes a staged

i. 10. Sylvia and the *paparazzi:* the descent of the goddess.

public relations gambit, its theatricality emphasized by the fact that Fellini shoots the sun's rays glaring through a round window right into our eyes, and then illuminating Sylvia, for all the world like a spotlight from heaven turned on Sylvia the movie queen. "Quiet" she commands in a stage whisper. "We're in church." When she shouts the religiously suggestive words, "Follow me, everybody," they all do. And again Fellini brings in the thematic spiral figure, as a subjective camera follows Marcello and Sylvia twirling round and round, covering many of the "more than 700 steps" up St. Peter's. The sweet life, we are beginning to know, is a life of false worship, of frenzied publicity, without privacy, solitude, silence, or order.

Clearly, the times are out of joint. The bizarre contrasts which introduced Maddalena's nightclub scene continue in Sylvia's nightclub scene. The first shot within the ancient Roman Baths of Caracalla is an incongruous close-up of a black sax player. The text describes some of the dancers in this grotesque ancient/modern nightclub. We see a "hideous dowager with a boy of twenty, and a fat old man with a Chinese girl." The waiter has a prosaic face with mustache and eyeglasses; yet he is wearing a classical tunic, and it isn't even correctly

Roman. For all of the frantic activity, for all of the false religion, for all of the publicity, and for all of the contrast, what we see is still boredom. The camera seeks out what the screenplay describes as "a middle-aged couple, utterly bored."

Both the boredom and the frenzy of the sweet life had been introduced in the Maddalena episode, and both are developed in the Sylvia episode, and throughout. So, too, does Fellini continue to show us various search reactions to this modern life, flights of both escape and pursuit, physical and metaphysical. We have seen something of the characters putting on their dark glasses to protect themselves against exposure; so do they take them off in their aspirations to discover others. Marcello had taken off his glasses when he searched for Maddalena, just as he now pushes up his glasses and peers under them as he searches for Sylvia. Similarly, Robert adjusts his glasses to look more closely as he tries to discover the meaning of Sylvia and Frankie's dance. On the contrary, Sylvia hides behind her sunglasses precisely as Maddalena and Marcello had hid behind theirs. The photographers, always wanting to penetrate privacy, to expose the self, shout to Sylvia, "Please, the eyeglasses. Sylvia, the eyeglasses! . . . Tell her to take off her sunglasses." Sylvia searches for a hidden Marcello just as the photographers search for a hidden Sylvia. Sylvia doesn't seem to see Marcello until she removes his sunglasses, which he had put on again as if to protect himself from her radiance. She only sees the surface: "For the first time she realizes that he is handsome."[26]

The frenzy, the boredom, the hiding, the seeking, all of this takes place on Marcello's turf. And it is all essentially connected with his job as a Roman journalist. Early in the Sylvia episode, Marcello is still the passive and objective journalist: "He's impressed, but he won't be one of the pack" who are chasing Sylvia. But soon the P.R. man in Marcello takes over: "We'll take her to St. Peter's and the Quirinal to see the guards. Leave it to me." And then the man in Marcello takes over: Under the influence of all the myths that adhere to Sylvia, he does join the pack. He becomes more participant than observer. His ecstatic pursuit of Sylvia up to the Dome of St. Peter's is accompanied by the pealing of the bells of Rome.

Fellini continually reminds us that Marcello's search is a city search, more specifically, a Roman search. In the nightclub, the orchestra plays "Arrivederci, Roma," and we take the required tours of the Baths of Caracalla, St. Peter's, and the Trevi Fountain. But we don't get the conventional tourist view. All of the sights are viewed through the very personal lens that pictures Fellini's Roma, the Babylon of his dreams. In his view of the Roman landscape, Fellini indulges his preference for mythic suggestions. When he himself first saw Rome, he tells us, "to my scared provincial eyes it wasn't even Rome—it was some fairy-tale vision."[27] Fairy tales and myths come easily in Rome. In the next episode, a strange prophetess figure will say, "Your Italy is a land full of ancient cults, rich in natural and supernatural powers." Fellini himself has said that "an Italian can never entirely shake the myth."[28]

Sylvia, dancing in the ancient Roman Baths of Caracalla, is extended by Fellini into a mythic symbol of all that Marcello aspires to find, both natural and supernatural. Her shadows are long, extending over everything in Caracalla as she dances in her ritual procession. Marcello, awed, says to her: "You are everything, Sylvia. . . . Don't you know that you are everything, everything." First she becomes Eve: "You are the first woman on the first day of creation." But Marcello aspires to more than Eve, so Sylvia becomes to him "the mother, the sister, the lover, the friend . . . an angel, a devil, the earth, the home." That is a tall order, even for Anita Ekberg. Throughout this strange night, filled with evocations of the ancient Roman past, Sylvia becomes to Marcello a kind of pagan goddess, and a mythic woman of nature. From the pagan past, with the walls of Caracalla lined with "huge heads of Roman emperors," Frankie enters the scene in a ritual dance. Frankie is "bearded like a satyr." He "advances across the floor, crouched like an ape and swinging his hips to the music." Sylvia picks up the tone from Frankie, and as they dance "they are sinuous and free, like two young animals." Sylvia "laughs with animal pleasure."

Sylvia is inclusive enough to incorporate within her ample self both Zampano's animal imagery and the gentle naturalness of Gelsomina. Her fur cape is lined with zebra. Along the Appian Way, Sylvia exclaims, "Oh Edna, look at all the chickens." And, a moment later, a flock of sheep seems to seek her out and "surge around Sylvia's car." Sylvia communes with animals. She howls with the dogs. She leads them in their baying to the night. Then all her care and attention are focused on a white kitten, who rides on her head. Suzanne Budgen summarizes Sylvia's connection with animals: "When she goes off dejectedly with Marcello, she is miraculously invigorated by a short spell of communication with the local fauna, suggesting renewal of a power at a deep pagan source."[29]

Sylvia is tireless, to the consternation of the journalists who cannot keep up with her. And, as part of her affirmation of life, she eats pizza and goes into raptures over spaghetti and cannelloni. She is herself associated with the carnal: A radio announcer comments, "What a juicy hunk of meat!"

Fellini takes all this exuberant imagery and he mixes it with Christian parody. As Sylvia climbs to the balcony of St. Peter's her dress is "an astonishing parody of an Italian priest." She wears a cardinal's hat, and seems to reign over the most mythic square in Christendom. At the Trevi Fountain, the water imagery goes beyond that of *La Strada*: In a cleansing ritual—a kind of Christian/Pagan baptism—she wades with perfect naturalness into the myth-encrusted fountain, a monument of the decadent baroque. Sylvia is now surrounded by her friends—Neptune and several tritons. Fellini well understood both what he had created in Sylvia and the mood of the myth-packed Sylvia episode. He praised his own creation, his own Sylvia: "This kind of Valkyrie, this pagan sex-goddess . . . seen with trembling admiration, as if one were in the presence of a supernatural event." "But at the same time," he added, "it is all rather funny."[30]

Just before dawn, all the images combine and Sylvia becomes Marcello's perfect Idealized Woman. The published screenplay describes what we see:

> She wades forward, lifting her evening gown as the water rises against her thighs. Then she drops the gown and lets it float on the water. She goes to the back of the fountain, where the water spills off a ledge of rock, and stands in the flow, letting the falling water bathe her face and breasts. She lifts her arms, and her head falls back in ecstasy. At the edge of the pool, Marcello stares at her in wonder. [i. 11]

Sylvia calls, "Marcello, come here." Marcello responds, "Yes Sylvia, I'll come too." Marcello mutters to himself, telling us what he has learned from this vision: "Yes, yes, she's perfectly right. I've been wrong about everything. We've all been wrong about everything." Marcello walks into the water after her. As he takes her into his arms, he asks, "Sylvia, Sylvia, who are you?" And then, the screenplay continues, "She lifts her hand from the water and holds it over his head, letting the drops fall like a blessing."

But of course by day the vision fades, and all those images disappear. In their topsy-turvy sweet-life world, things stop by day, do not begin at day. "The sound of the water dies away, and now it stops. . . . It is daybreak. . . . They step apart and begin to move slowly out of the pool." A bicycler who is just beginning his day stops to stare at these two mythic fountain creatures who are just ending theirs. In the real world of *La Dolce Vita* which Marcello now re-enters at daybreak, there is no mythical Sylvia for him. Instead of the mythic, the episode ends with the phony. Marcello is beat-up by Robert, in a fight arranged for

i. 11. Baptism in the Trevi.

the cameras of the photographers. Marcello probably never could answer Cerusico's mocking question that ends the episode: "Now Marcello, what happened?"

The Mistress

Maddalena and Sylvia had been antitheses, of ennui and activity, of perverse reality and of pagan, Christian, and natural illusion. But they had not been a fulfillment of Marcello's quest. Neither is Emma, Marcello's fiancée.

We meet Emma throughout the film. We get to know her in several scenes. As the woman with whom Marcello lives, the one to whom he returns, she is a part of his life and not just an episode. She first appears between the Maddalena and Sylvia episodes. Emma is neither perverse nor mythic. The environment of Emma is not a whore's bed nor Pagan/Christian Rome. Her setting is the unfinished newness of Marcello's apartment, with its hard and unrelenting verticals. (i. 12) And the setting of Emma is also the cold, blocklike, impersonal hospi-

i. 12. Emma in Marcello's apartment: the emptiness of the domestic.

tal, empty and echoing, where she is taken after she attempts suicide. In the hospital, even the lights stab out in hard diamond shapes. No evocation of the corrupt here, and surely not of the mythic. Emma is totally, even prosaically, realistic.

Emma also imposes herself into the midst of the Sylvia episode. The reality of Emma intrudes upon the mythology of Sylvia. Emma phones Marcello during the Sylvia press conference. With one ear, Marcello half listens to the naggings of Emma, while he scrupulously tries to take down on a note pad every word spoken by Sylvia. Emma threatens: "If I come there, I'll tear your eyes out." Emma pleads: "Marcello, why don't you come home now?" Emma offers the bed: "I want to make love." And Emma offers the kitchen: "Shall I make a nice dish of ravioli?"

In her several appearances, Emma offers Marcello the kind of love which, just because of its realism, appears to him as limiting, stifling, consuming. The first time that Emma appears, at the moment of her attempted suicide, we hear Marcello's frantic question, "Do you want to ruin me?" On the way to the field of the miracle, Emma mothers Marcello. Throughout the film, Emma longs for a child; and so she makes a child out of Marcello. She nags him to eat eggs when he doesn't like eggs; she forces him to eat a banana and even gives him directions on how to chew it. During the miracle scene, Emma treats Marcello like a possession, praying to the Virgin "that he be all mine." During their fight on the highway outside Rome, Marcello tells Emma: "I don't believe in this aggressive, sticky, maternal love of yours. I don't want it. I can't use it. This isn't love." But as the only stable force in Marcello's life, the only encounter which isn't casual, the only one to whom he continually returns, Emma is able to ask all the right questions: "What will you do with your life? . . . What do you want? What are you looking for?" She goes so far as to ask the Gelsomina question: "Who will stay with you if I leave you?" Emma explicitly connects Marcello with the quest imagery of the film, as she accurately diagnoses his trouble: "It's you who've lost the right path."

While fifteen bright lights from a tall tower shine down, Marcello and Emma begin to tell each other the truth. There is much illumination in the fury of their brightly lighted nighttime fight scene. Wise Steiner had told Emma that Marcello is not able to love himself. Now she tries to pass on that same wisdom to Marcello: "You haven't the slightest idea what it means to love somebody." "You have," Emma concludes, "a closed and empty heart." Emma is able not only to describe Marcello's current loveless condition, but she is able to predict accurately his future: "You'll end up all alone like a dog." But Emma's proposed solution is too narrow: "Marcello, when two people love one another, the rest doesn't matter." Marcello is looking for something broader than the realism of the bedroom and the kitchen, and so his response to Emma is fear. "I'm afraid of you!" he screams at Emma. "I'm afraid of your selfishness, of the poverty of your ideals! . . . Do you understand that a man who accepts a life like that is through?" Human, possessive, realistic love—narrowly domestic and inward turning—is not enough.

So three kinds of man-woman relationships are discovered by Marcello to be unfulfilling, to give no stable sense of private self in this world of public frenzy. He rejects woman as whore, woman as goddess, and woman as mother/wife. One of the wonderfully Italianate (and Felliniesque) aspects of *La Dolce Vita* is that as Marcello searches for purpose, beautiful women play the major roles.

The Miracle

But if not in woman, where else would an Italian—or anybody—look for meaning? Perhaps in religion? "Which way to the miracle?" is a line toward the beginning of the third episode. Marcello, Paparazzo and Emma approach the field of the miracle in Marcello's Triumph sports car. They find not a religious event, but a show. A workman pounds stakes into the ground. He is raising a tent. Performers, spectators, the lame and the halt, and especially the professionals of public exposure, are here in force. Can the true meaning of religion be found here in this false atmosphere? "Miracles are born out of solitude and silence," a priest responds, "and not in chaos like this." Chaos instead of silence is the stuff, this film has been showing us, of the sweet life. This is a life without privacy or solitude or silence. Without order. Certainly without real religion.

On a field in the country where one might expect the order of nature, Fellini creates astonishing visual chaos. Throughout this episode, the camera anxiously reflects the changing moods of the manipulated crowd. Fellini proves that his camera can manipulate us. It spirals its way up the stairs of the police station as Marcello's henchmen seek the miraculous children. It circles around in confusion as the giggling children continually change directions, chasing the media Madonna. Then the sun leaves and the heavens seem to comment on the falseness of the mirracle by dispersing the crowd with what should be a cleansing rain. The camera pans slowly as it surveys the scene. We don't just see an anonymous crowd. We recognize suffering individuals. As is typical in Fellini crowd scenes, we are arrested by a particular face, we notice an individualized gesture. But the camera coldly moves on. The rain becomes a deluge, a judgment. Fellini masterfully alters the mood from circus to hell. Where once the circus brought communal life, this circus brings only individual destruction and death. When the rain begins, a technician shouts, "Kill all the lights. Kill everything."

Even reality is destroyed during the miracle episode. Reality is shown as rearranged, rehearsed, staged. The Sylvia episode had first shown us that modern life and its emotions are mere performances. After Sylvia's first appearance on top of the steps of the airliner, Edna, Sylvia's public relations assistant, had commented, "That's good, smile. Smile." And then Sylvia and Edna had gone back inside the plane so as to perform the entrance over again for the photographers. Similarly, at the news conference, Sylvia had inquired, "What's the answer to that, Edna?" when she was asked, "What was the happiest day of your life?" The prepared answer, as one might guess, was "It was a night, dear." All of this artifice reaches its climax here at the miracle episode, for the miracle itself is an artificial creation of the media. (i. 13) We watch rehearsals of groups of actors brought in for the cameras; and we watch the performances of the mother, father, grandfather, uncle, and finally of the two children themselves. "Cry! Cry!" Paparazzo shouts to the mother as she speaks of her children. And

i. 13. Modern religion: the miracle as media event.

throughout the scene, the neon ad "Argon" flashes its commercial message in the background. The priest comments on the whole: "It's an indecent hoax." Emma is shocked at the manipulation of the innocent believers by the cynical merchants of the new chaos. She screams at the photographer, "You don't respect anybody." And she receives the expected answer, "I'm only doing my job." So is Marcello.

Religion has been replaced by publicity. The supernatural answer which once, in this ancient Italy, had been born in silence and solitude, no longer exists, at least for Marcello, the reporter of the sweet life. Marcello is not present when Marianne, the strange white-haired prophetess figure, says to Emma, "If you look for God, you find Him everywhere." Marcello is off taking notes on the miracle. In his wrong-headed aspiration, he climbs up a TV tower; the image is one of ascent, but he is surrounded by the press and the paparazzi who shout "Hold it!" at a world which they know can no longer be held, a world which zooms dizzily ahead and around. What the photographers capture when their pictures seem to stop reality is not reality; the frozen image is as much of an illusion as those several other illusions and aspirations that variously mislead Marcello.

At dawn after the miracle scene, we see the covered corpse, not cured by a miracle but killed by the chaos. We hear the priest intoning, "De profundis clamava a te, Domini." And the screenplay describes the conclusion of this episode: "Across the valley, the hills are dark against the sky. The field of the miracle lies deserted, but on the road a long procession of trucks, like a traveling circus, carries the television and movie equipment back to Rome."

The Saint

Marcello has not been able to find—either in the city or in the country—the realities of ancient religion. The fourth episode is to begin the examination of the new religion of secular humanism. Steiner's party—a quiet and natural and ordered secular celebration— follows the unnatural and chaotic miracle episode. Steiner becomes, for Marcello, a model of the secular saint.

In two separate appearances, in a church and at a gathering of friends, Steiner is, both visually and verbally, held out to be Marcello's best hope. Unlike the other characters, Steiner is not seen travelling; he is neither coming nor going. He has arrived where Marcello wants to be. He is found by Marcello in a quiet church, in the kind of place of solitude and silence in which miracles are born. And he is later found in his ordered artistic home, among loving wife, children, and friends.

Steiner first appears in a brief scene interposed immediately after the Sylvia episode. Within the frantic world of speed and flashing lights and mechanical noise, Steiner is discovered in mellow half-light, in a quiet church whose soft arches are the most gentle lines that we have seen so far in the film. In a whisper, Marcello and Steiner greet each other warmly, indicating the most genuine affection that we have witnessed so far in the film. The camera is as restrained as the church is quiet. The camera holds Marcello and Steiner in a perfectly balanced two-shot. Steiner carries a book, a permanent kind of literature, as contrasted with the ephemeral nature of Marcello's journalism. The antiquity of Steiner's book is emphasized: In the published screenplay, the book is a Sanskrit grammar; in the dubbed English version, the book is called "a very old volume, written by Italian monks." Steiner asks Marcello about his literature, not about his journalism: "How is your book going?" In reply, we see what the screenplay describes: "Marcello's face shows concern and unhappiness about his personal life, and it is painful for him to answer Steiner's questions about his work. But Steiner, with warm friendliness, expresses hope, and above all, kindliness." Steiner tells Marcello that he had recognized, in an article which Marcello had written, that which is "the best of you, that quality you keep on hiding but which is, after all, really you." Perhaps Steiner will be able to locate the "really you" of Marcello.

The camera, once more in that familiar searching and aspiring figure, spirals up the stairs, as it follows Steiner and Marcello into the organ loft. Steiner moves to the organ and plays music of pure and lovely organized form—a Bach fugue—patterned sounds entering the world which Marcello has viewed as formless and disjointed. These musical sounds are important, Steiner insists, precisely because they are natural sounds, "the sounds we have forgotten how to hear," sounds that come "from the bowels of the earth." A searching close-up of Marcello shows the intense effect that form and naturalness have on Marcello. He is as moved by the sudden order brought by the music as was Gelsomina by the sudden music of the tiny band that appeared in the sunny field. But Gelsomina moved along, spontaneously following the music, dancing with the music, which seemed to appear just for her. Marcello cannot move. His joy at the ordered sounds apparently turns to disappointment at the disordered reality of his life, and he turns his back on Steiner and his music. This short scene ends when the screen fades into black. But we do remember that Steiner had invited Marcello to come visit him in his home. Marcello had told Steiner, "I trust you." We wonder now, as this scene in the church fades out, what Steiner will do with that trust.

Perhaps in Steiner's own home Marcello will be able to find that which proved elusive in the church. Steiner was only a visitor in the church. He is at home amidst his family, within his gathering of friends. When Marcello goes to Steiner's home, Steiner is again, both visually and verbally, connected with order and form. The first shot after the miracle episode is the beautiful smiling face of Anna, Steiner's wife, who opens the door and admits us, along with Marcello and Emma, into the lovely apartment. Anna welcomes us directly, looking right into our eyes. No speeding vehicle has introduced this episode. The door simply opens, and Marcello exclaims, "What a beautiful apartment!" The first background sounds that are heard are the chanting notes of the lovely Indian woman. The Steiners' apartment is another visual confirmation of Marcello's growing assurance that here, in this natural, ordered, intellectual, traditional, artistic, family group is the answer to life's meaning, and his real self. Except for the church, where Steiner appeared for the first time, and this apartment, where Steiner appears for the second time, all the rooms that we see in this film are either old, in which case they are crumbling, rotten, decayed, or they are new, in which case they are unfinished, bare, flooded. But the Steiners' home, on which the camera lingers lovingly, is warm, comfortable, ordered. Anna, as hostess, gets everyone comfortably placed. The guests become as perfectly ordered as the furniture. The camera pulls back to admire the patterned scene. (i. 14)

The party itself is a work of art, with Anna guiding the placement of the people, and with Steiner guiding the conversation. All of the guests—identified as a painter, a poet, a traveller—seek the certainty of art. Steiner remarks, "One might say that art has left nothing to chance." In this atmosphere, so antithetical to everything represented by the sweet life, so antithetical to everything that we have seen and heard so far in this film, Marcello shows his first enthusiasm. It is an enthusiasm that reawakens Marcello's search. He puts aside his typical bored observer stance. "How I envy you," Marcello says to Repaci, one of Steiner's guests. "How I'd like to travel too!"

The solutions posited by Steiner's guests not only involve the order and certainty of art and the adventure of the journey, but also the purity of nature. "We really have a great deal to learn from these magnificent Oriental women," declares Repaci, "because, you see, they have kept close to nature." Steiner admires that same natural quality in Repaci himself: "He still has the freshness of a child." Just as, in the church, Steiner and Marcello had admired the primitive natural sounds of the organ, so now, at the party, they all admire the primitive natural sounds on the tape recorder. "Why did you record them?" asks Mar-

i. 14. Steiner's party: the harmony of the secular saint.

cello. "Because I found them beautiful," is Steiner's simple reply. As the sounds of thunder, of the sea, of the birds at daybreak, of wind in the trees, are repeated on the tape recorder, Marcello bows his head, moved, just as he had been at the similar sounds of Bach on the organ. Then Steiner's children appear, as if summoned by the sounds of nature. Steiner's little son seems to be the creature of nature: "When you give him a flower he turns it all around, looking at it, and then suddenly he laughs." And thus is Steiner's daughter the creature of reason: "What she loves best are words and the construction of phrases."

The high priest of all this secular perfection is Steiner himself. The guest named Iris tells Steiner: "You are the true primitive. Primitive as a Gothic steeple. You're so high that our voices grow faint in trying to reach up to you." It is *that* toward which Marcello aspires. And those key words are repeated on the tape recorder, just as the sounds of nature are, so that we can hear them twice. We will eventually hear them a third time, and we will begin to doubt their truth, just as we will be forced to rethink this whole scene. But for now we are made to believe the words, the sounds, the people, the mood, as Marcello does.

Marcello, in this Steiner scene, seems to be close to the truth about himself. As in the church, he is once more asked about his literature. "Have you finished your book," Anna wants to know, "yes or no?" Marcello expresses doubt about his journalism: "Now I'm doing work I dislike." He asks himself, "Will I ever accomplish anything?" Toward the end of this episode, Marcello concludes, "I'm wasting my time." The lesson that Marcello now learns from Steiner is explicitly stated: "I should change my environment," Marcello declares. "I should change so many things. You know, your home is a real sanctuary. Your children, your wife, your friends—they're all so wonderful."

In the final scene of the episode, Marcello follows Steiner as he visits his sleeping children. On the soundtrack, we hear steady heartbeats. Marsha Kinder and Beverly Houston express well the mood of this moment: The children are peacefully sleeping "behind filmy gauze curtains, as if to shelter them in perfect sanctuary from the hidden danger of chaos."[31] The audience expects, along with Marcello, that the model life, one in which the self can be discovered in peace and safety, has finally been found in the human virtues of Steiner. Marcello has been given his opportunity to follow that model. Steiner has offered, "If you want me to help you change your circumstances, I can introduce you to people. . . . Would you like to think about that?" We do think about that. But does Marcello? He seems to know that he must investigate a few more possible roads. We cut away from the Steiner episode so that Marcello can hear a message from the provinces. But the film will return to Steiner and to the climactic message that this secular saint—one of the many Fellini messengers—finally brings to Marcello.

The Provinces

The fifth episode brings Marcello's father from the provinces to Rome. The episode opens on the Via Veneto, the new *strada*. This is the Rome of the sweet life. The camera seems both overpowered and exhilarated by it. It looks around excitedly, like an outsider who can't take in quickly enough all of the Via Veneto's glitter. Fellini has written:

> In the screenplay for *La Strada*, there was a sequence which I never used, which expressed my highly personal view of Via Veneto. Zampano's motor-bike arriving from the Pincio sweeps down the slope of Via Veneto, sputtering and popping; from inside, behind half-open, swaying curtains, Gelsomina looks out, wide-eyed, at the lights, the illuminated signs, the palm-trees and the cafes.[32]

We watch now, in *La Dolce Vita*, with Gelsomina's eyes, as the Via Veneto performs its magic in front of us. All is pandemonium: a crush of people fills the sidewalk; a crush of cars fills the street; the camera searches for individuals through the mass of people and through the cars, moving and parked, three deep. The published screenplay describes the scene: "Via Veneto is full of people and lights. . . . It is the same crowd, always changing, always the same."

Somewhere alone within that crowd, Marcello is told, sits his father, waiting. The provincial innocent, like Gelsomina, like Marcello/ Moraldo once was, has come to the city. Marcello finds his father. In order to explain why he no longer sees nor writes to his parents, why he seems to have lost connection with his past, Marcello explains to his father something of the frenzy of his current life, as symbolized by this Roman street: "The trouble is, there's always so much going on around here." Marcello's work gives him no more stable point than does his personal life. The Via Veneto is the street of work as well as the street of play. "We work right here," Marcello explains. He points out the instability: "You know, father—my kind of work takes me all over, keeps me on the run all day long."

If Marcello is too busy running, within the bustle of the sweet life, to return to the provinces, then the provinces, and Marcello's past, now come to him. In the midst of all this movement, we expect to hear an idyllic picture of the simple life of the provinces. Perhaps, in the simpler days of *La Strada*, that would have been the message brought to Marcello by his father. But no more. The episode of the father's visit tells Marcello, instead, that he can't go home again. Home isn't really there. In a gently emotional example of the changes wrought by time, Marcello and his father briefly touch, each feels a sympathy for the life of the other, and yet each returns to his own place of isolation and boredom.

The simple sadness of this episode seems to be Fellini's own. Marcello's father is indeed patterned after Fellini's father: "His character is faithfully reproduced in *La Dolce Vita*," Angelo Solmi tells us. "It is a portrait which reflects Italian provincial sanity, its traditional common sense and modest desires."[33] The episode of a father's visit from the provinces was in Fellini's mind for a long time: it comes straight from the plan for "Moraldo in Citta."[34] Fellini, Moraldo, and Marcello all meet their father in Rome.

Marcello's father loves the excitement of the Via Veneto, and compares it with the deadening boredom of the provinces, where "at this hour everything is dark, so sad." At home, the father concludes, "there's nothing to do." The Kit Kat nightclub seems to Marcello's father more exciting than even the Via Veneto. At the Kit Kat, which he had visited in his youth, he meets the charming Fanny, and what seems to him all gaiety and life. Fellini's camera is more objective. We see the nightclub as sleazy and sad. We hear Paparazzo's muttered comment about the Kit Kat: "It looks like a tomb." We see that the sparkling lights are caused by the cheap spangles in the plastic decor.

And yet, on this night, the Kit Kat is a place where the sad and the gay mix; just as it is a place where age and youth meet for a moment, where the provinces and the city touch. (i. 15) The Kit Kat is the world of the circus, introduced by magical Nino Rota circus music. We watch and listen while "the clown walks slowly, playing his sad song." We see the loneliness and loss on the face of the clown, but we hear his pretty tune. We may well agree with Fanny's apparent contradiction: "He's so beautiful. I always want to cry when I see him." The clown is reminiscent of Gelsomina; as he plays his trumpet, kicking up his heels in a perfect Gelsomina gesture, he greets Marcello with a wonderfully knowing and understanding look—sad but surrounded by balloons. The clown introduces early the wistful note on which the episode of the father's visit will end.

i. 15. Fanny and Father at the Kit Kat: youth and age; city and provinces.

In this old nightclub of the happy and the sad, the search imagery begins again. Marcello tries in still another sense to find his father. When he was a boy, Marcello tells Paparazzo, he almost never saw his father. And now, he complains, "I hardly know him." Perhaps tonight will start something new: "How happy I was tonight to see him." Marcello treats his father with kindness and with care. He is proud of him, but worried about him. He seems to be approaching him.

The father, too, is seen as a searcher. For a moment, the Kit Kat does make him young again. It brings back his days in Paris, and the days when he travelled, selling champagne to half of Italy. The chorus girls even seem to cooperate in his fantasy. They come bouncing out, wearing the flapper dresses and cloche hats of his youth. Fanny says that she cannot believe that he could be Marcello's father: "You're too young." He seems to agree: "I could show these boys a thing or two." Fanny tells him that he is, indeed, like his son.

But the sadness of the setting, the faded joy of the sleazy nightclub, wins out. Neither Marcello's hopes, going toward the future, nor his father's nostalgia, going toward the past, can bring them together. Reality penetrates even the Kit Kat. The father remembers that he is no longer a traveller: "Do you know what makes us old? Boredom! When I travelled, I felt like a lion. . . . But when I have to sit home—then I feel like a man 80 years old. The life of neither father nor son has anything to teach the other; boredom is at the center of each. The two searchers—father and son—pass as they come toward each other. They may touch briefly, but they are unable to know one another. The father decides to go to Fanny's apartment; the son decides to go to work.

The fifth episode ends with intimations of mortality. Fanny meets Marcello on the street and tells him that his father is ill. Marcello spirals up the stairs toward Fanny's apartment, worried about his father, hoping to encounter him still. But the camera tells us what to expect instead. It catches Marcello through bannister slats, separating, distancing. Inside Fanny's apartment, the suddenly static camera frames the father within an enclosing doorway. He is sitting in a chair, looking out toward the now-dark city. With his back turned toward Marcello, the father says, "Put out the light." He has had a heart attack. The composition is all vertical and horizontal, all static. As Marcello approaches his father, they don't face each other, and they don't face the camera. We see only their backs. They are separated from each other. We, too, are shut out. Marcello tries to make contact. He pleads, "Stay here with me tomorrow—please. We can be together all day and talk. We never see one another." But the father can only reply, now that he has tasted the sweet life of the city: "I want to go home." Home may stave off eternity: "I'm still in time," he insists with desperation. "Yes, yes, I've still got time." He asks for his watch. The tick-tock of time is heard loud on the soundtrack.

The nearness of death sends Marcello's father back home, to another kind of death, from another kind of boredom. As father and son leave Fanny's apartment, the camera catches two shadows withdrawing. Just at daybreak, Marcello is left alone, still not having known his father, his present in no way illuminated by his past, the city in no way cleansed by the provinces. Shrunken by a high camera shooting down from Fanny's window, Marcello stands small and isolated as his father's taxi pulls away. Marcello is x'd into the cross-streets of a dark and empty section of Rome. He is far from the glitter of the Via Veneto; he is in a deserted section of Rome generalized by its name of "Italia." Marcello is as alone here as his father was in the crowd scene that began this episode. Fanny had said in jest to Marcello's father, "Take him back home." But Marcello knows that there is nowhere to go.

The Revels

And so he goes to a party. That is good Fellini doctrine. Parties are communal celebrations; like processions, perhaps they can give a relief from isolation. The sixth episode will take Marcello on a journey to a party in an old world which is new to him. His father's impending death, and thus Marcello's separation from his own past, increases his urgency to find something durable. This journey starts from the same spot as the last journey. It ends not in Marcello's provincial past, but in the strange and exotic world of the aristocrats of Rome. It is a trip through their present and their past. Perhaps the old aristrocratic order can bring something lasting to Marcello.

The first sound that we hear in this episode is a gong—with the Via Veneto's "Air India" sign blinking in the background—suggesting that this will be a long and exotic trip. Marcello, looking out the window of a Jaguar, goes along for the ride. Marcello, the beautiful blonde Swede named Nico, Oliviero, and assorted other aristrocrats enter the grounds of the Castle of Bassano di Sutri in their fancy new car, which spirals up the drive toward a decaying monument to the dying, old aristocracy. To lend reality to this highly symbolic scene, Fellini cast several real but tired-looking aristocrats—Prince Vadim Wolkonsky, Doris Pignatelli, Eugenio Ruspoli—as representatives of the remnants of their class.

Marcello is now embarked on his second-to-the-last episode. In the haunted surroundings of Bassano, the death imagery, which was an undercurrent in the episode with his father, finally comes to dominate. Marcello, in his search, is getting closer and closer to death. As their car approaches the castle, Oliviero announces, "The parties at our house are like first-class funerals." And, indeed, when they arrive, "The party is almost dead."

During what is left of the party, death and the lost past continually are invoked—in the person of the guests, in the talk, in the events, and in the images. Antequera, the sinister-looking man with the black patch over his eye and the black cloak over his shoulders, who will later be compared to Torquemada, the grand inquisitor, is introduced while enthusiastically describing a peasant funeral. Ghosts become the main topic of conversation. "Come on, darlings," shouts Jane, "We are going to hunt ghosts." In a most Felliniesque parody of a religious procession, the acolytes carry elaborate baroque candelabra, spreading flickering light over half-lit castle, garden, and neighboring villa. (i. 16) It is a much more sinister procession than the one in *La Strada*. Earlier, Nico had told a story about ghosts attacking her. Doris had told of an apparition in her sister-in-law's castle. Ivenda warns Irene to run into his arms if they see a ghost. In the séance, Ivenda invokes the spirit of Sister Edvige, "who walks through these rooms all summer with her head in a dish." Federica, "in the throes of possession," screams out her fear of death.

The images are of the past. Looking on in the background as the aristocrats lazily dance by are "massive busts of ancient Roman senators and emperors." The setting is a modern Baths of Caracalla. These deathly ghost-hunters of today are the successors of the ancient Roman dignitaries. This is the family which has had two Popes among its ancestors. A long corridor in the castle is filled with paintings of dead "grandmothers and great-great-grandmothers." Maddalena appears, with the same eyes as the ancestors in the paintings. Another woman, bizarrely costumed, is told by Marcello: "It's as if you had just stepped out of a painting." Marcello is hunting for sources: "What language are you speaking? Where are you from?" he had asked Nico with some anxiety. In a playful mood, as if answering his question, Nico later appears in a knight's helmet, making ghostly sounds and announcing: "I am your ancestor." Eric Rhode's description of the decaying castle setting is accurately evocative:

> The castle at Bassano di Sutri, shrouded by night, with its Roman busts and its hollow stone rooms, is the scene for a cult of the dead. . . . Aristrocrats, some of them slumbering, some of them dancing as though drugged, rise up like totems— enchanted, burdened by some abstracted despair for which their ancestors alone know the reason.[35]

i. 16. Hunting the ghosts of the past: the aristocrats spiral up the stairs at Bassano di Sutri.

The current aristocrats and their current setting partake of the corruption and decay which underlie the death imagery of the past. Because Maddalena is one of them, she is able to introduce the other corrupted aristocrats to outsider Marcello: "Federica the she-wolf . . . she likes to suckle the young. . . . The Gonfaloniera. . . . They own half of Calabria and the finest whorehouses in Rome. . . . Little Eleanore . . . 80,000 acres, two attempts at suicide. . . ." As Maddalena speaks, the aristocrats float by Fellini's camera, as though on a treadmill. Irene talks ironically about "the stupid and corrupt aristocracy." And Giulio, the heir to the castle, knows himself and his guests and their kind: "There's rats and bugs here, snakes, and even vampires. And now it's full of whores." The most beautiful Maddalena, whose own corruption we had seen in episode one, recognizes her connection with this place. She compares herself with the architecture. "The villa," she says, "is architecturally the most beautiful. But it's empty. And I too am empty."

A mock religious procession winds its way through the night to the nearby abandoned villa. A spiraling camera mounts the stairs. The villa matches the people who now invade it. In one mere paragraph of description, the words used in the published screenplay to characterize the villa are "decay," "dark," "cobwebbed," "neglected," "rotted," "mildew," "dust," and "empty." The camera shows all that. The Prince, the owner of the villa, concludes metaphorically, "What a ruin. Everything falling to pieces." The aristocrats have no durable answer for Marcello, or for themselves.

Within this deathly setting, Marcello and Maddalena try again—hopelessly, of course—for some permanent relationship. Maddalena tries to speak to Marcello. But to do so, she places him in another room, floats away from him, in a beautifully unreal gliding motion, and then speaks toward him, through a fountain, from her separate room. This is "the chamber of serious discourse." She tells him that she wants to marry him. She tells him that she loves him. And he responds with hollow echoing words of love. He concludes, "I'd like to be with you always," the words bouncing against the bare marble walls in the empty room. But throughout this stunning scene, as we hear these words of intimacy, we see Marcello alone, and then Maddalena alone, and then the one, and then the other, each in his separate room, speaking the words of love into empty air.

Maddalena tells the distant Marcello that she has "lost the power of choosing." In 8½ and in *Juliet of the Spirits*, as he had done in *La Strada* and had planned to do in "The Free Women of Magliano," Fellini tells us that choice is the saving human quality. Without choice, Maddalena

concludes, "I'm nothing but a slut. That's all I am. I'll never be anything but a slut." And she sits passively as she is pawed by a handsome
newcomer, proving it.

Before this aristocrats' episode, we had seen Maddalena one more
time after she and Marcello drove away from the whore's house in the
first episode. When Marcello was trying to find a place to be alone with
Sylvia, he had phoned Maddalena, wanting to use Maddalena's house
precisely as, together, she and Marcello had used the whore's house.
We saw, when Maddalena answered the phone, that her imagery was
imprisoning. She sat enclosed behind bars in a deep fishnet of a chair,
her eyes searching out toward the camera. Now, at the aristocrats'
party, Maddalena's eyes are again searching, but she herself is seen
again as imprisoned. But now ultimately so. Marcello says, "I don't
understand you." Maddalena replies, "I don't understand myself."
When we first met Maddalena, she was restless. Now she has de-
scended into total passivity: "It's as if I no longer existed." When
Maddalena speaks these words of final negation, she is starkly enclosed within an inverted "V" of light, pinioned against the wall in the
harsh glare.

Marcello is moving toward the condition of Maddalena. He says to
the empty air, intending the words for Maddalena, "I truly need you."
As Maddalena drifts off with the handsome newcomer, Marcello says,
from his isolated chamber, "You'd be a marvelous companion because
one can tell you everything." She isn't listening to what he is telling
her. Maddalena has disappeared. "Maddalena" he calls, "Can you
hear me? Answer me." After a halfhearted effort to find Maddalena,
Marcello joins the others, and he forgets his need. "Who is Maddalena?" asks Oliviero. We will never see her again. It's as if Maddalena has truly ceased to exist.

Marcello tries to pick up Doris, the woman who looks as if she had
stepped out of a painting. Then, during the séance, Jane, who is
popular because of her dirty stories, leads Marcello to fornication on a
broken dusty old bed. Marcello's imagery becomes as imprisoning as
Maddalena's had been. By the faint light of a match, we see the
shadows of bars behind the linked hands of Jane and Marcello. And the
design on their decaying four-poster bed is a spiral, leading only to
darkness. The single faint light goes out, as Jane blows out the match
that had led them to the abandoned bed.

At daybreak we see once more a procession of the worshippers of La
Dolce Vita. The Dies Irae now sounds out most clearly from Nino Rota's
conflicting tunes. We see the cult of those who live in the death of the
night. The scene is described in the published screenplay:

> The first light of morning is in the sky, and a fresh wind brings
> the sound of distant bells. In the park of Bassano di Sutri
> hooded figures may be seen in solemn procession . . . their
> heads bowed in meditation like members of some silent sect
> . . . The guests of Prince Mascalchi are returning from their
> all–night revels.

The procession of one ancient cult is soon mirrored by the procession
of another ancient cult. The Prince's mother, with priests and altar
boys, leads the Prince and his three sons off to morning Mass. We are
left with a shot of the rotting bridge, separating the two processions.
Earlier, the Prince had warned: "Giulio, tell them to be careful. You
know the little bridge is rotted through." Marcello stays behind. He
separates himself from both liturgies. He has one more ritual to fulfill
before he comes to the end of his journey.

Death

The Steiner episode is divided into three parts: the church, the party,
and now the suicide. As in *La Dolce Vita* as a whole, the time in the
Steiner episode is alternating: the three parts take place at day, at
night, and then again at day. Within this structure, Marcello's last and
best hope begins, grows, and dies. Death entered *La Dolce Vita* as a
suggestion of a fact to come. It was first connected with faithful
miracle-seekers and then with a simple man from the provinces. Then
it spread to sophisticated aristocrats who combined in themselves the
corruption of ancient and modern Rome. Now death is pervasive. It
becomes literal as well as figurative.

Part three of the Steiner episode begins with Marcello and Emma in
bed together. It is the morning after their fight in the road. And with
the dawn comes the news of death: the phone rings. Steiner has
murdered his two children and has killed himself.

Marcello rushes to Steiner's apartment, and he begins, like always,
to spiral up the stairs. Then suddenly he stops and looks up: "The
staircase curls around and around like the shell of a snail." That
striking composition, as it is described in the published screenplay,
tells us that the film is at a climax. Closed in at the dead center of the
spiral, as Marcello looks up toward Steiner's apartment and anonymous faces look down on Marcello, is a single fact. Steiner's suicide
awaits Marcello at the top of those stairs. That death becomes the
central fact of Marcello's life. And it is thus the central fact of the film.

i. 17. The stairs leading to Steiner's death: the end of aspiration.

The movements and the counter-movements of the film stop. The frenzy, the zooming camera, the quick cutting all stop. Fellini holds us for a long static moment on the new design: The spiral of the curling staircase has turned itself into an enclosed unmovable spot. (i. 17) The film shows no more aspiration. For over two hours, Fellini has built up a rhythm. That rhythm now comes to a halt. No motion. The single fixed fact is that Steiner has killed himself, and he has thus killed Marcello's hope. Steiner has killed his children, and he has thus killed both nature and reason. All the motion of the film, and all of its quests, have lead Marcello and us to this dead end. It is an unmoving spot.

Once inside the apartment, the stunned Marcello walks again to the terrace where Steiner and he had talked privately during the party. Behind them, when Steiner was alive, searchlights had stabbed the darkness and had intersected. The sounds of nature had filled their ears. Visible on the screen, and clear and obvious to us, was the illumination, nature, order that Marcello saw Steiner to be. Now that Steiner is dead, in the distance behind that same terrace looms strange and forbidding futuristic architecture. A water tower looks like a mushroom cloud. The only sounds are some kind of electronic or metallic clatter. Fellini doesn't even bother to explain the source of the noises. Here at the climax, as in the framing scenes that begin and close the film, Fellini moves away from realism. Marcello turns away from the terrace to see the disorder and publicity of death. The chaos in the apartment now is in stark contrast to its harmony when last we saw it. Now Marcello sees the scrambling policemen, a white-coated medic, photographers, detectives, going through Steiner's books, reading his manuscripts, listening to his tape recorder. The camera, distracted and disordered, cuts people in half, doesn't seem to know—in its uncertainty and dread—where to focus.

The death of Steiner is the fact of the film that holds most firmly in our memories. "Why did Steiner kill himself and his children?" This is the question most asked of *La Dolce Vita*. Surely Fellini doesn't want that question to be easily answerable. The life of the secular saint is the answer that our society at its best most often posits in response to our baffling quests for meaning. We want the life chosen by Steiner to be the answer. It is hard for most viewers of the film to accept the fact that, for Fellini, it is not. The suicide seems so arbitrary. Some facts of life, Fellini seems to suggest, are most puzzling simply because they do seem arbitrary. A deep mystery, and our protests, must remain. In our response to Steiner's suicide, we must share some of Marcello's bafflement and despair. Marcello says: "We'll never know."

Yet Fellini has been careful to plant some hints toward explanations. When we try to puzzle out the suicide and the murders, we begin to remember the hints that suggested to us that in Fellini's view Steiner was not the perfection that Marcello took him to be. Through the device of the tape recorder, Fellini has let us hear three times Steiner's own insistence that he was not the perfect model that his friends took him to be. Three times we have heard what his guests think of him: "You are the true primitive. Primitive as a Gothic steeple. You are so high that our voices grow faint in trying to reach up to you." They do think of him as a model high above them, seeing him as a true primitive, surely a good thing in this film's world of grotesque sophistication. They do think of him as a Gothic steeple, an admirable symbol of an ordered harmonious whole and of a period of time when life had meaning. A Gothic steeple is fulfilling shape—diagonals meeting at a point atop and above a world of disjointed, unstable, spiralling movements. But should we believe Steiner's guests? Some of them struck us as insincere. Some of them did remind us of other frightened people along the paths of the sweet life. Steiner's lady poet, who had insisted, "Don't choose," was soon to be echoed by Maddalena, who had found, "I'm not able to choose."

If we hear three times what Steiner's guests think of him, we also hear three times what Steiner thinks of himself: "If you saw me as I see myself, you would know that I am not any taller than that." When Steiner first appeared in the quiet church, he identified himself as the devil. Steiner had specifically warned Marcello not to do what he had done, not to "take refuge in yourself." The mere self is too little. Steiner had warned against the danger of being enclosed in the safe and certain, attractive as that might seem to be in this otherwise disordered and dangerous world. "Any life," Steiner had warned, "even the most miserable, is worth more than a sheltered existence in a world where everything is organized, everything is practical, everything has its place." That kind of world is the world of the sterile intellect, of the excessively planned, and thus not the real Fellini-endorsed world of vitality. Steiner's world is the world of nature transferred onto magnetic tape and thus isolated from the world of real nature. The perfection of Steiner's abstracted life is finally enclosing. In his search for order, Marcello was warned by Steiner not to enclose himself in *anything*, not even in the attractive order of Steiner's own life. That would be a withdrawal from life rather than an engagement with life. That would be to stop searching.

Steiner had told Marcello that he envied the freshness and optimism of Repaci; and when Steiner had said those words, his own face revealed a profound sadness, and a fear. After Steiner's death, when we are most deeply trying to puzzle out its reason, we are reminded—in the conversation on the street between Marcello and the police commissioner—that Steiner had been afraid of life, of himself, of us all. Perhaps Steiner was sad and fearful because he recognized that his little self was enclosed within virtues that he knew to be only limited human virtues. Steiner knew that he lacked the transcendent. Steiner's most solemn advice to Marcello was that "we should come to love one another outside of time, beyond time." Even with the perfected but still limited human virtues of the secular saint, there seems to be no salvation within time.

In the kind of life that Steiner held out as the ideal, rather than the life that he himself lived, we would expect to find some sort of answer: to be open, unenclosed, fearless, to continue to encounter, to continue to search for something durable, yet spontaneous, something outside of time. Fellini is not yet ready to show us anyone who is able to *do* that. He has not yet worked it out in his life and art, in Fellini's own search. He gave up "Moraldo in Citta" because he hadn't found the answer yet: "I did not make this film and I don't think I ever will, because I have not yet found this meaning of life myself and therefore I don't know what the conclusion of Moraldo's history might be."[36] Fellini did make *La Dolce Vita*, although he still was not able to show us conclusively how Marcello's history might end. To watch Fellini move closer toward a conclusion, we will have to watch him work through the agony and joy of *8½*. Then we will see Guido learning to do what Moraldo and Marcello didn't know how to do, what Steiner wanted to do but failed to do. In fear, Steiner had stopped searching because he saw himself enclosed in the orderly; in despair, Marcello is about to stop searching because he sees himself enclosed in chaos. Is there anything except these two kinds of surrender, these two kinds of death? We won't know until the final moments of this film. And we won't see the discovery of choice—of both freedom and life—until Fellini's next film.

In the meantime, Fellini keeps up his attack on the paparazzi who hover around the place where they expect Mrs. Steiner to arrive. Metaphors of devouring had already been used in this film to describe the photographers. The published screenplay had called them jackals; Emma had called them hyenas. Now the screenplay says, "They are waiting like vultures for the arrival of Mrs. Steiner." Fellini tells us that, as he planned the film, he "spent many evenings with the photographer-reporters of Via Veneto . . . getting them to tell me . . . how they fixed on their victim."[37] When Mrs. Steiner gets off her bus and steps into the cold, glaring, exposed geometric world of the EUR section of Rome, the paparazzi find their vulnerable victim. Flashbulbs go off in her face, and also in our faces. We seem to be as exposed as the vulnerable Mrs. Steiner. The photographers are taking pictures of us, invading our privacy too. There is no longer a place of escape or privacy or quiet. There is no longer a place for miracles, or even a place to mourn. A new weapon has destroyed another frontier. As Paparazzo comes toward us, his camera hangs at his hip like a gun in a holster, and the weapon fills the entire screen as the final third of the Steiner episode ends.

The End

In the script of "Moraldo in Citta," Fellini planned to have Moraldo despair after two key events: after a visit in Rome from his father, and after a party which fills him with disgust. After the party, Moraldo was to ask, "What am I looking for? What am I? What am I waiting for? What do I want?"[38] As the seventh and last episode of *La Dolce Vita*, Fellini now sends Marcello to such a party, where such questions would surely be in order if Marcello still cared enough to ask them. The party follows immediately upon Steiner's death and shows the desperation born of despair. Steiner's artificial rational order is succeeded by the orgy sequence. Paradoxically, the sexiest scene in international cinema up to 1960 is made into the most clearly boring in effect. "Having lost contact with the spiritual and natural world," explains Edward Murray, "having attempted to rationalize all experience, man has been left weighted with boredom."[39] When Fellini plumbs vice to its depth, he finds a glazed eye and a yawn.

The orgy episode begins more frantically than did any of the previous six. This time not just one speeding vehicle but "a pack of five or six cars are racing through the night." The screenplay describes the race:

> A white Thunderbird convertible pulls into the oncoming lane and races abreast of the lead car. The driver swings in close and the cars almost sideswipe, swerve wide, and come together again. The drivers shout and blow their horns as the first car drops back and the Thunderbird takes the lead. Now a Ferrari comes up on the outside and passes the whole string.

In the speeding cars, according to the screenplay, are "lawyers, dancers, millionaires, transvestites, hangers-on and whores, and they are racing down to Fregena for an all-night orgy in a beach villa." The denizens of the sweet life have all come out to play.

Marcello, no longer objective and no longer an observer, leads their games, as participant and even as organizer. The camera too is now involved, with lots of close shots and pans, and with no cold tracking shots. After Marcello breaks down the gate and throws a rock through the window, he offers his toast to get the party started: "A toast to the annulment of Nadia's marriage, to the annulment of her husband, to the annulment of everything!" In the scene that follows, everything is indeed annuled. The party celebrates the movement toward nothingness.

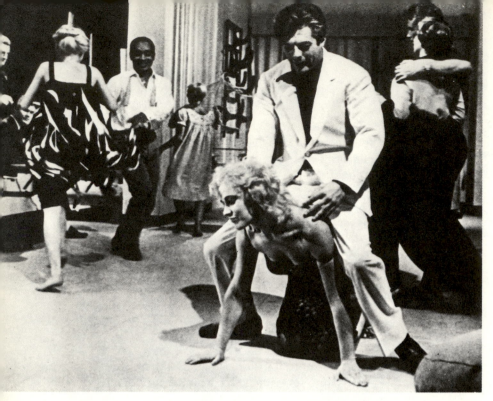

i. 18. Marcello as master of ceremonies.

Nadia, the guest of honor, is also the chief entertainer. Her striptease is boring and mechanical. Marcello, as master of ceremonies, announces the general mood: "I never saw such boring people. This party is a bore!" And Marcello is the most bored, and boring, of the lot. He seems not even entirely present: the edge of the screen cuts Marcello in half as he picks up the mink stole, looks at the naked Nadia lying beneath it, and gestures a mixture of disinterest and contempt. Similarly, the lawyer, not even looking at Nadia as she strips, and speaking of cars, comments as chorus, "It's a beautiful machine."

Themes and images from the earlier episodes reach their fullness at the orgy. We saw the theme of women metamorphosed into animals in the Kit Kat nightclub, when the clown with a whip forced a line of women in tiger costumes to perform their routine. We see the same theme now in the degradation of the girl from the provinces—from a place near Marcello's own hometown. She came to Rome to find her fortune. She tells us what she has found in Rome: "Nothing." Marcello rides her like a horse. (i. 18) He then asks, "Shall we make a beautiful big chicken out of you?" "I don't care, I don't care," the girl from the provinces whimpers as Marcello plasters her with feathers. "He's making a chicken out of this lady!" joyously shouts the dancer from Spoleto. The chicken lady howls like a dog.

Thus also does the degradation of Marcello continue. Laura, one of the girls at the party, calls Marcello a worm, repeating the word that Emma had used to describe him. Marcello's attitude toward himself just about matches that accusation. The lesbian dancer paints Marcello's face on a balloon; Marcello, in self-loathing, smashes his effigy with an empty liquor bottle. Marcello's career has degenerated. He once aspired to write literature. He had been a journalist. Now he calls for everyone's attention and makes an announcement: "I have left literature and journalism. I'm a publicity agent now." Laura editorializes for all: "I know that to make a living you have to take what comes along, but this is squalid." Marcello then proves how squalid it is. In the Sylvia episode, Marcello had refused rising bids to sell facts about Sylvia. Now Sernas, Marcello's master, makes his puppet dance: As Sernas continually raises the bid, Marcello suggests the succession of lies that he would be willing to tell, in an effort to sell his client. Toward the end of the party, held in a headlock by Sernas, Marcello delivers his drunken farewell: "I want to make a speech, thanking all my friends for the wonderful career they've helped me to achieve."

The composition in this episode shows us that the journey is ending. Marcello spirals up no stairs. Instead, he is frequently shown squeezed beneath a hanging staircase. He and the others are shown trapped by the strong vertical lines of a cagelike room divider.

Sacramental imagery, too, comes to a climax. The final orgy is a series of liturgies, as the baptisms, processions, dances, and parties have been throughout the film. During the orgy we see, first, confession. Nadia's lover, Ruggero, sits in a hooded wicker chair, "confessing Lucia" through a small, confessional-like hole in the side of the chair. Then, baptism. This time the sacrament of new beginning announces an ending, an annulment. Appropriately, the baptismal celebration is arranged by Marcello, the priest-celebrant throughout the scene: "The first strip will be in honor of our dear Nadia, to baptize her in her new life!" The orgy ends when each person dances a ritual recessional, dismissed by Marcello with a benediction of feathers. Nino Rota supplies the liturgical music. As always, he makes a major contribution to a Fellini film. His music for the recessional picks up once more the "sweet life theme," lush overripe music with the sweetness of decay.

As always, the episode ends when day breaks. Dawn, always returning but without showing progress, is, once more, a dead moment. Domino, one of the transvestites, sums up the Fellini view: "The light reveals all our flaws." He has the last word in the narrative part of the film. A kind of coda is about to begin.

The Visionary Frame

The inhabitants of La Dolce Vita now stand, in clumps, yet scattered, separated by pine trees, with sunlight casting long shadows on the ground. Something has happened. The tone is different. The light is less realistic. The characters leave their automobiles, they turn to the right, they turn to the left, they begin a dance to the sea, inter-weaving, asking questions as they move rhythmically toward the source of life. This is the last procession in the film. The words we hear most clearly are again those of Domino as he scampers along: "I've lost all interest in life. . . . I feel I must do penance. . . ."

The members of the ancient/modern cult now reach the sea. From the sea, a group of fishermen haul ashore a huge flabby fish, described in the screenplay as "a strange bloated monster that stares at us with dead, accusing eyes." One observer responds, "Oh, horrible!" Another responds, contradictorily, "My God, the splendor!" One says, "He's alive!" A fisherman says, "He's been dead three days." They ask questions of this mystery. They wonder where the fish came from. They wonder which is the front and which is the rear. They wonder if it is male or female. They ask, "Who knows?" But they receive no answers. Together "they look down on the fish and it seems to stare back at them with its round, dead eye." Marcello makes his first comment about the monster: "What is he looking at?" And a while later Marcello finally comments uneasily: "He's still staring."

Fellini is now beyond the stark black-and-white magazine-style or newsreel-like neo-realistic exposure of the seven episodes. The lighting, the rhythms, the mysteries of event and dialogue, all reach out into symbolic extension. The storytelling of the seven episodes is completed. Fellini gives us symbolic comment here at the end, just as he gave us symbolic comment at the beginning. The entire narrative part of the film has been framed by a symbolic foreword and a symbolic afterword.

But what does it all mean? Verbalization won't really do. The beginning and ending are almost entirely visual. Fellini chose to make them so. Fellini himself has warned us: "A film cannot be described in words."[40] And neither can a film be fully explained in words. But that is all we have just now, so let me at least try to describe and to explain what we see on the screen. Let us go back to the beginning. The first shot, under the credits, is a beautiful picture of the eternal and empty sky. The camera moves searchingly, and we are located in place: in Rome, in ancient Rome, at the ruins of the San Felice aqueduct. We are back 2000 years in time, and the structure is crumbling. An incongru-

i. 19. The symbol for the whole: a mediation between the old and the new.

ous modern sound is heard. A helicopter comes into view. Enclosed together into the same shot we see the old, the aqueduct, and the new, the helicopter. (i. 19) Contrast is thus established at the very beginning of the film. We immediately see old/new; we will soon see day/night, natural/unnatural, provinces/city, quiet/frenzy, order/chaos. And we remember the similar contrasts that helped set up the choice and give meaning and extension to *La Strada*. Suspended between the old and the new, and as if in mediation between them, is a statue of Christ, arms outspread in blessing. The blades of the helicopter form a kind of modern halo over the statue. The graceful arch of the ancient aqueduct is replaced by a series of stark verticals of modern buildings. A few ragged people down below chase the image of Christ and the shadow of the image. They reach up to it. But of course they cannot reach it. Yet nothing can stop it. A modern apartment building looms up and blocks the passage of the shadow; it races up the building toward the sky. Marcello is in an accompanying helicopter. We see at once his interest: not the Christ suspended below him, but scantily clad girls, still further below, sunbathing on the roof.

This famous and controversial introduction has, of course, many possible interpretations, all of them too blunt when stated verbally. What is certain is that the entire film is placed into this context: Ancient

Rome, Christian Rome, and the modern world. We cannot do without these givens. That is the triple locale within which Marcello will carry on his search. Other, less certain, more speculative, interpretations come to mind: "This is a kind of second coming of Christ, as foretold in the Apocalypse." "This film is the story of what Christ would find if He did come back to earth." "Christ is now out of reach of His people." "This unreal hideous image is our substitute for the living Christ; only idols now remain." All of this, and more.

Then the shape of St. Peter's Square, thronged with pilgrims, is echoed by the shape of the stage in a nightclub, thronged with inhabitants of the sweet life. A close-up of the face of the statue—a mask in that Christ's real face is hidden within this image of Him—fades into the mask of the Siamese dancer; and we are thus placed into the world of the grotesquely contrasting false images that fill modern-day Rome. We are about to look at a series of images as part of "a fresco of the society we live in," as Fellini once described this film.[41] That metaphor from art is a good one. For the Fellini world is a world of artifice, of images, of masks. We are about to see a series of masked people, hiding from themselves as they search for themselves. Disguises, costumes, role-playing, image-making—all attempts to deceive others and to deceive the self—will play before our eyes. As always in Fellini, we are asked to question images which we see through the illusionistic medium of the cinema itself. In life and in art, Fellini has played with the circus and the photo-novel, with vaudeville and caricature, on his way to the powerful and playful illusions of the cinema.

The staring fish with its unblinking eye is, at the end, like the statue at the beginning, an image of Christ. But both are parodies of images of Christ, just as the film itself has shown so many parodies of Christian sacraments. Traditional iconographies make a fish into Christ and an eye into God the father. The Christ/God appears in the film, after the seven episodes, as a monstrous, yet splendorous fish, about which nothing is known, except that it stares accusingly. This Christ/God is enclosed in bonds; we view this fish symbol through the bars of a fishnet, so like the many networks and cages which have imprisoned the people of the film. And, at the end, we are not sure whether this fish, or the people, are alive or dead. Whether or not this Christ has been dead three days, He surely will not be resurrected. This God will not respond. This is all that the sea as the source of life, the sea which spoke so eloquently to Gelsomina, and so healingly to Zampano, can now say to Marcello.

So what happens to Marcello? What happens to the modern traveller whom we have watched as an observer of and then a participant in the modern world of La Dolce Vita? One final image comes to him. Marcello understands nothing of the fish. Its message means nothing to him. He simply wanders away from it, and from its accusing eye. But he hears a voice, and turns. Paola, the girl whom Marcello had met briefly in dappled sunshine on a bright day at the seashore, is calling to him. Paola had first appeared at an emotional high point, right after Steiner's party, when Marcello's hopes were up. She appears now at the end, as if to call him back to hope.

Paola is a girl from the provinces, from Perugia, a young girl whose beauty and innocence had reminded Marcello of an image of an angel in an Umbrian church. But she is not only a vision; she is also a reality. Gilbert Salachas is right to insist that Paola is *really* there, as person as well as promise: "Her feet are planted firmly on the soil of this century; she is a waitress but would like to be a secretary; she enjoys the rollicking, seductive music that is part of contemporary folklore. She is not a spiritual apparition, but a real girl."[42] Such an image of real and natural beauty, from the seashore, extended in meaning into an angelic messenger outside of time, still had force and effect in *La Strada*. It changed Zampano. But Marcello, on his knees, is less alive than Zampano. Zampano turned to the sea and to the sky, and perhaps understood. Marcello turns to Paola and can only mutter, "Me? I don't understand. I can't hear." Fellini recognizes that Marcello is "very similar to Zampano." Fellini acknowledges that both of them are seeking clarity by searching within the self.[43] But Zampano's movement was circular. Marcello's movement is downward along the spiral. Marcello at the end is where Zampano was at the beginning: beastlike, isolated, without communication. Gelsomina spoke and was heard; Paola speaks but cannot be heard.

The theme of failed communication reaches its climax. In a pantomime during the opening scene of *La Dolce Vita*, there was communication without hearing between Marcello and the girls on the roof. But throughout the film, his powers of communication weakened, even though communication is his profession. He talked to Sylvia in a language she didn't understand. He could not, in spite of his pleas, talk to his father. Just before Maddalena disappeared, his words to her echoed into nothingness in an empty room. And now the film closes, as it began, with a pantomime. But this time the pantomime is without communication.[44] We see the tide running between Marcello and Paola, separating them. The sounds of the sea and the wind drown out their voices. Marcello repeats his words of failed communication, this time pronouncing them slowly and hopelessly, as if knowing that his voice cannot ever reach the ideal/real messenger of hope, so great is the distance between them: "I don't understand. I can't hear. I cannot hear. I can't hear."

The search is over. Lisa, one of the girls from the final orgy scene, holds out her arms. "Come, Marcello," she says, and beckons to him. That Marcello can hear. "I'm coming," Marcello says to Lisa, as he turns away from both Paola and the sea. These words, "I'm coming," are the last words of the film, and Marcello is shown locked in an embrace with a member of the sweet life, now fully a member of it himself. Like Maddalena, Marcello cannot now choose. He does not even hear or understand the components of a choice. He has slipped into a modern death. The prophetess at the miracle scene had said that if a person looks for God, he will find Him. But Marcello is no longer searching for anything, even his self, let alone God.

The final shots of *La Dolce Vita* are described in the published screenplay. What they show is not a Marcello search:

> He gives a weary little shrug and turns away. He walks slowly toward Lisa, then stops and looks back. Paola has not moved. She smiles and waves to him. Lisa puts her arms around Marcello's shoulders and they walk away. Paola's eyes follow Marcello. She is smiling. We see them smaller in the distance now. And her smile . . . [i. 20]

Marcello had hidden his face with his hand, and had half-waved goodbye. Behind Paola are several little children frolicking in the sand. And behind the children is an ordered, harmonious structure. All of that is one possibility. Behind Marcello is the other possibility. Behind Marcello are the inhabitants of *la dolce vita*, scattered, moving on to another episode in the night. Fellini has called the one world "hope," the other world "folly."[45] Between Marcello and Paola is the tide, and his failure to hear, his inability to understand.

In spite of the fact that Marcello's search for self ends with negation, it is Paola's smile that remains on the screen after Marcello disappears: "And her smile . . ." Paola turns her smile from Marcello, and smiles, instead, directly at us. Paola looks at us steadily. The close-up of that smile, addressed to us, is not only the last, but also the most long-lasting, image in the film. That smile remains on the screen even longer than the enclosed unmoving spot that had announced the death of Steiner. We cannot know precisely what that smile means. The assurance with which Fellini ended *La Strada* is now gone. Fellini puts the burden of search onto us. But Fellini is always Fellini, and so, whatever that smile may mean, it is an affirmation. It is a radiance. And surely a goal. Something worth searching for exists. Even in his story of the sweet life, Fellini's bitterest film, he ends with that vision of a goal at the end of an unknown road.

i. 20. The Paola smile: a call Marcello neither hears nor understands.

ANGELO SOLMI KNEW WHAT to expect after Fellini finished *La Dolce Vita*. It was a familiar Fellini pattern: "After every film, his creative activity has been troubled by doubts."[1] But this seemed to be never more true than it was now, when everyone—Fellini, friends, critics, fans—had reason to doubt. Marcello's quest had ended in negation; only Paola's smile remained to suggest that something worth searching for continued to exist. Marcello—and Steiner, his guide—had given up. The question was whether Fellini, who had identified himself with Marcello, would continue to move along Fellini's road, or, like Marcello, would drop out. For months into years, no new film came. But Fellini knows himself to be a "man who feeds on doubts."[2] So perhaps everyone should have been confident that the delay, the very doubts, would engender new search, and thus new films and new film forms.

Two years after *La Dolce Vita*, in 1962, Fellini contributed "The Temptations of Doctor Antonio" to Carlo Ponti's anthology film called *Boccaccio '70*. But Fellini's short film, featuring Anita Ekberg as a huge billboard come to life, was not the film to resolve doubts about Fellini's future. It did continue Fellini's thematic concerns for freedom, for the natural, for the full life. In hindsight, we can see that stylistically "The Temptations of Doctor Antonio" did look forward. It blended fantasy with reality; in a dream sequence, Dr. Antonio sees an enormous bier which is surrounded by all the people of his life. But the film wasn't really Fellini. It was made to someone else's order. It was an interlude. It was not a further step in Fellini's personal/artistic development; it was not a continuation along the road that had led from the first neo-realistic films, through *La Strada*, to *La Dolce Vita*. While filming "The Temptations of Doctor Antonio," Fellini explained his continuing doubts: "It is possible that the same sort of thing is happening to me as happens to Marcello at the end of *La Dolce Vita*."[3] Fellini predicted of his next film: "It will be an attempt to study what the little girl says with her enigmatic smile to Marcello at the end of *La Dolce Vita*."[4]

Fellini emphasized that the new film was developing out of *La Dolce Vita* when he asked Marcello Mastroianni to play once again his searching alter ego. But the new protagonist was not to be a journalist. In *this* film, Fellini wanted to get even closer to his current self. "You must choose a profession you know well," Fellini explained in retrospect, "and I had thought of an art director, someone whose job resembles mine. At the beginning it seemed too bold to depict a film director."[5] Fellini next moved a little closer to himself, and his hero changed from an art director of films to a writer of films. Fellini wrote a long letter to his collaborator, Brunello Rondi, detailing a film in which the hero was a filmwriter quite like Fellini.[6] This career shift was in fact Fellini's own autobiographical career journey: from journalist to filmwriter.

Plans continued. But so did doubts. Even when Fellini was finally ready to begin shooting, he admitted: "I know very little about this film myself. It is still in its embryonic stage, and sometimes I have a feeling I'm an astronaut shot out into space."[7] When Deena Boyer, who had been asked to be on-set press officer for the new film, asked Fellini with some impatience, "But what's the film about?" Fellini responded by detailing that same search metaphor. The setting had come to Fellini in October of 1960, when he took a cure at a health spa in Chianciano, north of Rome. The hero of his scenario similarly goes to take a cure at a spa:

> He starts thinking about his life. . . . Well, *just anyone* was no good. He had to have a profession. . . . a writer, going through a crisis, a general crisis, in his work and in his private life. Commissioned to write a scenario, he imagines a sequence in which man abandons the earth. . . .
>
> It's a way of saying that his own troubles are part of a much broader crisis that touches everyone, and that under these conditions, there's nothing to do but abandon the earth and start over elsewhere. So all humanity, thousands and

> thousands of men, women, and children, the Catholic Church
> in the lead, piles into a gigantic spaceship.[8]

By the end of *La Dolce Vita*, Marcello had explored all the roads of both aspiration and escape which are to be found on this earth. So to the new protagonist only one grand escape and one grand hope was left to beckon: abandon the earth entirely and begin again.

Fellini has never hidden the fact that "my work coincides with my own life."[9] And while preparing his new film, Fellini spoke, as he has often done before and since, about "the autobiographical vein that is in all of my work."[10] But obviously something new was happening. Perhaps recalling the atmosphere in which Emma was told that miracles are born, Fellini told Deena Boyer that "I feel that for once I have to have silence." This film, he told her, was to be more personal, more introverted, than any of his previous films. This film would be his *own*.[11] He even promised Angelo Solmi: "This film will be the ultimate in autobiography; it will be a kind of purifying flame."[12]

The crises, both professional and private, that are suffered by the filmwriter in Fellini's projected film sound continuing autobiographical echoes. The film continued to move inward as it formed in character, theme, and setting, so that it was no longer "too bold" for the filmwriter to become a director. Fellini gave to the new protagonist, a film director called Guido, his own characteristic doubts. About Guido: "He is stalling because he hopes from one minute to the next that somehow he'll find out where he is."[13] And about himself: "My own private world is a muddle, constantly changing."[14] That stalling, that muddle, that changing, had to find its way into the very form of the film.

The form of the film, Fellini insisted, must be "a magical kaleidoscope."[15] For the new film, neither a linear nor a cyclic nor a spiral design would do. The kaleidoscope inside the head of the director was to be shown through episodes which would exist at once in the present, in memory, and in fantasy. "I am making a film," Fellini said while working on the new film, "in which parts of the past and imaginary events are superimposed upon the present. I want to take a precise moment in a man's life—a day, an hour, a unique moment, and show how it is lived on three different levels."[16] Fellini once told a friend that he was interested in film form that could be compared to a piece of sculpture, but a sculpture broken into pieces so that he could examine the pieces one by one.[17] The kaleidoscope and the sculpture are appropriate artistic metaphors to describe the form of Fellini's new film. This new film would eventually make an important statement about the very nature of art.

The new form would not be easy. "What is it to make a film?" Fellini asks. And he answers his own question: "It is, naturally, a question of trying to bring order."[18] But what if Fellini himself, as director of the new film about a film director, does not possess a clear sense of order? Then, he says, "it would be dishonest to give it to the characters of my movie." And it would be equally dishonest to give a sense of order to the viewer. Honesty demanded that he "leave in the viewer a torment that can engender meditation."[19] Obviously speaking of both art and of life, Fellini said, just before filming 8½, "I haven't found a final solution myself, and I would consider myself finished if I had found it."[20] Instead, the search for the solution is the whole purpose of the process of creation.

Fellini's road is to continue to probe mystery: "For me, the key to the mystery—which is to say, God—is to be found at the center of the successive layers of reality."[21] So Fellini, the characters, and the viewers will *share* the initial disorder; but they will also share the tormenting but liberating creative process of probing the several layers of reality, of ordering the parts into the whole, of shaping chaos into form. In a most perfect piece of collaborative art, we—and Fellini—will work our way through the successive layers of the new film form, to find what we can at the center.

The making of art, which we share with Fellini in the new film, is his metaphor for the process of life. Every life is put together out of pieces. Every life tries to bring the pieces into order. That is every man's job—not just the artist's job: to find a harmony, a form, finally a meaning, which will hold off chaos, which will bring us to a center. That common life process of finding form is the reason that the artist's "own troubles are part of a much broader crisis that touches everyone," as Fellini would have it. The universality of that broad crisis keeps Fellini's most personal film from becoming a private film. "When I speak for myself," he said, "I feel that I have spoken for everyone."[22]

Fellini's next film after *La Dolce Vita* turned out to be not the spaceship film, but rather a film about the making of that film. The completed film in fact combined—as never before in Fellini and perhaps as never before in cinema—the search for meaning in life with the search for order in art. Critic Ted Perry, summarizing the views of Christian Metz, perfectly described the completed film: "8½ is a film by a filmmaker making a film about a filmmaker trying to make a film about himself as a man and as a filmmaker."[23] For a similar meditation on life and art, critics were driven to comparisons in André Gide, Marcel Proust, and James Joyce.

Life and Art

In May of 1962, filming began, with a partial script only two weeks old and with no definite ending. The working title suggested just how personal this film was to be, and how closely, in the film, life and art were to be interconnected. Fellini's developing film was temporarily called "8½" because it would be, when finished, Fellini's opus number eight-and-one-half. Fellini had created six full-length films: *The White Sheik, I Vitelloni, La Strada, Il Bidone, The Nights of Cabiria,* and *La Dolce Vita*. He had collaborated with Alberto Lattuado on the direction of *Variety Lights*, and so that film counted as one-half. And he had contributed one episode to each of two omnibus films, *Matrimonial Agency* and *Boccaccio '70*: and those counted as two halves. Therefore the Fellini total was 7½ films. This would be 8½.

Although the working title of the new film while it was being shot was "8½," Fellini's collaborator, Ennio Flaiano, suggested that the title should be "La Bella Confusione." Rumors circulated that the final title would be "The Labyrinth."[24] Actually, the expected final title was to have been "Asa Nisi Masa." Perhaps as much as "8½," that projected title emphasizes the true nature of the new Fellini film. Fellini's early scenario included a scene in which, in flashback to Guido's childhood, several children, including Guido, would be seen stomping on grapes and chanting "Asa Nisi Masa, Asa Nisi Masa, Asa Nisi Masa." When Fellini was a little boy, he played an Italian word game, similar in intention to our pig-latin, in which the vowel of each syllable in a word is repeated and an *s* is inserted between the two vowels. So "Asa Nisi Masa" turns out to be "A Ni Ma," the Italian word for "spirit" or "soul." In the actual film, Fellini found a new place for the introduction of the special word, so as to give it accented symbolic meaning. In the nightclub scene, the Magician looks into Guido's mind to discover his preoccupation and comes up with that word "Asa Nisi Masa," as a magical memory from childhood. The lost innocence of Guido's childhood had been on his mind; his own "anima" or soul is the obvious goal at the end of his journey.[25]

As Guido searches for his soul, as he tries, through his art, to come to grips with his whole self, the film intermixes the problems of life and art, of the real and the ideal. Some of the techniques, maybe even tricks, invented for *La Dolce Vita* are carried further here. Actors again retain their actual names in the film. This is true of Guido's three major assistants: Bruno Agostini, who plays the production supervisor; Cesarino, who plays the production director; and Conocchia, who plays the general factotum. Rossella Falk, Nadine Sanders, and Mario

i. 21. Reflections: Marcello Mastroianni playing Guido Anselmi in disguise, complete with false nose and Fellini's hat.

Pisu all keep their first names. Several people in *8½* actually play themselves. Claudia Cardinale not only plays an actress named "Claudia," but that actress is an international star identical in every way with Claudia Cardinale. The young American girl named Carolyn who plays the secretary of Claudia Cardinale is actually a young American girl named Carolyn who is the secretary of Claudia Cardinale. "Jacqueline Bonbon," the wonderful name used in the film for the aging chorine, is the stage name of the real vaudeville showgirl. A reporter from *L'Espresso* came to see the first shots of Fellini's new film, and the director sat her down in camera's range to play a reporter who had come to see the screen tests for Guido's new film. Similarly, several extras who play reporters asking questions in the press conference scene are actually reporters who were told by Fellini to ask their own questions in the scene. During the shooting of *8½*, the Rome newspapers reported that Fellini was going to create a part for a starlet named Edy Vessel. Neither Edy nor anybody else knew what part was going to be created for her. So Fellini made art follow life: Edy appears as "Edy" in Guido's film, as a girl whose role is to wonder what part is going to be created for her.[26]

The confusion between life and art gets even more inventive, as it connects Guido with Fellini. Much of the dialogue concerning the fictional Guido is just as much about the real Fellini. A special part of our delight in the film comes from the self-mocking lines which Fellini writes for other characters to use in attacking Guido, whose films evoke the same set of questions and criticisms that Fellini's do. And not only dialogue. Guido often appears on the screen of Fellini's film wearing the famous hat that the publicity shots show Fellini wearing while he directs his films. (i. 21) And as Deena Boyer watches Fellini's mannerisms, she reports: "Often, between shots, when he is sitting with his legs crossed, I see the nervous jiggling of the raised foot that he tried to make Marcello imitate."[27]

Many of the events in Guido's life began as events in Fellini's life. But, as Fellini films them, reality becomes something else. Alberto Solmi describes the process: "Sometimes he has amused himself by padding out real episodes with imaginary ones and at other times he has inserted true facts into fictitious happenings . . . ending up by losing sight of the real nucleus in the fictional superstructure."[28] Fellini himself admits that "it is true that inevitably all the episodes in *8½* refer to my life, but some of them gradually became distorted, while others took shape during the shooting."[29]

The fiction/reality confusion is shown with most complexity in Fellini's fantasy use of Claudia. In reality, even before he knew how he would use her, Fellini hired Claudia Cardinale, apparently hoping for a kind of inspiration through her. So in the art, even before he knew how he would use her, Guido hired "Claudia," an internationally famous Italian actress, who he hoped would help him to bring his confused ideas into order. In both Fellini's film and in Guido's film, Claudia Cardinale plays Claudia, in intersecting levels:

1) Claudia becomes Guido's idealized woman. She floats into Guido's life, serving his every masculine desire. She presents him with healing waters; she serves him meals; she brings him illumination; she makes his bed, enters it, but remains pure and unsullied and forever white. She is dreamily ethereal, sexually unthreatening; and yet she is full-bodied, full-lipped, deeply sexual. She asks for nothing. She is

pleasure, without responsibility or commitment, in contrast to Guido's demanding mistress and demanding wife. She is nurse, mother, muse, and lover. She is the Ideal. If this combination heaven/earth creature can so serve Guido's fantasy life, perhaps she can serve his art.

2) Claudia becomes a character in Guido's film. "What if I make her a symbol of purity, of sincerity?" Guido asks himself. As he thinks of Claudia, Guido becomes mockingly Felliniesque: Claudia becomes a funny emblem of innocence as she floats along, smiles into the camera, puts a white veil over her head, transforming herself into a chaste bride; and then the camera pulls back to show us a beautifully ordered, harmonized shot of Guido's hotel room, as patterned as Steiner's apartment had been. That artistic image gives Guido an idea about how Claudia could specifically serve his art: "Yes, there could be a museum in the village, and you could be the curator's daughter. You've grown up surrounded by classical art and beauty." As if responding to Guido's thoughts, Claudia goes to the typewriter, looks intellectual, reads a book; but then her composure breaks and she puts her head between her knees and laughs at the inappropriateness of the manner in which Guido seeks to use her. She knows that this is awful art. Even his visions won't behave; characters take on a life of their own. It is as if Guido's, and Fellini's, fictional characters are themselves searching for their true selves, as are their creators. Guido tells Claudia: "You're right to laugh." But then Guido becomes Fellini again, and Claudia comes to him and declares her purpose as he wants it to be: "I want to create order. I want to create cleanliness. I want to create order." We know enough about Fellini to know that any woman who could really do that would surely be his own dream girl, as well as Guido's. (i. 22)

3) Claudia becomes an actress named Claudia who has been hired by Guido to play the museum curator's daughter in his film. This Claudia first appears while Guido is watching screen tests in a painful effort to decide who is to play the *other* parts in the film. Claudia has already been cast. At least his Ideal is certain. The real actress appears all in black, in contrast to the white dream version of herself. She appears as a salvation figure, precisely when she is most needed, when the viewing of the screen tests has disintegrated into chaos because of Guido's confusion. Appropriately, she appears just after Guido's wife accuses him of not knowing the true from the false. Claudia's bright

i. 22. The ideal: Claudia the illuminator, one of her many roles.

and true smile fills Fellini's screen. "You came just in time," Guido declares. He begins to describe her role in the film, which really means that he begins to explain her function on several levels, in both his own life and in the life of the hero of his film: "He meets a girl at the springs. She gives him water to heal him. She's beautiful: Young, yet ancient. Child, yet already woman. Authentic. Complete." Guido doesn't have to explain that she is to be Anita Ekberg/Sylvia transposed from one film to another. Yet Claudia is to be Gelsomina and Paola as well as Sylvia. Guido tells the actress: "It's obvious that she could be his salvation." Earlier, Guido had said about this Claudia, "There is no doubt that she is my only hope." His hope is in all these Claudias: the image of purity and love who will serve Guido's imaginative life, the image of order who will serve his artistic life, and the actress who will make it all real and true.

4) Claudia finally becomes Claudia Cardinale who was hired by Fellini to embody all of the several levels of meaning. When Guido explains the film to the actress named Claudia, she puts her head between her knees and laughs precisely as the Claudia character in Guido's film laughed at Guido's imaginative projection of her artistic role. We realize that this is Claudia Cardinale laughing at Fellini's imaginative projection of *her* artistic role. It is now Claudia Cardinale speaking not to Guido but to Marcello Mastroianni, who is dressed to look like Federico Fellini. Claudia says to Mastroianni precisely what Cardinale would in reality say to her friend Marcello: "How funny you look with that ridiculous hat and your black clothes and all made up like an old man!"

All four of these Claudias see through to the central problem beset-ting both the hero of Guido's film and the hero of Fellini's film. "That man you describe," Claudia concludes, "he doesn't love anyone." An actor named Marcello hears the same accusation that in another film a character named Marcello had heard. Three times Claudia repeats, while lighted as though in a spotlight: "He doesn't know how to love." Each time she says that, Guido tries to substitute a less painful cause of the hero's problems. The camera cuts quickly from Guido to Claudia and back again, emphasizing their separation. Claudia persists in her explanation: "He doesn't know how to love." Claudia, the most unreal of Guido's creatures, carries to Guido the most real truth.

But *does* Claudia exist? Can one woman bear all of a man's hopes in life and art? Claudia the actress answers that question when—speak-ing for all the Claudias—she concludes: "You swindler! So there's no part for me in this film." Guido concedes: "You're right. There's no part for you in the film. . . . Nothing at all."

Stasis

The film begins in a dream. At first it all looks realistic enough. In the initial shot we are inside a car, next to Guido, looking through the windshield at a traffic jam. Not only are we inside a car, but our car is inside a tunnel. Nothing is moving. This film of quest begins in stasis, the antithesis of the search that has informed all of Fellini's films. We see no Gelsomina walking diagonally across the screen toward the sea. We see no helicopter flying through a free and open sky. Instead, mobile modern man is trapped in a traffic jam. Vehicles of motion are so complexly interrelated that nothing can go anywhere. No one can move. At the still center is Guido, looking out with our eyes, stuck. He is the center of attention. We see everyone around him, in cars, in doubledecker buses, staring at him. They seem to expect things of him. They seem to accuse him. But Guido himself now can hardly see. The atmosphere is suffocating. Guido seems bottled up. Steam, or maybe Guido's own breath, begins to cover the windows. Guido picks up a rag and tries to wipe off the steamy obscure windshield. The traffic jam turns into a prison. We see a faint light at the end of the tunnel, but Guido can't get to it. He is enclosed in the dark, as trapped as any Marcello, but still struggling. He frantically starts pounding the windshield, with fists and feet.

The film begins in absolute silence. Then, in Guido's isolation, the only sound is his own heartbeat. Now the sounds that we hear are the echoes of Guido's panting, and his fingers squeaking and scraping along the enclosing glass. The camera starts its own frenzied struggle for freedom, moving quickly from side to side. From outside, faces continue to stare at Guido; they are isolated from him, not only by panes of glass, but by indifference to his struggles. Among the people staring at the entrapped Guido is Carla, Guido's mistress, who is being pawed, in another stalled car, by one of Guido's assistants. We, of course, are ourselves trapped in confusion because, at this point in the fractured time of the film, we have no way of identifying any of these characters, of understanding their roles or their meaning.

In the film's first definite break with reality, our confusion increases as the soundtrack goes silent, and the camera shows Guido's back, mystically ascending out of the car, and then floating freely above the crowd, away from its accusations and indifference. He soars into a brightly lit sky, between heaven and earth, as now the sound of wind fills the soundtrack. Stasis has turned to euphoric movement, entrapment to freedom, dark to light, closed-off tunnel to free and open sky over sparkling sea. Guido floats past a ruined tower, which looks curiously like a rocket launching pad. Like Christ at the beginning of *La*

Dolce Vita, Guido floats high above his whole domain, surveying it, in power and perhaps in benediction.

Deena Boyer watched the entire film being shot, and she describes, from her vantage point at the actual shooting, what we now see on the screen, although we still have no way of interpreting the people or the images which we see:

> The agent of Claudia, the actress, is now a medieval knight, . . . his ordinary clothes covered by a cape of a gray cloth that looks like aluminum. Round his forehead is a band with a pendant. He is on horse back. Claudia's press agent lies in the sand, tugging at a rope that seems to come down from the sky and crying, "I've got him! That does it!" The medieval knight looks at a document: "Bring him down! For good!"[30]

Later we will understand that Claudia's agent does indeed possess the power to bring Guido down to earth with a crash. "Don't try to hide," the agent will warn Guido. "We'll always find you." Like most of Guido's demons, the agent has pursued him into his very dreams. So does the medieval church have power over Guido, with its documents and its doctrines of guilt. The rope is tied to Guido's leg, preventing him from soaring any higher; he struggles, but when the agent tugs on the rope, down Guido falls, easily manipulated by men on the earth. A high camera watches Guido plummet sickeningly down. He has escaped suffocation only to be plunged down toward drowning in the sea. Timothy Hyman sees this initial Guido dream as an archetypal circle of Crisis, Liberation, and Fall.[31]

In retrospect, we can understand much of the meaning of the artist's dream which begins the film. The creative man is the one who must move on, who is most trapped when stopped. The traffic jam is a Fellini nightmare. His characteristically mobile camera—a mark of his constant curiosity—is seldom so restricted as it was in the claustrophobic space of the small stalled car. Edward Murray comments about the thematic function of Fellini's mobile camera: "If one technique can be said to recur in Fellini's pictures, it is the moving camera. Since the world remains 'open' and 'multiple,' this procedure seems ideally suited to convey the twin ideas of spaciousness and manifoldness."[32] Fellini thrives in processions, in dances, in motorcycles, in speeding sports cars, in movement toward a goal. And it is so, he has told us, in his life as well as in his art: "My natural condition," Fellini has said, "is to be in motion, on the move. As a matter of fact, I feel very well in a car, with the images rushing by outside the window."[33] In the first scene of *8½*, no images rush past. The artist is stalled. When he seems to break free, that is only an illusion, and a prelude to disaster.

Healing Waters

In the spa, Guido is in reality. The time is now. But Guido wakes up as enclosed as he was in dream. Doctors and a nurse surround him, probing a personless body on an examination table. We see a hand, legs, a torso, Guido as a dismembered object. During the examination, a doctor carelessly throws Guido's robe up over his head. He is faceless. He is hemmed in, as he was in the traffic jam, by people who look at him without really seeing him, without seeing *him*, nor his intertwined personal and artistic difficulties.

In a mocking way, the dialogue begins to connect Guido with Fellini: "Well, what are you working on now?" one doctor asks. "Another film without hope?" The writer comes in to talk to Guido about his script. He keeps his distance; he looks at Guido accusingly. The doctor announces a conclusion: "The organism is sluggish all right."

Guido gets up and goes into the glaring, coldly sterile shower room. He walks to a mirror. We see his face for the first time, at the same moment as Guido sees it. Guido confronts an aging baggy-eyed image of himself. Reflected in a mirror, Guido puts his hand on the small of his back, and stoops down in the bent posture of a decrepit old man. Mirrors will play an important part in the film as Guido continues to probe his own image for any reality or truth that might lie behind it, much as Fellini is doing through the character of Guido.

This scene in the examining room at the spa has started the actual plot, in actual time. We have learned from good expository dialogue that Guido is a famous and Fellini-like director who is taking a cure at a spa. And we have learned from the visual imagery that he is trapped, unwhole, accused, sluggish, introspective, and aging.

As "Ride of the Valkyries" swells on the soundtrack, we switch from inside to outside the spa. John Russell Taylor introduces the new episode suggestively: "When we start with a blanched, ghostly panorama of the springs themselves, with dozens of mysterious figures in black standing out in hallucinatory relief, many of them extremely strange and grotesque, are we in dream or in life?"[34] In a wonderfully ironic Wagnerian procession, aging and trivial faces— shot in heroic Germanic close-ups—parade past the camera on the way to the healing waters, all in time with Wagner's oversized and heroic music. The music is controlling the camera, and seems to be creating the film. A helpless Guido—and we—are just part of the aging mass. The haggard faces look at us as they are looking at Guido. It is a Fellini procession of faces. (i. 23) They present themselves to Guido, staring at him as did the faces in the dream, expecting things, making mute demands. It is a mock liturgy. The images are old faces, but also

i. 23. Faces at the spa: demanding, accusing, and indifferent.

trembling hands, stringy hair, unsteady feet. It is a dance of death by decaying Valkyries. Each face, each costume, each gesture, is unique within the mass. Fellini the caricaturist is individualizing with broad strokes. They are all there at a spa for a hoped-for "cure." Perhaps the healing waters of the spa will be sacramental, renewing the dead into full new life.[35] Guido, of course, is there for renewal. In this film that clings so closely to Guido's point of view, we usually see with his eyes, and those eyes often turn inward. These exhausted and depleted people are expressions of himself.

We feel in the spa procession the funny futility which is a mark of the film. For there is in this film a cinematic playfulness that explains why the title page of the original scenario carried at the top the designation: "A Comedy."[36] And it is a comedy. The occasional heaviness and sometimes self-conscious seriousness of *La Dolce Vita* have been supplanted in this more personal film by an almost sweet mixture of irony, compassion, and self-mockery.

Fellini switches the rhythm and the mood as the spa orchestra, which we discover to be the source of the music, changes from Wagner to Rossini. The sunny overture to "The Barber of Seville" introduces close shots of several ancients hopefully and rather gaily quaffing big cups of mineral water. Guido walks into camera range, wearing sunglasses, looking around as if searching for something, smiling in tune to the spirit of the Rossini. Suddenly Guido pushes down his sunglasses, and all sound stops as Claudia, all in white, lovingly centered within the shot, floats toward the camera. Claudia is freed from the earth. She glides toward Guido with her arms behind her, like bird who doesn't even need wings. She smiles beatifically as she hands Guido mineral water; but then, as suddenly as she had appeared, Claudia is replaced by a haggard woman insisting impatiently, "Senore, your mineral water!"

For a few seconds we had moved from the level of the real to the level of fantasy. We figure out that Guido's act of pushing down his glasses had been a signal. Apparently Fellini is trying to give the viewer at least some clues so that in this film we will be just confused enough, although perhaps not quite so confused and tormented by art as by life. Several times Fellini will use Guido's glasses trick. The basic meaning of the symbol—concentrated attempted sight, looking inward as well as outward—works here as it did in *La Dolce Vita*.

The levels of reality in *8½* are already more complicated than I have so far suggested. It was not fully accurate for me to have said that in the spa "the time is now." Now is supposedly 1962. And yet we notice that something is a bit off. Deena Boyer was confused, too, as she watched these scenes being filmed, for, in the spa scene, "all the extras are wearing the clothes of the 1930s." And, she continues, "As for the music, I have just been told that it is the kind one heard in every Italian spa in the 1930s." The careful viewer might have noticed that even the opening dream sequence existed in two times at once: in 1962, according to the models of the cars and according to Guido's clothes, but also in the 1930s, according to the clothes worn by the spectators. "All right," insists Boyer to herself, "let's recapitulate." She does so: "Guido is taking a walk in a spa in 1962. The people around him are dressed in the style of 1930." She conjectures: "It is a way of projecting into the present the childhood memories with which [Fellini] is obsessed at this time." After the film was completed, Boyer asked Fellini, "What gave you the idea of a 1930 background in the midst of a 1962 reality?" Among his replies, many of them typically evasive, was the rather straightforward: "My childhood memories go back to that time." During the filming, Boyer worries, "Will people understand these sutleties when they see the film?"[37] And yet must they understand them as the film is going forward? Perhaps it will be enough to be able to put all the parts together when the viewing of the film is completed. The theme of the film will eventually tell us that we don't possess the part of life until we embrace the whole of it; it is only fitting that the structure of the film say the same. That is one way by which we may be led to experience the "torment that can engender meditation" on both life and art.

It was also not fully accurate for me to have said that the scene in the examining room takes place "in reality." When Guido walks from the examining room to the adjacent shower room, we are struck for the first time with the startling flicker of very bright lights that will suggest several times in the course of the film that we are watching all this under the power of motion picture floodlights. And when Guido begins to take off his robe, a soundstage buzzer sounds, and he suddenly stops disrobing, as if he had just then realized that he was about to take a shower in front of a watching movie audience. Frequently Fellini will thus remind us that we are watching a film, or a film about a film, and that we are thus watching images of reality a few levels removed from reality itself. We are forced throughout to rethink the concept "realistic" just as we are reminded to rethink the concept "time" and the concept "art." But perhaps, for Guido and Fellini, who work on the level of the imagination, everything seems equally real, or equally imaginative.[38]

Space is as confused as are time and reality. We have no establishing shots. We therefore never know precisely where we are, or where one place exists in relationship to another place. The geography of the spa never does come clear. Many of Fellini's compositions feature parallel lines reaching into infinity. We must in our minds build up the space relationships in the spa and its environs and in the fantasy places; we must try to place the finite within the infinite, just as we try to order the sequence of events into a patterned whole. We no more know for certain where we are than when we are. Or if, for that matter.

But surely in all of these confusions Fellini faces a problem. If he wants us to be confused, as he surely does, Fellini might well have a difficult job keeping us patient, or in good humor, while he is confusing us. To solve this problem, he puts us into a good humor by mocking himself. Just when we may be about to become impatient with a film which is not explaining itself to us, Fellini brings in the writer, Daumier, who articulates to Guido at least some of our own feelings at this point: "Well, the main problem is, your script lacks a fundamental idea. . . . The film is merely a series of completely senseless episodes. Of course, the realism is quite amusing, but what is the writer's real intention?" As Daumier speaks these lines, Fellini shoots Guido trapped within the bend of the writer's arm. Guido seems caught, forced to listen to this rational attack on his own irrationality, an attack which he obviously feels may be all too true. Daumier's words do not make the film any clearer, but they at least show us that Guido, and perhaps Fellini, share with us the feeling of confusion, and thus the torment, and even the fun, of the attempt to order all this into something whole.

To Guido's artistic confusion, Fellini adds a personal agony: the process of aging becomes an insistent theme throughout the film. Guido begins to be hounded with the recurring question: "When will you finish this film?" He is continually warned that he doesn't have much time. A good middle-age crisis is all Guido needs. This film, which is so much about time, begins to ask the question: *Is* there time enough? We have seen the wizened faces and the twisted bodies mutely trying to march like Valkyries. Now comes Guido's old friend, Mario Mezzabotta, who fights his aging through the transparent self-assurance given him by Gloria, his new sweetheart whom Guido takes to be his daughter. (i. 24) Guido sees the futility of Mario's attempt,

i. 24. Another middle-age crisis: friend Mario and his Gloria.

both now and in the later steamroom scene when the true age of Mario becomes most apparent. Age is on Mario's mind: When Guido first spots him, Mario pretends to be old and arthritic, as if mimicking the old-man posture that Guido tried out in the shower room. But then Mario straightens up and dances to Guido, exclaiming, "You've gotten a little gray, Guido old man!"

A Woman for All Seasons

If the aging Mario has his youth-seeking dalliance with Gloria, Guido has his with Carla. In an ingenious contrast, Fellini introduces us to Carla precisely when Guido is thinking about Claudia. The real mistress is surely a far cry from the ideal dream girl. Guido is sitting in the railroad station, waiting for his mistress, as he reads the mocking notes of Daumier: "The capricious appearances of the girl in white, what do they mean? An offer of purity?" Carla, at least, is more obvious than that. In a theatrical appearance, train platform as a stage, Carla—ostentatiously bundled in furs against the Italian summer—steps front and center into Guido's life. She appears, all the fleshy pounds of her, not in Claudia's simple white, but in a magnificently vulgar costume that becomes her trademark throughout the film. Deena Boyer describes Carla's costume, as worn by the delightfully awful Sandra Milo: "Black velvet redingote, open over a pink crepe dress with a generous *décolletage*; white ermine collar, muff and pillbox; white gloves; a little silver evening bag; violets at her bosom."[39] As a greeting to Guido, Carla dips and makes her little comic book noise, something like a "Sgulp!" Even Guido looks embarrassed.

Carla is, flamboyantly, another archetypal fantasy by the male. She is earth where Claudia is heaven. She is flesh, and warmth, and basic no-nonsense sex. She is another of Fellini's obsessions. We will soon see Saraghina, the enormous prostitute on the beach at Rimini, who was Guido's, and Fellini's, first experience with overpowering female flesh. But now, in Carla, we have a domesticated version of Saraghina. And more. She playfully serves many of Guido's needs. She teases him sexually; she babies him. So Carla can be both lover and mother. And thus she is, in her manifold female functions, still another version of Sylvia. Indeed, Fellini had talked with Anita Ekberg about turning Sylvia into Carla. But, explains Boyer, finally "he could not bring himself to have the key character, the earthmother, played for the third time by the same actress, however perfectly she embodied [perfect word!] his concept. He tested a number of unknown candidates, but in none of them could he find the big white-fleshed woman he sought—a respectable Saraghina, in sum—motherly of manner and simple of mind."[40] Finally, he put an ad in the paper, calling for his Carla: "A pink and white complexion . . . a Rubens body, very soft, flowery, maternal and opulent."[41] Sandra Milo was not quite all of that, so Fellini hired her and then made her eat bananas throughout the filming. She ended up just fine! "Carla is La Saraghina transposed to the time of Guido's manhood," concludes Boyer. "She is Anita, she is the subject of the sketches, caricatures really, of enormous women that Fellini draws almost unthinkingly during his conferences with the scenarist."[42] The more known about Fellini's films, the more personal this film becomes. We know about his fondness for picturing, in his films as well as in his sketches, the huge whore, the mountain of willing flesh.

Carla plays her many roles. In the train station, she is Guido's mistress: He asks her, "How's the equipment?" as he looks down at her round behind. Her response is an affirmative and assuring giggle. In the hotel dining room, she becomes Guido's mother: As the sound-track softly plays the lullaby that will be featured soon in a scene from Guido's boyhood, Carla baby-talks in momma-fashion: "Guido, be good. . . . Were you really a good boy?" The lullaby has come out of nowhere; it is clearly in Guido's mind. Then the lullaby turns into Saraghina's music, as Carla turns from mother to whore. In Carla's bedroom, Guido makes up her eyes: "Your makeup's all wrong. You should look more like—like a whore." He sends her out into the hall with instructions: "Pretend that you came into the wrong room, the room of a stranger." "Oh good," replies Carla, always ready for a new role, "We never tried that!" The several roles played by Carla distance her from Guido, make her, in his hands, an image more than a person. That is safer. He doesn't have to accept her as another person, to attend to her demands, or even to meet her. He merely plays with her, gives her roles. As he tries to do with everyone.

Tears and Guilt

Carla serves as the transition to the next fantasy scene, this one a combination of dream and memory. Daumier was wrong—at least if he meant Fellini—when he accused Guido of constructing a film made up of a series of senseless episodes. So were the several critics who accused Fellini of constructing an incoherent film. When we collabo-

rate with the film, each episode of 8½ can make emotional and intellectual sense in itself; and each episode becomes related to the
other episodes in the film. Each episode fits. Each is, at least by the end,
part of an ordered whole. Fellini even attends to transitions. He filmed
a transition shot for use at the end of the Carla bedroom sequence, for
the purpose of introducing Saraghina. The connection was to be
Guido's appreciation of nice round sex. "You're beautiful," Guido said
to Carla in this rejected shot, "because you have such a wonderful
round bottom."[43] From that, we were to move into the memory of the
excessively rounded Saraghina. But Fellini decided to introduce
Saraghina at a more appropriate moment. It would be clearer and
more coherent to introduce Guido's parents and wife before introducing a subsidiary character from his childhood. So Fellini used the
motherly nature of Carla, instead of her sexual nature, as the triggering
device into the next episode. Carla had recently compared herself with
Guido's actresses: "I wouldn't like the kind of life they lead. No, I'm a
homebody." And, as Carla lies in bed, an old woman appears, being a
homebody, washing the walls of the bedroom. Guido's voice whispers, "You're my mother, aren't you?" She nods her head, and as
confirmation of her characteristically Italianate motherhood, she
murmurs: "Oh, the tears I've shed, my son!"

Introduced with the tears of Guido's mother, who is dressed in
mourning, who is trying to cleanse the room as Guido lies in bed with
his mistress, the dream-memory episode in the cemetery is packed
with Guido's guilt. Guido is no less obsessed with guilt than is Fellini
himself, who speaks of his continuing childhood-induced "sense of
guilt, and embarrassment, of underlying corrosive fear."[44] For both
Guido and Fellini, guilt and fear are rooted in childhood and persist
into manhood. As a sign that his guilt is all mixed up between the past
and the present and seems to exist forever, the adult Guido is dressed
in the schoolboy uniform of his youth. The cemetery scene is shot in
harsh white light, in the glare of which Guido can hide nothing. A
mood of eternity pervades the cemetery scene. Space is as endless as
time. We see shots of long lines of tombs meeting together off in some
infinite space. Guido can hardly reach his parents within that infinity.
He finds it hard to talk with them. His father hides behind a crumbling
building as Guido says, "We've talked so little together!" And Guido
has to call out, "Father, wait? Father, I've so many questions to ask
you."

Guido's father is played by Annibale Ninchi, the same actor who
played Marcello's equally unreachable father. He won't answer any

questions. But he complains that the ceiling of his tomb is too low and pleads with Guido to do something about it. Guido's producer lets the father know of Guido's current artistic failure, adding another Guido-caused sorrow to his father's burdens. "It's sad for me to realize how miserably he's failed," is his father's quiet response. Guido's own hands lower his father—weighted down with grief—into his grave. The music is a dirge. (i. 25)

In a wonderfully Freudian parody, as Guido kisses his mother to console her, a motherly kiss turns into a passionate kiss on the mouth, and the mother turns into Luisa, Guido's wife, wearing the same mourning clothes as the mother. This is only the most obvious of the many times that we will watch Guido searching for some woman who will be an undemanding always-loving mother substitute. Remembering Carla, we understand Luisa's own reason for mourning, and know that Luisa's mourning adds to Guido's guilt. This moody dream sequence ends with a long sterile shot of the cemetery, and with a small Luisa standing alone, abandoned in the eternity of the crumbling tombs.

i. 25. Eternity: Guido at his father's grave.

The Parts

The next episode, in the hotel of the spa, takes place in current time. We share the confusing pressures all heaped upon Guido as artist and man. The scene features the recurring motif of elevators and stairs, as we watch Guido's ups and downs, descents and resurrections. Most often we watch a descent. Going down in an elevator, Guido encounters the Cardinal whom he will later be forced to consult about his film. Now Guido can only huddle in a corner like a small intimidated boy, as he is grinned at indulgently by the Cardinal's attendant, who, in Guido's subjective eyes, becomes a cross between a Cheshire Cat and Mephistopheles. This film will eventually tell us more about Guido's —and Fellini's—boyhood complexes, the kind of guilt and insecurity problems that a man spends a lifetime trying to integrate into a wholeness of life. Guido's boyish behavior in the elevator is still another characteristic which Fellini admits to be his own: "I'm still a little ill at ease because I have a complex about being a little schoolboy— intimidated but somewhat naughty; I'm not mentally free of this."[45]

Down in the hotel lobby, Fellini creates a bustling scene, which he packs with demanding people invading the space within the camera's range, and then darting out again, while the unrelenting camera keeps Guido trapped within its limited frame. Guido cannot escape from us, from the camera recording him, any more than he can escape from the people around him, or from himself. The entire scene is a masterful example of Fellini's filmic rhythms. Throughout the scene, the trapped Guido can only react, in bewilderment and frustration, to the bedlam of demands made upon him. He initiates no action. Guido is pressed to make a decision about which of several aging actors should play the role of the father. Like Fellini, Guido tries to choose actors on the basis of their faces. In real life, as in the film, the faces seem to accuse the filmmaker, demanding to be used, to be made a part of the whole. "It's as if they were trying to say to me," complains Fellini, " 'Look well at us, each one of us is a piece of the mosaic you are now building up.' "[46] A series of aged faces, forlorn, incredibly sad, pass in front of Fellini's camera, trying to be a piece of Guido's mosaic, as Guido asks each old man just how old he is. Once again, as Albert Benderson nicely puts it, "mortal numbers echo through the sound track as they answer in turn . . . seventy . . . sixty-four . . . sixty-eight."[47]

Guido is pressed to settle contract details with Claudia's agent, who has followed Guido all the way from his opening nightmare. Guido encounters the French actress, who demands to know the facts about her role. Hired to play the mistress in Guido's film, she knows only that she is supposed to eat spaghetti to gain weight, just as Sandra Milo, hired to play the mistress in Fellini's film, must eat bananas. Guido must answer questions obsequiously placed by a vulgar American journalist. Guido must deal with Carla, who sends a message that she doesn't like her hotel room. He must put off his producer, who descends the hotel stairs like a maharajah, dispensing gifts and hoping as he descends that Guido's ideas "are clearer by now." There is just one moment of peace in the whole wonderful, confusing, and funny scene. The hustle-bustle rhythm stops only once, when the air seems to clear as a lovely vision of a beautiful stranger walks gracefully down the stairs, turns and calls "Darling!" to a little girl who is accompanying her. The vision is dressed in the becoming clothes of the 1930s. Guido is stunned by the beauty of this stranger. Her identity remains, for a time, a mystery to Guido and to us.

By night as well as by day the pressures upon Guido continue. For Guido, this spa is surely not a place of rest, let alone a place of cure. The scene is now an outdoor nightclub at the spa, and all the characters in Guido's current filmmaking life cluster at tables around the almighty producer. Once more, the theme of aging is introduced. Out of the darkness appears a group of strange women, one chattering: "I saw her passport; she's fifty-two." She later reveals that she herself "would like to live another hundred years." An old couple dances by, and almost falls off the edge of the stage. Slow dance music changes to the twist, and the aging Mario Mezzabotta tries unsuccessfully to keep up with the gloriously healthy young Gloria. Mario indicates to Guido his uncertainty about his relationship with Gloria: "You must think I've lost my mind, right? I'm thirty years older than she is." In the midst of all these aging people, Guido's inner wish is externally pictured by Fellini. For no reason of plot, we are shown Guido trying to be someone else, wearing a disguise, a false nose, and Fellini's characteristic hat. But of course it fools no one. Disguise or no, Guido has to face his inner doubts and an external barrage of questions and duties. He cannot command, on demand, a comforting escape into wish or fantasy. The American newsman frequently interrupts to ask the kind of questions that Fellini is continually asked: "What's your position between Catholicism and Marxism?" "Is Italy fundamentally a Catholic country?" "Could you create something truly original on demand? For instance, suppose the Pope gave you a commission?" Conocchia, one of Guido's assistants, produces a paper showing the exorbitant cost of the launching tower. The agent of the French actress asks more probing questions about her role in the film. All this takes place while Carla sits at a table on the sidelines, threatening, as does virtually everything in this film, to intermix Guido's personal problems with his professional ones.

Asa Nisi Masa

Suddenly the music and the editing mood change from bustling realism to quiet mystery as a spotlight illumines the androgynous white face of Maurice the magician, another unearthly Fellini messenger, another of the long line of Fellini "clowns, who are the ambassadors of my calling."[48] This magic clown is assisted in a mind–reading act by an equally unearthly "Maya," sharing her name with the Eastern goddess with whom C. G. Jung associates what he calls "the projection–making factor."[49]

Now, in the nightclub of the spa where the adult Guido has gone to pull himself—and his film—together, Maurice the magician conjures a scene from filmmaker Guido's—and Fellini's—childhood.[50] It is when the magician reads Guido's mind, in the midst of the trivial and the consuming demands made on Guido, that we discover precisely what it is that Guido is truly seeking. As the magician will do again in the climactic scene of the film, he now helps Guido to cut through to the essential. Maya goes to a big blackboard to write down Guido's secret thoughts. Maurice puts his hand over Guido's head, and concentrates. Maya calls out, "I don't understand. I don't know how to say it." She writes on the blackboard the letters "ASA NISI MASA." The scene fades out as Maurice looks into the camera and asks all of us: "What does it mean?"

Guido's first dream had ended with a Fall; the second dream was a deathly fantasy of guilt. Now the magician brings Guido back in memory not to a guilt which he still feels but to the innocence from which he has fallen. The scene at Guido's boyhood family farmhouse—located somewhere in the never-never land of the Italian provinces where Gelsomina roamed and Paola was born—is the loveliest scene in the film. It is a reconstruction of Fellini's grandmother's country home at Gambettola, where he spent his boyhood holidays. It is a place of which he often speaks nostalgically.[51] The pure whites, the total blacks, the few tender grays of the scene evoke a

i. 26. Memory: the simplicity of childhood innocence.

remembered time of simple innocence and uncluttered beauty. (i. 26)
Probably no film has ever so perfectly pictured the idealized memory of
happy childhood, a time when a person's soul is clearly and unambigu-
ously whole and his own. We see here what Guido has lost, and what he
impossibly seeks to recover. The scene begins with a pure motherly
lullaby, with visuals of fluttering clean white sheets, and with a loving
grandmother calling little Guido to come join the family festival. He is
called away from his present nightclub isolation to the loving community of his youthful family. The camera surveys the scene from afar,
placing Guido in a spacious, open, freeing context. Amidst laughter and
softly caressing shadows, protective hands pick up little Guido, and
place him with cousins galore into a tub foaming with wine lees. The
children stomp with determination. Little Guido scampers under a
table, is wrapped in a soft towel, and is carried up and up—to the
accompaniment of the lullaby—winding, as he ascends, up a beautiful
stairway, into a kind of heavenly upper room, filled with memories of
two big soft beds, and healthy and wriggling children, a huge bed
warmer, kisses, and snuggles, and a childish chant of "Asa Nisi Masa."
Guido's mother comes in, much younger and more beautiful and bountiful than when we saw her in mourning in the cemetery. "Did you say
your prayers?" she asks comfortingly, adding, "My sweetheart. The
sweetest boy in the world." (She will repeat that line when she reappears in the fantasy harem sequence.) An aunt comes up, smiles, kisses
Guido.

After the lights are out, moonlight falls on an old picture behind the
bed. Some of the supernatural mood of the magician/clown act returns.
Grandma comes quietly into the room; she is wizened, ancient, but
not—as are so many other characters in the film—fearful or resentful of
age. "You can't fool me," she gently accuses. "You aren't sleeping."
The protective figure inspects all of the innocent faces, each of which is
feigning sleep; and as the flickering candlelight darts across their faces,
she pronounces a benediction: "Sleep well, my little babies." When
the children are alone in the dark room, a cousin jumps up and says
quickly: "Guido! Are you asleep? At midnight, the picture moves its
eyes! Say the magic words, and we'll be rich!" She then recites again
the mystic chant: "Asa Nisi Masa. Asa Nisi Masa." She flaps her arms
as she casts her magic incantation. A stooped and hooded old lady
dissolves into the picture, as the camera surveys the quiet house, its
courtyard, the shrines of ancestors, candles flickering before their
portraits, and a warming fire holding out against a threatening wind.
Slowly the simple memory fades into the harshly lit lobby of the
elaborate spa hotel.

Movie Matters

We are back in current time. The clock says 2:00 A.M. But even at this hour, Guido cannot find rest or peace. Mario is playing the piano; Gloria is nagging him to play "Mystification." The French actress wants once more to talk about her role. She offers Guido a drink, anxious to get through to him, anxious to establish a closer personal relationship than the distant one that is all the wary and self-protective Guido is willing to risk: "I need to feel close to my director." Guido is evasive: "I'm very tired. . . . I've got a headache." She tries to cure his headache, "with a magic fluid in my left hand." But he won't be cured. She turns on him in hysteric tears: "Why do you delight in torturing me?" Her specific complaint is uncomfortably like Guido's own: "I feel like I am a complete failure—in my life and in my career." Guido looks away, weary. The only peace in the scene comes when Guido sees again the vision of the beautiful stranger, this time talking on the telephone. The anxious camera stops and admires her beauty. We hear her say: "No, I'm not angry. . . . No. I forgive him everything." Guido, himself surrounded by angry people, himself seeking forgiveness, is impressed. He pushes back his hat in a gesture imitating Fellini. We suspect that this beautiful vision means something to Fellini as well as to Guido.

A hotel man tells Guido that there is a call from Rome. As Guido walks toward the phone, he passes an alcove in the set which is still under construction. Once more we are reminded that we are watching a film. Fellini left the unfinished construction in full view on purpose, explaining: "I wanted something temporary-looking in the hotel. That makes sense, doesn't it, with this character who doesn't know where he's going, who lives half in the past and half in his fantasies, all entangled in this film . . . ?"[52] Guido talks on the phone to his wife Luisa, invites her to join him, and thus precipitates a new crisis in his entangled life.

Before Guido goes to sleep, he stops by his production office and finds that chaos and insistent demands continue to surround him. He had just told Luisa, "I can't really rest while I'm working." The scene is shot in a tight enclosed room, with faces and objects forcing themselves onto Guido and us. One problem is money: "10,000 for set construction, and 70,000 for the steps!" Another is casting: "I couldn't get that German girl you wanted. She's in Paris with the circus. What should I do about her?" And locations: "About that farmhouse: I found the photo, but who knows where the place is? There's no address." And even hanky-panky: Two giggling girls in a bed; and Cesarino, in

his undershorts, introducing them as "my little nieces." In the confusion, the levels mix up once more. Which film is being made, Guido's
or Fellini's? We see a wardrobe woman pinning net material onto a
dressmaker's dummy. But it is not a fictional "costume"; it is the
beginning of the actual dress worn in the scene just completed by the
French actress who is to play the mistress, the character who is the
film's counterpart of the real Carla. And some of the dialogue applies
as much to Fellini as it does to Guido. One of the "nieces" passes on a
familiar complaint: "She says you can't make a good love story." In a
tired, amused, and half-despairing voice, Guido mutters, "She's
right." Reporters, too, will point out this defect in Guido's canon, and
Claudia will contend that it is a defect in Guido's life. Fellini, we know,
has never made "a good love story."

In a tunnel-like hallway outside the production office, Guido is once
again trapped by an attempt to establish a closer personal relationship
than he can now safely allow. Conocchia pleads, "Guido, do you need
me? Is there anything I can do?" Guido's reply is "Go back to sleep."
The bitter altercation which follows is an almost embarrassing further
revelation of Fellini himself. Sounding much like Roberto Rossellini or
one of Fellini's other neo-realist mentors, Conocchia explodes: "Listen,
I'm in this business thirty years. And I've made pictures none of you
would have the guts to try. . . . How you've changed, Guido my
friend." In a return to the aging theme, Guido shouts, "Stop shouting,
you old fool," and, in response, Conocchia warns, "Watch out, you're
not so young any more either." Guido is left alone, Conocchia's warning ringing down the corridor. As in the cemetery scene, the parallel
lines reach toward infinity. The scene ends with a long shot of the
isolated Guido, looking old: his current film, his past friendships, his
whole life are collapsing, leaving him with nothing but his empty and
hidden self.

Order and Disorder

In his hotel room, obviously unnerved by Conocchia's warning
about his fading powers, Guido tries to talk to himself, attempts to
assess the inward trouble: "A lack of inspiration. That's it." And then
he expresses a hope: "I suppose it's just temporary." But that strained
hope doesn't last long: "Guido old man, suppose you're really
finished, you uninspired, untalented fake?" Just at that moment, his
muse enters the room. Inspiration appears, in the person, as one might
have guessed, of Claudia, who means so much, on so many levels, to

both Guido and Fellini. The music of the muse is a gentle unearthly humming chord. She is all in white, as she was when she gave Guido healing waters to drink. Now she pushes the curtain aside, so that the lovely moonlight illumines Guido's bed. Claudia herself, her music, her whiteness, the moon, all give Guido the explicit idea of making her into a symbol of purity, of sincerity.

But, a moment later, he thinks better of it. That had worked in other Fellini films. Gelsomina and Paola had been symbols of purity. But can he just repeat himself? Does he not now have to move forward? The easy answers of the past clash with the new cynicism of the post-*La Dolce Vita* present: "But what the hell does sincerity mean anyway? Enough of symbolism, and those escapist themes of purity and innocence." Daumier had already ridiculed Claudia: "Of all the symbols that abound in your story, that one is the worst." Guido moves into the bathroom, where he parodies a self-anointing as he sprinkles a few drops from a bottle onto his head, as he asks the basic Guido/Fellini uneasy question: "Then what am I looking for?" Claudia reminds him that it *is* purity and innocence that he seeks, for all of his new cynicism, as he, obsessed with his "anima," tries to find a meaning in his life and art. Claudia becomes now the pure white bride, within a room of harmonized patterned beauty, and he decides to use her in the film as the museum curator's daughter. Guido turns upside down onto his bed, indifferently lying on top of many glossy photographic images of beautiful women. It is a good picturization of the way Guido thinks of all his women, as mere objective images. But the idealized Claudia is a special kind of object. Claudia, in her symbolic role, gently kneels at his side, picks up his hand, kisses it, kisses his face, as she reminds Guido of her necessary function: the creation of order in both Guido's and Fellini's films. The camera now pans to Claudia's face, and she is in bed, radiant, lying next to a quiet and satisfied Guido.

A ringing telephone interrupts the dream. The reality of the aging Carla, in bed with hot flashes, interrupts the fantasy of the ageless Claudia. In the middle of the night, Guido gets up and goes to Carla's bedside. Carla is as demanding as Claudia is giving. Carla demands his attention: "You leave me alone all the time!" And she demands answers: "Tell me the truth. Why do you stay with me?" But Guido has other questions, about other worries. With no transition, the scene cuts from Carla's bed to Guido's bed, and we hear Guido asking himself, "What will you say to the Cardinal tomorrow?"

We are now back to the problems of filmmaking. Guido needs to—but fears to—ask the Cardinal for some advice about his film. Within the plot of Guido's movie, his hero is to meet a cardinal in a mudbath, an undignified meeting which sorely distresses the clerical assistant with the Mephisto face. As Guido walks along a garden path toward the Cardinal, he is hemmed in, enclosed, pointed down the narrow way by a clerical assistant on his right and by a clerical assistant on his left. As is often true throughout the film, Guido is restricted by suspicious men around him. Guido explains to the Cardinal's assistants on both sides of him something about the Fellini-like background of the hero of his film: "Like most of us, he's had a Catholic education, and it has created certain problems, certain complexes." As Fellini is moving this scene forward, he is also getting us ready for the next scene, the Saraghina sequence, which will picture some more of those childhood-induced "complexes."

But now Guido, both as man and filmmaker, seeks advice from "an oracle of a truth he can no longer accept." Speaking about the hero of his film, but also obviously about himself and about Fellini, Guido explains to the clerics: "He looks for help, for revelation." But what does Guido get instead? An interview with an almost dead Cardinal, who unnerves Guido by asking irrelevant questions about his state of marriage and number of children. Instead of giving help, or providing revelation, the Cardinal goes off into transports at the sound of a bird, which, according to an ancient legend recounted by the Cardinal, sang a funeral chorus as Diomedes was carried to his grave. As the Cardinal talks of one legend, it is Guido's turn to be transported—by a memory, a legend of his own, a myth from his youth. When the Cardinal stops to listen to his bird, Guido sees a fat woman, exposing her legs, coming down a nearby hill. Guido mutters, as he stares at the woman's ample flesh, "Memories have so little respect." Guido looks over his glasses. We hear the sound of a whistle. And Guido is free from the Cardinal; and we are back into Guido's youth. We are about to see his fall from innocence.

The Fall

As the Steiner episode stamps itself on the memory as the central sequence in *La Dolce Vita*, so the Saraghina episode is the most unforgettable portion of *8 ½*. Fellini breaks out all his cinematic genius to imprint in the viewer's psyche his crucial statement—that in the search for the self, the child is the father of the man. In the cemetery sequence we saw guilt. In the childhood sequence we came to understand the mystic meaning of Asa Nisi Masa as Guido's search for soul and lost innocence. And it is in this second childhood sequence when we discover that Guido must accept and integrate into his current life not only the joys and innocence of his past but the guilts and traumas as well. Only then can Guido find a wholeness within his soul in the present. So central a statement will that become for Fellini that he will also make it the basis of his next great—and revelatory—film, *Juliet of the Spirits*.

The first voices of the Saraghina episode are those of a group of boys, playing soccer, and shouting: "Guido, Guido, we are going to see Saraghina!" We again see Guido as a boy, older than he was in the farmhouse scene, but wearing the same school uniform and long cape that big Guido was wearing in the dream sequence at his father's grave. Fellini remembers his own schooldays, "dressed in long black capes that came down to our feet."[53] Young Guido shouts to the boys in excited anticipation of Saraghina: "I'm coming!" In an eloquent Fellini composition, Guido is seen framed within the enclosing arms of a religious statue, which seems to be holding him back. But then, as we hear Nino Rota's wonderfully rhythmic "Saraghina's Music," compelling, sexy, and gay, Guido and the other boys all run away from the still camera, escaping from the embrace of the religious statue and thus from the authority of Church and school.

We see a long shot of little Guido and the other boys in the happiest of environments: in brightest daylight, free and open on the spacious windy beach, against the clear sky and sparkling sea—natural imagery central to every Fellini film. We hear only the music and the sound of the sea. Saraghina—as a kind of mythic sea monster—emerges from a bunker on the beach, all wild, with hair like seaweed, with undulating wavelike breasts and buttocks, powerful, inviting, overwhelming. Her music is now raw: "Saraghina, the rhumba, the rhumba," the boys call out. There is an abandonment and a kind of monstrous beauty as Fellini films Saraghina's dance. (i. 27) As always in Fellini, a dance is a moment of exaltation. Flashes of sunlight hit our eyes as Saraghina dances. She is overexposed on the film as she exposes herself to the boys. As Saraghina dances over to the bunker and fondles it, Fellini puts her out of focus and brings in clearly the limitless sea behind her. Saraghina backs into the camera, her huge bottom filling the entire screen. In pantomime, the boys jump up and down in ecstasy. In an orgasmic moment, Guido is lifted right off the earth: Saraghina enfolds him in her vastness, picks him up, high and higher, dancing with him dizzily.

Saraghina's dance is stunning in its impact: funny but terrifying, beautiful but truly monstrous. It is a little boy's quintessential first encounter with the paradoxical mysteries of sex. We can understand

i. 27. Saraghina's dance: Guido's fall from innocence.

why the Saraghina memory is so vivid to Guido that it intrudes at the incongruous moment of his audience with the Cardinal. And Fellini so films the encounter that it is unmistakably communicated as a vivid and personal memory of his own. No outside source of information is necessary to make us feel that this scene is as significant to Fellini as it is to Guido. But Fellini *has* explained the significance of the real Saraghina in his own life. Saraghina did exist. She was a prostitute who lived on the beach in Fellini's boyhood town of Rimini. She sold herself to the local fishermen in exchange for the dregs from their sardine nets. In the Romagna dialect, sardines are called "saraghine." So the boys took to calling their local prostitute "La Saraghina." Fellini has spoken many times about how inescapably this "troubling fabulous monster" was to cling to his memory.[54] To Camilla Cederna he described in cinematic sensory detail how, "with all its horrible force," the sexual power of this living myth from his childhood was first revealed to him. Once, when he was eight, Fellini went to Saraghina's concrete bunker with some older boys:

> The sun was setting after a storm. We were quivering with anticipation and fear. When we reached the beach, we began throwing stones at her windows. Finally La Saraghina came

out, screaming at us. . . . It was an unforgettable sight: there she stood silhouetted against a rough sea, screaming insults, huge, her clothes in disorder, her eyes as wild as a lion's, her head made even bigger by a mass of curls like those of Louis XIV. . . .

"We have the money," the older boys called. "Toss it over." she replied. . . .

I stood two feet away from her, trembling; near enough to smell her—a combination of seaweed, fish, tobacco, rotten wood and gasoline. La Saraghina counted the money, and then stared at us. As the sky turned purple, the ritual began. With a solemn gesture that almost bespoke respect for us and for herself, she slowly exposed herself several times. Then she turned round and did the same thing. It was an unbelievable mountain of white—a kind of Moby-Dick that didn't scare me at all, even though I couldn't talk for at least fifteen minutes afterward.[55]

Once Fellini, in this most personal of films, was able to face his La Saraghina once more, she was to appear in some form, almost as a Fellini trademark, in all his subsequent films.

In real life, Fellini was speechless; in Fellini's film, little Guido has no time to try to find his voice because a cadre of priests appears on the horizon, descending on the boys in a speeded-up slapstick Keystone Kops chase that ends when Guido runs bump against the biggest priest of all, and they all tumble in a heap. That tone is perfect, for the whole Saraghina episode is a delightful mixture of humor and pathos, of power and triviality. It is as if both Guido and Fellini were trying to soften their traumatic childhood memories through amused adult self-mockery.

The scene cuts from the beach, and little Guido is toted by the ear into the range of the camera, and back into the authority of Church and school. The school, like Saraghina, is taken from life. Fellini explains: "After primary school I was sent to a small boarding school run by monks at Fano. The stories about La Saraghina, the discovery of sex, the punishments dealt out to me, I have shown in 8½."[56] In La Dolce Vita, Marcello says that he too went to school in Fano. Fellini's obsessions with punishment and guilt, lodged in his childhood memory, are as much the point of this episode as are Saraghina and sex. Fellini supposes that his "four or five years in that school" are the reasons for "the feeling of guilt I drag around with me."[57] The rest of the schoolboy episode shows that after the initiation comes the guilt, and then the penance.

With an alarm bell tolling in the background, little Guido is led
down a long, dark, and enclosing stairway, past the staring and accusing eyes of all the old priests who, in portraits, hover in their black and
solemn frames along the hollow halls of the school. The whole tradi-
tion, all of history, is accusing Guido. The last of the accusing faces is
the most terrible of all, and only when it moves do we realize that it is
not a portrait but a living priest, the last of a long line of disciplinarians
bent now to the single task of punishing Guido for his sexual sin. His
accusers are all themselves sexless creatures, actually men played by
women with cropped hair and bodies hidden inside priests' shapeless
flowing unisex cassocks. The accusations against little Guido seem to
rise out of the ground: "For shame." "It's a mortal sin." "For shame."
"I can't believe it." "Look at your mother." Guido turns to look, and
another shame is added unto him. His mother, dressed once more in
the mourning outfit that she wore in the similarly guilt-laden cemetery
scene, adds her lamentations to all the rest: "O Lord! What shame!
What pain! What pain!" And behind the mother, above everyone, is
the angelic picture of the pure boy saint, Dominic Savio, the model
Italian schoolboy, so obviously superior at this moment to the sinner
Guido. (i. 28)

i. 28. Guido at school: after the initiation comes the guilt.

Guido's shame continues into the classroom, as Guido walks in, wearing a dunce cap on his head and a sign reading "Shame" around his neck. "I was shown to all the classes," Fellini remembers, speaking of the time at Fano when he wore such a sign of guilt around his own neck.[58] In the dining hall, the contrasts between sinner and saint continue. The reading during dinner is an instruction concerning a saint pointedly different from Guido: "But what the pious Luigi abhorred most throughout his life was any contact with women. He would flee the moment a woman came into his presence." Guido, for penance, is forced to kneel on a pile of kernels. "One of the most frequent punishments," Fellini remembers, "was to have the pupil who had committed some small fault remain kneeling on large kernels of corn for half an hour or an hour."[59]

The rituals of guilt and forced penitence go on. Guido covers his eyes as he is forced to look at the mortal remains of a mummified saint. Just after facing the corruption of the body, the guilt-ridden Guido attempts to purify his now-corrupted soul, his tarnished anima. The camera with determination seems to march along with Guido toward a black and ominous confessional box which looks like a consuming insect. Inside the tiny enclosed space, Guido is isolated from the priest and everyone, as the Confessor moans aloud: "Don't you know that Saraghina is the devil?" And Guido weakly replies, "I didn't know; I didn't know," as the Confessor sighs in sorrow.

Once outside the black beetle box, Guido kneels down to say his penance. He looks up for solace toward a lovely, forgiving, and generous statue of the Virgin Mary. And suddenly we understand the role of the mysterious vision of the beautiful stranger who has been appearing in fantasies to the grown-up Guido. The consoling statue of the Madonna has the face of that beautiful stranger. By its impact on the film as a whole, that face seems to be as personal and important to Fellini as is Saraghina. And indeed it is. But that particular face means much not only to Fellini, but to his generation. Deena Boyer explains why Fellini called from retirement a beautiful stage actress out of his past:

> Fellini wanted a real "character out of the 1930s" for his film, and, to a man of his age, Caterina Boratto is precisely that: a lovely memory of adolescence come back to life. Thousands of Italians will be startled when they see in this picture the woman who, in the last years before the war, was the incarnation of the "diva." Goddess or apparition—one is much the same as the other, is it not?[60]

Having hired Caterina Boratto to play his memory of the Virgin
Mother, a consoling and loving figure from his youth, Fellini dressed
her in the clothes, hair style, and makeup of that period in his life. And
he gave her face to his Madonna.

The Saraghina episode ends with neither Guido's shame nor with
the consolation that he receives from the lovely and loving, although
elusive, Madonna. Now the initiate, having confessed and paid his
penance, Guido returns to the life he has recently entered. The initi-
ated Italian male finds another kind of Madonna. The scene dissolves
from the face of the statue to the bunker on the beach. We hear
Saraghina singing. The scene is not now a mixture of beauty and fear. It
is now pure. It is a memory fantasy solely of seaside beauty and peace.
Saraghina is sitting in a chair, with her back to us, a long white pure
scarf fluttering gracefully in the sea breeze. Guido kneels to worship
not a devil but a new Madonna. He waves his cap to Saraghina. She
smiles, whispers gently "Ciao," as a kind of benediction, and continues singing. Even this lovely coda is from life. Fellini says: "One day
I cut school for another look at this legendary, exciting monster. She
was singing a rhumba. . . . I said 'Good day, Signora. How well you
sing.' Then I ran away, waving my cap to her."[61] Neither Guido nor
the adult Fellini found it so easy to run away from the memory of his
legendary monster.

When the Saraghina episode ends, Fellini cuts back to the Cardinal.
But time has now jumped forward. The interview in the garden is over.
The Cardinal and his entourage are now sitting at a table in the spa
restaurant. At the next table, Guido overhears their joking conversation, as Daumier intones into his ear his rationalist criticisms of the
images and sounds from Guido's film which we have just witnessed
on Fellini's screen:

> What does it mean? It's just another episode from your child-
> hood memory. Do you want to make a serious film about the
> Catholic conscience in Italy? In that case, you must lift every-
> thing, to work at a sophisticated cultural level. You must use
> stringent, unassailable logic. These tender innocent scenes of
> your childhood are entirely negative. They are drowned in
> nostalgia.

The writer concludes his very familiar anti-Fellini attack by asking
the question that several critics of the completed film will take as their
own. Daumier's final challenge is: "Don't you see the confusion, the
ambiguity?" Like a latter-day Shaw, Fellini delights in thumbing his
nose at his critics. Fellini has his own explanation of his behavior: "This

is a side of my character that comes from Romagna. The man who has been laughed at goes arrogantly ahead."[62] He will gladly commit the sins of which his critics accuse him, even those critics whom he himself creates. And so the next scene is one of the most wondrously confusing and ambiguous scenes in the film.

Inferno

The steamroom episode returns our attention to the Cardinal, and is totally without stringent and unassailable logic. It begins in current time, as several spa inhabitants, all robed in white sheets, begin a descent into the steamroom. The light music at the restaurant turns into ominous marching music when the descent begins. Pace the producer continues the needling which Guido has been suffering, as he shouts out warnings similar to those which were begun by Daumier. Without stopping his own downward movement, Pace calls to Guido over his shoulder: "I understand why you want this film. You want to show the confusion that man has inside of himself. Just be sure that what interests you, interests everybody. Remember that the audience has to understand the film." Guido hears these words which he fears are true. When he most needs consolation, it comes to Guido as if from heaven: the lovely stranger walks down the stairs, apparently for the precise purpose of taking the sting out of Pace's words. She turns to exhibit her beautiful Madonna face, just for Guido's admiration and peace. At the bottom of the stairs, Pace continues his attack on Guido, continuing to speak accusations which Guido obviously both fears and believes.

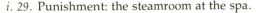

i. 29. Punishment: the steamroom at the spa.

The scene begins to look to us as it must feel to Guido: it has become a descent into hell. (i. 29) The words which have been spoken throughout the film about aging and death and punishment are here transformed into a panorama. The benches are packed with wizened old men, drooping like corpses as the steam rises as if from an an invisible pit. The pure white sheets which wrapped the youthful Guido and his wriggling cousins at the farmhouse are now shrouds draped on aged and still bodies. The music echoes the cemetery scene. Guido sees Mario Mezzabotta, eyes closed, looking his true age.

As Guido sits alone in this inferno, his glasses steam over. Once more, his vision turns inward. The level of meaning shifts. A gorgeously husky female voice, which we don't yet recognize, announces a possible ascent out of this hell. From a loudspeaker, the beautiful voice booms out: "Guido, His Eminence is waiting for you!" In a wonderfully confused scene of demanding chatter, each assistant asks Guido for a personal favor to seek from the Cardinal, as they prepare him for his audience. We watch Guido approach the real Cardinal with whom he has already had an interview, as if that Cardinal were the Cardinal in Guido's film. The representative of the Church sits in the steam, deep under the earth, in a bath of mud, acting out the scene from Guido's film which Mephistopheles has already condemned as inappropriate. The camera, and apparently Guido and his hero too, floats into the mudbath room through a tiny hinged window.

The fictional Cardinal is as unhelpful to Guido's hero as the real Cardinal was to the real Guido. In a Latin that only strengthens his isolation, the Cardinal three times intones the classic Church doctrine proclaimed by Origines: "Outside the Church there is no salvation!" Another of Guido's—and of Fellini's—complexes from his Catholic boyhood now rises to the surface, and Guido must worry about salvation. Clumps of mud in the foreground might well be ironic editorial comments about the worth of the Cardinal's words, but the sentences are chanted with power and filmed with troubling impact. The solemn warning about the loss of salvation, placed in this episode of hell, is clearly not trivial to either the fictional or the real filmmaker. We don't see Guido at all; the Cardinal speaks a line for everyone, a line that generalizes the quest structure of the entire film: "This is a time to determine your task in life." With a cinematic gesture of respect or fear, the camera backs out the way it came, quietly retreating through the little window, which closes slowly behind it, shutting out the Cardinal's final frightening warning: "That which is outside the City of God belongs to the City of the Devil."

Spirits

We hear "Blue Moon," the music apparently not of *civitas dei* but of *civitas diaboli*. We are now in a busy street at the fashionable resort spa, seeing what Guido sees as he strolls down the avenue, quite in tune with the lightness of the music. Fellini treats us to another quick contrast in mood. Guido sees a fakir, breaking endurance records for enclosure within a transparent booth. That visual metaphor for Guido's—and Fellini's—condition as filmmakers has also been expressed as a verbal metaphor by Fellini. Just before filming *8½*, he spoke of the "fakir's wall" within which he needed to hide in order to protect himself from interference when he was, like Guido, besieged by producers and others.[63] The already besieged Guido sees Luisa, and a new crisis is added to his life. Guido greets Luisa in front of a travel poster of a wide and expansive sea, with troubled waters. At best, the prospects are uncertain. We, too, meet Anouk Aimée; and we see the opposite of Sandra Milo. Guido's wife is thin, proper, and plainly dressed. His tastes in wives and mistresses are obviously as contrasting as the moods and styles of this film.

The scene shifts again. Luisa and Guido are dancing, always a festive event in Fellini. "We haven't danced together in years," Luisa reminds Guido. When Luisa asks him how his work is going, Guido's honest admission dampens the festive mood a bit: "I don't think I've made much progress." As the whole production group prepares to drive to the launching tower, the grand white elephant in Guido's stalled film, Luisa suddenly turns icy. Because, throughout the film, we share Guido's limited point of view, we also share his confusion about the reason for Luisa's sudden coolness toward him. Luisa's accusing attitude is an added burden weighing on Guido as he is forced to face the barrage of questions and ridicule hurled at him during the subsequent launching pad episode.

To ominous music, the scene dissolves into a hand-held lantern, then blinding car lights, then the hulking other-worldly launching tower itself. The mood now is one of science fiction, that blending of fact and fancy that fits this film as well as any. The viewer has not, of course, read the scenario of *8½*, let alone the scenario of Guido's film. He doesn't even know what Guido's film is supposed to be *about*. Luisa had just asked Guido explicitly: "What's the film about? What's on your mind this time?" He didn't answer her, or us. This sequence provides some answers.

A voice somewhere in the background announces: "This is the launching pad. The most important scene in the picture." We now see, in front of the launching pad, a photograph of a long parade of the populace, led by the Church dignitaries, to the escape rocket on the site of the launching pad. We actually saw this photograph once before, unobtrusively behind the giggling nieces in the production office scene. We ought to know by now at least that Guido is trying to make a film of escape.

As the visitors climb the tower, continuing chatter helps us piece together the plot of Guido's film—precisely as we have been in the process of piecing together Fellini's film. One voice asks, "Is your husband playing with science fiction?" Another voice explains, "You see, the earth is ravaged by nuclear war." As Guido speaks down below to Luisa's friend Rossella, more voices tumble down from high up on the tower. Some of the voices continue with explanations that help the viewer: "Then in an attempt to escape atomic pestilence, the survivors try to flee to another planet." The meaning of the photograph of the big procession—a wonderful eschatological twist on the characteristic Fellini ritualistic religious procession—thus finally comes clear. Other voices rehearse Guido's mounting problems with the film: "You see you have to be crazy to listen to this director." "We're behind schedule." "That madman made us spend 80 million new lira on this construction!" "We need 10,000 extras; maybe 15,000."

If we can hear these voices both of explanation and complaint, we must assume that Guido, down at the base of the tower with Rossella, can hear them too. Guido's guilt, caused by all those artistic problems, now combines with his recognition of Luisa's anger. All of this together provokes what Deena Boyer, sensitive to the sacramental moments that are so important in Fellini films, calls "Guido's confession."[64] The setting of *this* confession is not the devouring insectlike box of Guido's childhood memories, but rather the shadow of the useless tower, the insistently visible symbol of Guido's artistic failure, that tower which is now crawling with demanding and consuming insectlike people. Perhaps we can remember now that that abandoned tower was the first object that we saw when Guido floated freely above the earth in the dream of attempted escape that began the film. And as the many voices, speaking many languages, ring out from the tower, we might well realize that, in his aspiration to rise above the earth and its cares, Guido has tried to build his own Tower of Babel. Alberto Solmi tells us that Brueghel's painting *The Tower of Babel* had, indeed, been the inspiration for this scene and its symbol.[65] The confession scene is rightly placed within all this radiating symbolism. (i. 30)

i. 30. The launching pad: Guido's Tower of Babel.

Fellini has created the interesting character of Rossella so that she can hear Guido's confession. When we first met Rossella, Pace, Guido's producer, had been afraid to shake hands with her because "she reads your soul through your finger tips." She had been connected with "mysticism" and with "spirits." For this important role, Fellini found the wonderfully beautiful actress Rossella Falk, an amazing look-alike of the young Greta Garbo, herself an important kind of priestess to that decade of the 1930s which is continually recalled throughout this film. In her priestly role, Rossella first explains to Guido, and to us, about Luisa: "She's confused. She wants one thing today and another tomorrow." Rossella has thus told us that wife is not so different from husband. Now Rossella proceeds to read Guido's soul. First Rossella tells Guido about his "guilty conscience," and about his evasions to avoid facing that conscience.

In response, Guido confesses his failures, as accusing words continue to rain down from the tower. He wanted his art to solve the problems of his life. Therefore, "in my picture, everything happens! I'm putting everything in." But art, like life, involves *choices*, and Guido has refused to choose one thing to the exclusion of another. The result has been confusion: "I thought everything was clear in my mind. I wanted to make an honest film: no lies, no compromises. I thought I had something so simple, so simple, to say. I thought it would be helpful to everybody. . . . No. I'm totally confused now. And with this tower on my hands. . . ." Guido walks away, stooped, with his back to the camera; he is crushed beneath the weight of that tower and by the weight of those people, from both his professional and personal lives, all hovering threateningly above him. He asks poignantly: "Where did it all go wrong?" And his final grim words of confession are delivered in a self-taunting sing-song chant: "I really have nothing to say." But, more soberly, and with a kind of resolve in his tone, Guido adds, "I want to say it just the same." Perhaps he has something to say or to show which is beyond words, something to do with the very crisis of choice which he is now enduring. Guido asks Rossella for her response. She passes on to him the simple advice of her spirits. Rossella speaks the spiritual message that implicitly was told to Gelsomina and Zampano, and that explicitly confronted Maddelena and Marcello. Rossella says to Guido: "They say that you are free. But you *have* to choose. And you haven't much time left." Voices call to Guido from the top of the tower, asking the appropriate question in this quest film of descents and ascents: "Guido, are you coming up or not?" We are left with the question.

Simple and Complex

Guido has been after something "so simple, so simple. . . ." But he hasn't found it yet. It's one thing for him to be told to choose, but quite another for him to know *what* to choose. If the spirits say that free choice exists, they still don't tell him what he is to do about it. And most immediately he must face the problem of Luisa vs. Carla. What is he to choose to do there? Problems of filmmaking give way for a while to problems of living.

The film cuts to a shot of Guido alone in bed. He pretends to be sleeping as Luisa comes into the hotel bedroom. We can tell by the mobile face of Anouk Aimée that Luisa is about to give up on Guido. She notices a glossy photograph of a beautiful girl and glances accusingly at Guido. The girl in the photograph is more Luisa's rival than she knows. It is an image of Luisa herself, as she is to be transformed by Guido's art into something more acceptable to him. It is in fact a photograph of the girl whom we will soon see playing Luisa in the screen tests, who is to thus become Luisa in Guido's attempt at artistic reconstruction of their lives. Guido keeps on his dresser not an image of the real Luisa but an image of the imagined one.

In the furious argument which follows, Luisa articulates their true-life relationship: "I know that we've been at a dead end for years." She visualizes their separation by turning her back on Guido; he, in turn, in his separate bed, does the same. Back to back, the argument continues. Luisa identifies the exasperating characteristic which Guido, in this quest film, exhibits in both his life and work, the characteristic that still separates him from the despairing Steiner: "But you, always wanting to start over again!" Luisa has identified a characteristic for which Fellini often mocks himself. He speaks of his "slightly absurd hope of making a clean slate in order to start again from the beginning."[66] In a weary voice, Guido suggests that perhaps that characteristic is exhausted in both film directors: "I don't want to start anything over again."

In the next scene, with Guido, Luisa, and Rossella in the outdoor spa cafe, Luisa specifies one reason for her current anger at Guido. Carla arrives in a coach, all bells and light music and magnificent vulgarity. Luisa says to the shrinking Guido, as he hides behind his newspaper: "Relax. I already saw her. Last night, soon after I got here." Now, realizing why Luisa had suddenly turned cold and then had turned furious, Guido characteristically tries to lie his way out of this new problem: "I'm really insulted. Would I go with a woman who dresses like that?" Luisa's complaint is as much about his lying as it is about his infidelity. She complains that when she is with Guido she herself can't tell the true from the false. "Is it possible that *you* can't tell the difference?" Luisa asks of Guido. Perhaps the imaginative artist can't tell the difference, perhaps that could be his strength as an artist; but perhaps it is just an evasion as he tries to find his self but is afraid of what he might discover. At any rate, when the lie doesn't work, Guido switches to fantasy, and the true does blend into the false.

While Luisa carries on, as she puts it, "like a scandalized housewife," Guido puts on his dark glasses, looks into the camera, raises his eyebrows, sighs, mutters, "And yet!" As Guido smiles blissfully and snuggles down into his chair, we hear Carla singing like a lark. Luisa approaches her with warmth and accepting love, saying, "What a lovely voice you have, Carla." Luisa adds, as they exchange a sisterly kiss, "I've been wanting to meet you for a long time." In the background, Guido, his legs up on a table in perfect comfort, smiles approvingly at Luisa and Carla, and applauds their togetherness. To help us realize that this is fantasy, not reality, Fellini has removed Rossella from the scene. She and her spirits are all too real to Guido; he can't fantasize them into cooperation with his desires. Luisa and Carla dance away together, Guido's imagination adopting in their dance Fellini's favorite symbol for festivity. "How elegant you look!" Luisa says graciously to Carla as she eyes her costume. "Oh no," protests Carla humbly, "I'm a bit overdressed." Indeed she is. But how like Guido's ego to wish that tasteful Luisa couldn't notice Carla's vulgarity. (i. 31) The camera rhythmically follows Guido's wife and his mistress as they dance away together into a dissolve. Ever the movie director, Guido constructs his fantasies as if he were constructing a film, molding intractible women into pliant servants of his wishes. This wishful fantasy of how Guido's women *should* behave triggers the most hilariously wonderful portion of the entire film, the renowned harem episode. Rossella had asked, "Aren't you ever going to grow up, Guido?" Wouldn't it be nice. . . .

The Harem

Carla and Luisa's two-step dissolves into a warming flame, glowing within the lovely farmhouse kitchen which we had seen in Guido's earlier boyhood memory. Within that site of a past loving family community, Guido projects his present wishes for the future. It's a perfect Freudian fantasy, fitting Freud's own definition: "A fantasy at one and the same moment hovers between three periods of time . .

i. 31. The plain and the fancy: wife and mistress.

past, present, and future are threaded, as it were, on the string of the
wish that runs through them all."[67] In the wish, Luisa, hair covered by
a cloth, is costumed in the long black dress of the Italian peasant
woman, kept pure by a crisp white apron. She removes from the flame
a steaming bucket of hot water and begins, in perfect harmony with the
classic male stereotype of the dutiful housewife, to scrub the floor. Just
then a bevy of women run to the door with the excited greeting, "Here
he is!" We see all the women in Guido's life, many of whom we know
by now, many of whom are strangers to us, all of them transformed
from the real to the ideal. Only Claudia is missing, for she is already
Guido's fantasy of the ideal woman. He doesn't have to work on her.
As Guido's women move in and out of this scene, so do the musical
themes that have been associated with Guido's episodic life. All blend
into harmony as Guido's fantasy takes control.

Like a Santa Claus, generous and loved and expected, Guido enters
the interior warmth from the blizzard raging outdoors, scattering
gifts to squealing and appreciative women. Among the recipients of
Guido's largess is Luisa's sister, whom we had seen earlier to be
bitterly opposed to Guido. She is now dusty and dishevelled from
housework, gratefully receiving not only Guido's gift, but his kiss.
Mario's Gloria is there, always the pretend intellectual, now solemnly
playing the harp as she receives her gift. Later, a ladylike Carla,
vulgarity evaporated by fantasy, will also play the heavenly harp in
this wistful episode. The French actress looks at Guido trustingly,
without a single inquiry about her role. She now knows her role. It is to
love Guido unquestioningly. The vision of the lovely stranger receives
as her gift Luisa's own tiara—a crown more fitting for the Queen of
Heaven than for a mere wife. And for the first time the stranger actually
speaks to the man who venerates her. Luisa surveys the scene, looks
into the camera, and—perfect wife—editorializes for all the others:
"He's such a darling!" Now it is Guido's turn to receive a present.
Hazel Scott, a sexy black American dancer, is presented to Guido as a
gift from Luisa. Hazel does a little dance to show her stuff. Her
accompanying music is Saraghina's rhumba, but the dance is now
refined by skill. Some of Guido's amateurs have turned pro. Liking
what he sees, Guido turns to his wife and murmurs with complacent
gratitude: "Thank you, Luisa. Very thoughtful of you."

Guido shifts his role from Santa to little boy. The women now
prepare his bath, in the very tub of his childhood. Luisa's sister takes
off Guido's coat; Carla blows on his cold hands; they all remove his
pants. Guido's mother sends Gloria off to get the talcum powder. As
the vision of the lovely stranger prepares to wrap him up in one of the

huge pure white sheets from his childhood, he asks her: "Will you tell me just one thing, lovely lady? Who are you?" He doesn't know what he remembers. We understand that this Madonna figure, always mysterious, hovering, unattainable to Guido, is an idealized moment out of his Catholic boyhood, a remembered Madonna not able to be a permanently consoling reality to the adult Guido. But he can only take a bit of pleasure in her momentary presence in his memory. She replies: "My name doesn't matter. I'm happy to be here. That's enough."

The camera tilts up and shows Rossella as an observer of all of this. She sits next to a trapdoor over the tub, in precisely the position occupied earlier by another spiritualist—the little girl cousin who chanted "Asa Nisi Masa" during the childhood scene. Rossella is present in this roomful of Guido's women in a very special role. As in life, she is to him the outsider, the priest-observer of Guido's soul, the messenger of special spiritual force. When Guido sees her, she explains that she is there "like Pinocchio's nagging conscience," thus

i. 32. Rossella chaperones a small part of Guido's harem: A relative, Momma, another relative, the French actress, the Danish stewardess, Edy the starlet, and Jacqueline Bonbon, as Carla kneels before Guido.

reminding both Guido and us that he lies as outrageously in his fantasies as he does in his life. Rossella explains precisely what we are seeing: "So you finally got your harem, King Solomon." We remember now the words that must have played a part in initiating this fantasy within Guido's mind. Soon after Luisa had arrived at the spa, her sister had commented bitterly, "Look at the harem that this director travels with!" The producer had asked, "And is this lovely mystic part of the harem?" And Rossella had responded, "No; I just came along as a chaperone." (i. 32) Even here in Guido's harem fantasy, Rossella remains the chaperone. "Can I stay?" Rossella now asks. She adds: "I just want to observe you." But, as always, Rossella also carries a kind of warning for Guido. "Tell me," she asks, "aren't you afraid?" "Of what?" asks Guido, innocently secure in his fantasy. Guido concludes: "Everything is perfect."

And for a while everything does remain perfect for Guido. Hovering women bathe him now, as hovering women bathed him when he was a boy. They whisper, "Isn't he the sweetest boy in the world?" Saraghina admires his legs, as he had once, in his way, admired parts of her. The black girl juggles. The apparition carries the old-fashioned oil lamp that we first saw banishing the shadows from the boyhood farm house. As Guido sits in his tub, he folds and flaps his arms just as his cousin did when she chanted "Asa Nisi Masa." For a time, back in his innocent childhood, a satisfied Guido thinks of himself as self-possessed once more. Fellini has bluntly told us about reality: "I'm not at all self-possessed."[68]

Several new women are introduced to us. One is a cute little starlet-type who continually appears throughout the scene in new dresses and new hats; we can imagine the role the aspiring young starlet has played in the life of famous director Guido. Famous director Fellini intrudes himself again into Guido's fantasies. This is the starlet, called "Edy" in the film, who is actually the aspiring young starlet Edy Vessel, to whom, the gossipy Rome newspapers had reported, Fellini had promised a part in his film. But no one on the set knew what she was to do as the harem scene was being filmed.[69] In the film, Edy now leans out over the vat and asks, "Do you like this dress, Guido?" Puzzled, Rossella calls her back and asks, "Who are you? What are you doing here?" "I don't know," responds Edy, on camera, making the fantasies of art follow the rumors of reality. "He said he would give me a part in the picture."

Another new woman is introduced to us as Guido turns to a tall sexy Scandinavian-looking stewardess and asks, "Nadine, what did you say in Copenhagen?" Her reply makes clear how Guido came to know *her*: "We invite all our passengers to be our overnight guests in Copenhagen. . . . All expenses will be paid by the company. We wish you a delightful evening." Guido closes his eyes in ecstatic memory of the delights of that particular Copenhagen evening. We recognize Nadine's voice, as she speaks into her microphone, from its previous throaty announcement that the Cardinal was ready to see Guido in the mudbath. Guido's memories and fantasies are quite wonderfully and inextricably and irreverently intertwined.

Rossella's warning query, "Aren't you afraid?" now becomes prophetic. Even in his fantasies, Guido has trouble keeping order. Guido's women won't stay in place any better than his art. Trouble begins with a shout from the basement. "Who is screaming?" Guido asks warily. In comes Jacqueline Bonbon, in all her feathered and bejewelled finery, a quintessential buxom burlesque showgirl, a Fellini woman *par excellence*. Jacqueline protests that she is too young to be banished to the upstairs, where Guido's women must go when they reach a certain age. "All those old hags upstairs are older than me," she protests. "I'm only twenty-six!" Jacqueline shouts: "Look at my legs! Who's got a bosom like mine? Who has such a nice behind?" As she talks, she displays each extravagant (but aging) part. It is a bittersweet scene of great charm and pathos. The mood affects the characters in the fantasy as strongly as it affects us. We feel Guido's injustice as Jacqueline pleads, "Guido, Guido, I beg you, don't send me upstairs!" A rebellion begins. Boyer describes how it looked as it was being shot:

> Jacqueline rebels, encouraged by the stewardess. Soon all the women want to shed their chains. "That's an order made by someone whose own life isn't in such good order! . . . You're a monster!" Edy comes on in another costume. "What are we, lemons for him to squeeze and throw away?". . . . But Gloria, the contrary intellectual, dissents: "I adore monsters. We're all women created by his imagination, so it's right for him to devour us." The Negro dancer leaps on to the table and seizes a sheet hanging from the ceiling. "Down with the tyrant! Down with Bluebeard!" She swings Tarzan-like across the room on her sheet. . . . Meanwhile, "Fiesta" has given way to "The Ride of the Valkyries."[70]

Still confident, Guido puts on his hat, like the one Fellini always wears, looks, bored, at his fingernails, and insists to Jacqueline and her rebel supporters, in a voice filled with Hollywood cool: "It's the house rules." But only the family now wants to keep to the rules of Guido's house. When Jacqueline announces firmly, "I won't go!" Guido's

Mother responds, "She's crazy! We shouldn't have taken her in."
Guido's aunt, annoyed, insists: "Jacqueline, you know the rules." The
French actress announces her objection: "It's an absurd rule!" Nadine
agrees: "We shouldn't accept it!" And Saraghina quite simply intones,
with a growl: "It's not fair!" "A real man," the French actress adds,
"wouldn't make such a rule." Guido now turns into Humphrey
Bogart, curls his lip, and sneers: "Get off my back!"

One rebellious voice articulates right out loud Guido's fear of aging:
"What makes him think he's still young?" And then comes the crusher:
"He's a lousy lover." Poor Guido. His fantasies reveal not only his
masculine desires but his classic masculine fears. Luisa had earlier
commented sarcastically to Guido about his "vaunted virility." And
the full truth now slips out from one of the crowd of women, any one of
whom should know: "Let's make no bones about it: You don't know
how to make love. Caresses, sweet talk—and then you fall asleep."
Stung, Guido shouts back his defense: "I don't sleep! I think!"

Guido, who has already been Santa Claus, little boy, Solomon and
Sultan, Bluebeard, Cowboy and Tough Guy and Fellini, now becomes
Latin lover. He picks up his huge whip, cracks it, and attacks the
women one after another. And they love it. Carla giggles, Gloria sighs,
in ecstasy, "Delicious!" Edy, in a new hat, cries out with pleasure.
The screen is filled with a tall shadow of Guido, whip dominant. The
lovely vision's attitude is not sexual but solicitous: "Darling, you're
wounded!" And Mother sums up her traditionally maternal defense of
her boy: "He's too good for you." The excited camera races to keep up
with the action. The music builds to a crescendo. Hazel runs in a circle,
makes catlike inviting noises toward Guido, turns toward the camera,
blows Guido a gentle kiss, like a lion subdued by the forceful whip of a
lion tamer. Then all the women, formed into a surrounding circle,
break into applause at Guido's splendid performance. Guido stands
quietly, whip now limp, and accepts their admiration.

Luisa has not been part of the rebellion. She has been hostess. She
has been making dinner, setting the table. She has gone on, quietly,
dutifully, being the ideal wife. She has been bringing about the order
that ideal woman Claudia claimed as her special province. To Jacqueline, Luisa quietly reasserts the basic principle: "It's the house
rules." Luisa watches Guido have his fun, only insisting that he hurry:
"The soup is getting cold." At the end of Guido's performance, Luisa
exclaims admiringly: "What an extraordinary man!" Rossella looks
astonished, but Luisa explains: "He likes excitement. He does this
almost every night."

i. 33. Banishment: Jacqueline's farewell dance.

Nadine announces into her microphone that the revolt is over. "Dear Jacqueline," she says on behalf of the assembly, "We're happy to have had the pleasure of your company, and we wish you good luck on the upper floor. We know that you were the first artiste in Guido's life, and he grants you permission to give a final performance of your act." "Gratia!" responds a grateful Jacqueline, with a spotlight on her face. She starts to sing a sad and sexy farewell song, dancing awkwardly, as her feathers and her pearls scatter around the room. Women enter and exit Guido's life in ritual dances. As Hazel danced her way in, Jacqueline dances her way out. Jacqueline's career is over. (i. 33) The spotlight slowly follows her up the stairs. Mother and aunt close the barred upstairs door. The spotlight goes out. The music stops. An unconcerned Guido admires himself in a mirror, held up for him by several of his still-young women.

A quiet sadness follows. The vivacious camera is suddenly still. Now no people, no objects, no fluttering cloths fling themselves into the camera's range. All is meditative. We see Guido's thoughtful face. His real self must wonder, we speculate, where the upstairs exists to which he can exile Carla—who had visited "those poor lonesome girls up there," who had sympathized with Jacqueline, and who is much like

Jacqueline in many ways. Is there an upstairs for Carla, now that she is having hot flashes, now that she is continually nagging at him in a rebellious way? Guido must wonder how he can get Luisa to behave in reality as ideally as both Luisa and Claudia behave in his fantasies. Guido admits aloud that even this escapist harem fantasy didn't work the way he had hoped: "I thought this would be such an amusing evening. . . . We would have been happy, hidden away here, far from the world. But what went wrong?" The beautiful stranger, ever consoling and compassionate, and knowing all about Guido's capacity for guilt, says sadly to the others, "Now we've made him feel guilty!" But Luisa, still the cheerful and protective wife, tries to save the day: "But it's been a wonderful evening!" The hostess turns to all her guests: "You shouldn't feel sad."

Luisa stands up. "You can all go to bed now. I still have some chores to finish up. There's the laundry, and the dishes to wash." Luisa picks up a scrub bucket. She is photographed now in stark black and white, no grays in this fantasy which momentarily returns to clear perfection as Luisa begins to scrub the floor. She concludes with conviction: "It's nice living all together like this, Guido. At first I didn't understand. I didn't understand that this is how things *should* be. But now, don't you see how good I am, Guido? I don't bother you anymore. I don't make demands. What a fool I was. It has taken twenty years to learn." A spotlight has switched on, reminding us at this crucial moment that we are watching art and not reality. Luisa turns to Guido with love in her voice, as she remembers "the day you became my husband and I became your wife." A long dissolve fades out Luisa, on her knees scrubbing the floor, as we begin to see, in real time, the face of Guido taking to himself: "If you could be patient with me a little longer, Luisa. But maybe you can't anymore." His clear and rational thoughts are as hopeful, and as doubting, as the fantasies which we have just seen. And we remember once more the advice of Rossella: "You have to choose. And you haven't much time left."

The Screen Tests

The next episode, the screen tests, shows that choice is precisely what is now impossible for Guido. Yet the necessity for choice is the central point of the sequence in which Pace insists that Guido now make the final selection of actresses for the important roles in the film. No one mentions any actor for the *central* role. Guido is living that one. The producer describes how much is hanging on Guido's capacity for choice: "We are the joke of the film industry. Everyone is waiting to pan this film. You don't have any friends left."

Guido and his associates are sitting in an almost empty film theatre. Daumier launches an attack on Guido, voicing opinions which, as usual, Guido only too strongly suspects are true: "You've come here this evening trying to do the impossible. No actor could breathe life into the banal characters in your script." Guido smiles ruefully as he nods his head in agreement. The writer quotes Stendhal against Guido: "The self-centered man who cherishes himself alone will end by strangling on his own emotions." Apparently the word "strangling" gives Guido an idea. He puts up his hand, signals to two assistants, who obediently surround the writer, put a hood on him, stand him up, walk him up the stairs, pick up a noose, put it around his neck, tighten it, and hang him from the rafters. As the screen tests begin, the viewer is disappointed to realize—when Daumier is again seen seated in his regular place—that the unhappy end of Guido's severest critic was just another unannounced wish fantasy.

The screen tests bring the viewer's confusion—and Guido's—to new heights. We now see on the screen a succession of several earth-motherly actresses who are costumed in the dress and hat that Carla has worn since her first appearance in Fellini's film. Each screen-test Carla is seen in a room much like the hotel room in which Guido has installed the real Carla. Each screen-test actress imitates some of the mannerisms of Sandra Milo, the real actress who is playing Carla in 8½. The screen in the theatre in which Guido is sitting becomes the screen in the theatre in which we are sitting. We have previously been lead to believe that the French actress, Madeleine LeBeau—and she really is a French actress—was going to play the part of the mistress. So why are they still testing actresses who dress like Carla? Guido seems to have lost the track. Life and art melt together like never before. We realize again that Guido's entire life is built on the principle of imaginative projection; more and more what we call reality and illusion are coming to look the same to him.

A woman quite like Anouk Aimée, with glasses exactly like Luisa's, now appears on the screen, both screens. She is the woman in the photograph in Guido's room. A directorial voice says to her, "Sit down exhausted. This is a defeated woman, no fight left in her." The actress testing for the part of the wife begins to recite her lines: "I'm offering you your freedom. You don't need me anymore. I'm only in your way." Suddenly we are watching not the actress but the real Luisa, who is biting her fingernails, watching the actress. The actress on the screen has now picked up Luisa's own insistence that Guido must at

least be honest: "I don't care what you do! But just be honest about it!"
The distance between Luisa the wife of Guido and the actress testing
for the part of the wife of Guido's hero has already been destroyed. But
then Rossella makes an incidental-sounding comment that increases
the distance, that starts in our mind a chain of Chinese boxes dizzying
in its complexity. Rossella interrupts the screen test with, "Oh, now I
recognize that actress. I know her!" So where are we now? Rossella,
Fellini's fictional character, tells us that she recognizes an actress who
is playing the screen-test role of the wife of Guido's hero, and that wife
has in Fellini's film been identified with Guido's wife Luisa, who is
watching the screen test, and who is played by Anouk Aimée; and that
wife has in Fellini's film also been identified with Fellini's wife, who is
herself an actress, Giulietta Masina, as everyone knows. As we are
working all that out, or being unable or unwilling to, Guido whispers
to his wife, who is watching the screen test, "Luisa, I love you." He
says that as if in apology for his depiction of her. And, as if in response,
the woman in the screen test, who is playing Luisa, accuses, "You lie
with every breath!" Luisa's sister, also in the theatre watching the screen
tests, breaks the chain, yet, objectively, responds to the screen, in
confirmation of what it has just said: "Oh, he *is* a liar!" We take "he" to
mean Guido's hero, Guido, and Fellini. But by now we are so weakened
by confusion that we might well take the "he" to mean that the husband
of the actress recognized by Rossella is also a liar.[71]

In order to create, on his screen, this magnificently confused feeling
of endless and inextricable blending of life and art, Fellini cleverly
contrived to create the same feeling on his set as his film was being
shot. He feared that the dialogue and images wouldn't be quite enough
to establish sufficient confusion. He tried to plant the confusion in his
actors and workers and watchers. First of all, he shot the screen-test
episode at the very beginning of his filming schedule. Thus the screen
tests *in* his film were shot immediately after the actual screen tests *for*
his film. And the screen tests that Fellini incorporates into his film were
virtually identical with the actual screen tests that Sandra Milo and
Edra Gale, among others, had undergone for the roles of Carla and
Saraghina. The first person to appear on the set when filming began
was an actress named Olympia Cavalli, who was to play the part of one
of the actresses testing for the role of the mistress. In the film itself, we
see the clapboard announce: "Test: Olympia." Boyer describes the
consequent confusion on the set:

> She is wearing the same costume Sandra Milo wore in her test
> for the role of Carla in Fellini's film. She is the first of a number
> of actresses who, in Guido's film, will be tested for the part

of—let us say, to compound the confusion, Signora Carla. . . . The first shot of the picture is no different from the tests we have been making during the past weeks. . . . Second shot, second Carla: an identical copy of the first: the same mouth, the same wig, the same coat, the same hat. There is something at once terrifying and exhilarating in so strong a resemblance. For those of us who have just watched Fellini testing actors for those same roles in the film, the repetition and screening of the same tests as a part of Guido's film gives a bewildering sense of *dejà vu*.[72]

But still more: As Fellini tested actresses for the role of Saraghina, even before shooting began, he was already confusing levels of reality. During the actual tests, he recreated the situation which he had actually lived when he was eight years old—the same situation which he would recreate in his film. Fellini called out to his actresses testing for the role of Saraghina: "Saraghina! Look over here! I am the boys! They're calling you." Then he quoted from life: "Saraghina, come on out! We've got some money!"[73] We hear those same words during the screen test in Fellini's film, words spoken, therefore, in Fellini's real life, in the real screen tests for Fellini's film, and in the reconstruction of those screen tests for Guido's film as shown in Fellini's film.

The tests go on, as one actress after another tries for the roles of the mistress, the wife, Saraghina. Guido's indecision grows into panic. He hides his face, as if he can't face these awful imitations of people he knows to be much too real. Luisa grows increasingly restive as she sees Guido's limited version of *her* self now appropriated into *his* self-serving art. Luisa walks out. Guido catches up with her, and asks, "Did the screen tests offend you? It's just a movie." "Oh, I know it's just a movie," responds Luisa. And the real Luisa repeats the accusation of the Luisa in the screen tests. Guido continues to live, and to film, a lie: "You show only what suits you! The truth is another matter!" Luisa's return to the theme of truth makes us wonder, at this point in our confusion, whether truth is ever recoverable. Luisa continues the attack: "You're lucky I don't have the nerve to tell the world what you really are!" Guido and Fellini seem themselves to be trying, within hopeless confusion, to tell the world, and in so doing to discover for themselves, what they really are.

Guido assents to Luisa's every word, and, quietly and anticlimactically, he affirms a choice: When Luisa says contemptuously, "Go, make your movie!" Guido responds, "No, I'm not going to do it." The search, and Guido's film, seem to be over. For the first time, Guido seems to have chosen to give up. We know now what he meant when he said that he wasn't going to start anything over again. As a parting shot, Luisa adds: "What can you teach other people? You're not even honest with the woman who shares your life. . . . You asked me to come to a final decision. My mind is made up now. You can go to hell!" Luisa, too, has come to the point of choice. She walks away.

Abandonment

Left alone, Guido stumbles back into the screening theatre. The tests are continuing. "How about this one, Guido?" demands Pace. Under his breath, Guido groans, "Don't you see? I can't answer." How can Guido choose actresses to play these roles when he is surrounded in life and in memory by all the originals? On the screen, a series of different Carlas, all dressed like the real Carla, accuse Guido of abandoning them. One after another they say, "You always leave me alone," and "You should come right away," and "I'm tired of waiting." The images in the screen tests all jumble together. Saraghina and Carla appear on the screen, chasing one another, fading, blending, as they have done in Guido's fantasies, but now mixed with the Cardinal, with little boy Guido, and with the actors playing them. Big Guido himself now appears on the screen, in the midst of the tests. Pace shouts, "Somebody better give an opinion here!" As total disorder descends, a man comes up to Guido and announces a reprieve: "I'm Claudia's press agent. . . . Look, she's here." "So you finally came!" Guido exclaims hopefully to Claudia, as Claudia Cardinale walks, as if by magic, into our screen, with a burst of light on her face. Now the entire screen is filled with her smile, like the smile of Paola.

Claudia drives away with Guido. The actress who has been hired to play the part of the inspiring figure who comes to bring order is now behind the wheel; but she has to ask "Where are we going?" and she has to admit "I don't know the road." Guido at least knows clearly his direction. "Straight ahead!" he demands. A bit shaken by her indecision, Guido brings up the problem of choice. He asks her, "Could you choose one single thing and be faithful to it?" Evasively, she turns the question back on him. "Listen," he responds, "the springs are nearby." Once more Guido connects Claudia with healing waters. And he tells her the explicit role that her character must play in his film, how she must serve the hero: "She gives him water to heal him." As Guido describes what Claudia's role must be, he explains instead his own need, through his description of the central character in his film: "He doesn't know how to give up anything. He changes course every day for fear of missing the right road." As he speaks to Claudia, he may as well be reciting a monologue; his words come out of the darkness. We can't see him speaking. Claudia stops the car. She has driven him into a small enclosed square. The road has reached a dead end.

In the lonely little town square—deserted, as is usual in Fellini— Guido projects Claudia acting out her services to him: All pure, in white, Claudia brings to the darkness the light of a lamp, the same old-fashioned oil lamp that we saw in his boyhood memory and that the apparition had brought to Guido in his imaginative projection of her during the harem scene. Claudia the light-bringer is herself wise. "I don't like this place," the actress says to Guido, adding: "It doesn't seem real." She at least knows the difference. And of course Claudia herself is not real, for none of the Claudias, not even Claudia Cardinale, not even all the Claudias added together, could ever do all that Guido has demanded of her. In fact, she *has* no role. There is no part for her in the film. Claudia knows that Guido has lied even to her: "You've been lying to me. This part doesn't even exist." Guido admits to Claudia what he had declared to Luisa: "There's not even a film. There's nothing." This time even Claudia hasn't brought order. We might have known that the real Claudia could not serve as had the ideal Claudia. The real Claudia is mere woman; as woman rather than muse, she criticizes him and makes demands, like mother, wife, and mistress. Guido tells Claudia, in exasperation: "What a pest you are, just like all the others."

If Guido has given up, the film's producer hasn't. Suddenly Claudia's face is illuminated, not with an old-fashioned lamp but with Pace's automobile headlights, as the announcement is shouted, echoing throughout the square: "A cocktail party at the spaceship to launch the picture!" Guido's ability to choose is temporarily taken away from him. The picture will continue. In spite of Guido, in spite of all, the search goes on.

The motion of the producer's car blends into the motion of Guido's car, as Guido is carried along to the final setting in Fellini's film. The first shot of this sequence is reminiscent of the first shot of the film: converging cars. But in that shot the cars were stalled; in this shot the cars are speeding. Suzanne Budgen nicely describes this effective transition: "With all the cars moving together, it seems as if the whole theatre were going forward into the frame, giving a renewed sense of participating directly in the action, this time in the final, unifying sequence."[74]

The cocktail party/press conference sequence begins with the hopeful announcement: "Guido, we're finally in business!" But the business is hype, not art. It's the fastest and most furious scene in the film. Throughout the scene, the cuts are harsh; objects and people pop into the camera without motivation; the camera speeds around, not knowing where to look, and often missing the central action. The music is frenetic. We see organ, drums, cymbals, faces shouting questions into Guido's face, and thus into both the subjective camera and into our faces. If we know where we are, we are confused as to when we are. Time telescopes meaninglessly as Pace shouts to Guido: "We've been waiting for you for three days. It's winter already." Paparazzi right out of *La Dolce Vita* once more shoot their flashbulbs into our eyes. We half expect Sylvia to appear. We don't know what film we are in. We don't know whether this is fantasy or reality. We are approaching the final scene where reality and fantasy blend inextricably with present and past, where Guido's integration as a person is marked by the final integration into wholeness of all these still-diverse elements. But we are not there yet. The elements *are* still diverse.

As Guido approaches the press, his legs give out; and he is dragged along by two assistants, just as he had been dragged to his disciplinary court by two priests in the aftermath of the boyhood Saraghina episode. In the crowd, we recognize Claudia's press agent, Daumier the writer, Conocchia, Pace the producer—all as if they had come to

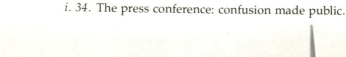

i. 34. The press conference: confusion made public.

witness a public execution. Only Maurice the magician waves a greeting of "Ciao, Good Luck!" Daumier looks superciliously at the whole
public relations display. Real journalists fling into the camera the kinds
of questions with which they always hound Fellini, both before and
after 8½: "Don't you take yourself a little too seriously?" "Do you
believe in God?" "How can the story of your own life interest the
public?" Amidst gales of derisive laughter, a scornful American female
face shouts, in English, Guido's own previous self-accusation: "He has
nothing to say!" As if in response, Conocchia pleads to Guido: "Say
*some*thing!"

The film production crew is now all seated at a raised mirrored table,
visible to the throng. (i. 34) The accusing faces are reflected in the
mirror, multiplying their impact. Rightside up and upside down,
everyone converges on Guido. As all of Guido's internal and external
doubts swirl about him, Pace hisses out his ultimate power: "Answer
them! I pay the bills for your confusion! Make this picture or I'll ruin
you!" But, firmly, Guido shakes his head. He has no answer, and no
film. We have just seen that Guido's marriage has ended, that Luisa
has left him, that he has given up on the film, that Claudia could no
longer inspire him to continue either his personal or artistic quest. So
he has no answer. Bereft, he mutters for succor: "Claudia, where are
you? Where are your spirits now, Rossella?" But it is Luisa who
appears, pure and demure in her wedding gown, like Claudia, as he
would have her be. But even the idealized submissive Luisa asks
questions before she fades away into unattainability: "Won't you be
my husband anymore? Won't I be your wife?" Obviously, the answer
to these questions is also "No."

At a signal from Agostini, who has always tried to smooth out
Guido's problems, Guido crawls under the table, past a series of now
suddenly menacing silhouettes. We remember when, in an entirely
different mood, little Guido crawled under a similar table, playfully
chased in a game by his mother. And now Momma suddenly reappears, apparently a fantasy within a fantasy, not young as she was in
the boyhood scene, but old as she appeared in the cemetery scene. She
is standing along the shore of Fellini's beloved and usually saving sea.
But she turns and runs toward the camera, away from the sea, shouting accusingly, "Guido! Guido! Where are you running to, you
wretched boy?" The camera in a long and quick retreating shot zooms
away from the suddenly horrified mother as we hear a gunshot. Up
close, Guido's head sinks to the ground. The camera stops its movement. All sound ceases. We see the launching tower, now half destroyed. We think of similar constructions that have stood out symboli-

cally in other Fellini films, especially the ordered construction behind
Paola. The abandoned launching tower is not ordered or harmonious.
We know that Guido's film is over. For the third and apparently final
time, Guido has given up.

Guido's fantasized suicide suggests that he has in a way killed
himself when he killed his artistic search. That gunshot and the ruined
tower are the auditory and visual confirmation of what Guido has said
to Claudia: "There's not even a film. There's nothing. Nothing at all."
The stark picture of the ruined and abandoned tower brings back again
the image of the Tower of Babel; as once it was the sign of aspiration,
now it is the sign of failure. Fellini had previously shot a scene in which
he suggested Guido's despair by showing furniture being crated up in
the production office. [75] But Fellini found this better symbol, the abandoned tower, and gave up the first and less powerful attempt at the
expression of failure. Now there is nothing left for Guido to do but to
supervise his own destruction. In a subdued mood, Guido, standing
before the remains of his escapist tower, says to the workmen, "Take
everything down, boys." If he is no longer searching, he is no longer
escaping. "We're not making a picture," Guido concludes. He walks
off left.

At this most negative moment in the film, the camera pans to
Daumier, the perfect voice of modern negation, the kind of cynical
critic who has always attacked Fellini's irrational and continual search-
ings for affirmation. This modern critic, whose intellect never could
understand Fellini's intuition, affirms only Guido's suicide; he remarks on the rightness of Guido's despair: "You did the right thing.
Believe me, this is a good day for you. . . . Why add disorder to
disorder? . . . It's better to destroy than to create what's unessential.
Besides, what is clear enough, valuable enough, to deserve to sur-
vive?" We see a close shot of Guido's dejected face, listening to the
voice of modernity as parts of his launching tower crash to earth in the
background. Daumier continues: "We are already suffocated by
words, by sounds, by images which have no right to exist, that emerge
from the void, and return to the void. Any man worthy to be called
artist should swear one oath: Dedication to silence!" We can hear in
these words the kind of modish secular hopelessness that might explain Steiner's suicide. All of Guido's explorations into his own past,
with its complexes, guilts, and fears, and with its joys and innocence,
and all of Guido's explorations into aspirations, dreams, and fantasies,
as well as into his wishes for escape, have brought him artistically and
personally to the state of Marcello at the end of La Dolce Vita: to silence.
The journalist—or the artist—when he learns that he has nothing to
say, refrains from saying.

Acceptance

Only after silence comes the miracle. Only when Gelsomina was abandoned did the circus music play. Only when Marcello was isolated did the smile of Paola appear. Only after Guido's suicide is resurrection possible. When Guido's miracle occurs, he—like Zampano but unlike Marcello—does hear and understand. The miracle begins through a Fellini clown, through the medium of Maurice the magician, who had reintroduced Guido to his boyhood and to a consciousness of his quest for Asa Nisi Masa. As Guido sits in his car listening to Daumier's dissertation against creation, the clown-artist—the spirit of creation for its own sake—runs up to Guido, tips his hat in salute, and exclaims, "We are ready to begin!" He escorts someone into the camera's view. She turns, and we see that it is Claudia, once more all in white. She is barefoot in a lovely field, a setting reminiscent of the Italian provinces in the films of early Fellini.

That dreamy vision of Claudia is contrasted with the harsh words in the continuing speech of Daumier: "There was no need to leave a film behind you, like a deformed footprint of a cripple." The words "deformed" and "cripple" strike our ears as perversions as the beautiful image of Claudia strikes our eyes. And then Claudia is not alone.

i. 35. Purified memories: Young Momma, the Cardinal's assistant, Old Mother and Father, the Cardinal, Carla, a priest disciplinarian from school, the beautiful stranger, Saraghina, Jacqueline.

Guido looks over his glasses and sees, also all in white, his young mother, his aunt, little Guido, Saraghina, his mother and father as happy and contented old people. All of these components of Guido's fractured life smile acceptingly at Guido, as if to answer the next question of Daumier: "Why piece together the tattered pieces of a life, the vague memories, the faces, the people whom you never knew how to love?" Claudia, too, had told him—three times, we remember—that his problem was that he did not know how to love. Perhaps he can learn. Carla, Luisa, dozens, even scores of other people in Guido's life, all purified now in his memory of them, and in his acceptance of them, all dressed in white, walk across the foreground from left to right. (i. 35) Claudia, who had been the first to appear in the field before Guido, is now the only one who leaves. The Ideal may have inspired Guido, but that is an evasion. It is the real people of his life whom he needs, and now accepts. Claudia knew that she had no part in the film, as she had no part in the harem, and will have no part in the final circle. So the Ideal moves off toward the left, toward the sea, and smiles a goodbye to Guido. Unlike Paola, Claudia walks away, aware that she is finally not needed. Paola was a real girl; Marcello could have chosen her road had he still been searching. Claudia was not real. She walks away so that the still-searching Guido might choose a reality.

Guido pushes his hand through his hair and murmurs his recognition of the sudden and simple miracle: "What is this sudden joy?" That is Guido's epiphany. Guido asks, "Why do I feel strengthened and renewed?" His answer is in his subsequent words of repentance: "Forgive me, sweet creatures. I didn't understand. I didn't know." Understanding and knowledge are what Marcello had sought in *La Dolce Vita*. Guido finds them here by simple acceptance of the simple. He has heard, understood, and accepted the message of Paola. Fellini *has* hade a film which explains the meaning of Paola's smile.

Rossella, in the background, watches like a white-clad guardian angel. Luisa, as if returning to Guido, walks toward him, and he says to her: "I do accept you. I do love you. How simple it is." Now Guido can speak the words of freedom: "Luisa, I feel that I have been freed. Now everything seems worthwhile, meaningful, true."

The intellect of a Daumier could never, of course, understand this Fellini message of grace. Guido himself wishes that words would do: "Ah, how I wish I could explain. But I don't know how." Fellini has many times before and after this film rejected the *necessity* of explanation: "I don't believe that rational understanding is an essential element in the reception of any work of art."[76] The art of this film, quite beyond the rational, is leading Guido, and Fellini, to their own kind of imaginative understanding.

Guido now tries to tell Luisa what this imaginative review of his life—that is, the film till now—has taught him:

> All the confusion of my life has been a reflection of myself.
> Myself as I am, not as I'd like to be. This no longer frightens
> me. The truth is that I do not know. I seek. I have not yet
> found. Only with this in mind can I feel alive, and look at you
> without shame. Life is a holiday. Let us live it together. That is
> all I can say, Luisa, to you and to the others. Accept me as I am.
> Only then will we discover each other.

Guido recognizes by those words the paradox of simultaneous dis-covery and continued search. Guido, within that paradox, is now filmed in lights and shadows; the characters of his life, as they appear to him, all stand in stark white light. For all the brave affirmation of Guido's speech, the shadows, and our memory of the whole content and form of this film number eight-and-one-half, show Fellini to be as profoundly unsure as is Luisa, who, smiling nevertheless, replies: "I'm not sure that's true, but I can try, if you'll help me."

The Fellini concerns and themes which we have traced through three central works of Fellini's art all come together in Guido's speech to Luisa. But the great filmmaker must not just tell us; he must contrive to show us. Fellini needs to confirm visually Guido's acceptance of what he is, of the people of his life who have caused him to be that, and, most important, of his decision to go on from there. He must, that is, find a way to complete his film. Fellini has described what is for him a frequent problem: "I don't know how it's going to end. I really don't know—that is, I know what I want to express, but I'm unable to see any images." These doubts, this agony of indecision, Fellini insists, is some-thing that he really does share with Guido: "This indecision of mine is not part of my deceptions; it's not a slightly superstitious mechanism that I put into motion to stimulate creativity. It is a real, concrete abyss that I reach every time, with the risk of breaking my neck."[77]

Up out of the abyss, the images began to form. Fellini first tried to visualize the search structure of the film by setting Guido's speech to Luisa in a moving train. Here is the scene as it was described in a scenario along the way:

> *Dining Car.* As the train rolls across a quiet countryside, Guido
> once again enters an unreal world. Around him, the other
> passengers become people out of his life. They smile sym-
> pathetically at him. He recognizes that he cannot deny them.
> Greatly moved, he rises and searches for a way to tell them
> that, at bottom, he can be happy this way. The waiter and

Luisa are dumbstruck. The dream breaks. Guido takes Luisa's hand and tries again, with his eyes, to "tell her something," while the train rolls on through the night, comforting him with its sound."[78]

When he filmed that dining car sequence, Fellini gave to Guido words which tried to explain in sufficient detail to the people of his past the fact that "he cannot deny them." The words of Guido's acceptance in this rejected speech are interestingly similar in intention and meaning to the final words that do appear in the actual film. Fellini clearly *did* know what he wanted to express. The whole film, and its entire conception, had been leading up to this. Here is the language of Guido's final speech to Luisa in the dining car, filmed but never used:

> For a moment, I felt as if I had been set free. For an endless moment I felt at peace with everyone. I felt myself—as I am, not as I wish I were. I would like to kiss you all, and ask your forgiveness. I didn't realize: it's easy to take you as you are and love. It's wonderful. Luisa, I can't say anything different to you. I don't think there is an ending. . . . It's back again, this endless confusion. But I don't have to hide it now, or disguise it. It's myself. Tell the truth, admit what I don't know, what I'm still looking for or what I haven't found yet—that's the only way I can live, breathe, look you honestly in the face, Luisa. Take me as I am.[79]

In both versions of Guido's final speech, a sense of sacramental freedom, strength, and renewal follows repentance and confession. In both versions, Guido finds that acceptance of all the past—that which he has reviewed and which we, through the film, have shared—is finally simple and easy, a question of choice. But to accept the past means to accept himself as he is now, with all of his failings, and as he is in the process of becoming, with all of his aspirations, and with all of his consequent confusion; and to ask his loved ones to accept him, as he is now able to accept both himself and them. Guido's own continuing search for self now goes beyond self-concern and into other-concern. It is as if Zampano had discovered in time his concern, and need, for Gelsomina. "Only then," as Guido says, "will we discover each other."

Some better visualization is obviously necessary to moderate the patness which results from the bald verbalization in these speeches. When we only hear the *words*, these speeches may ring of complacency and even simple-mindedness. When Guido concludes in one version, "Take me as I am," and, in another version, "Accept me as I am," we must not think of him as complacently ending his own continuing search for himself. Precisely the opposite is Fellini doctrine. Looking back on the film, Fellini admitted that "8½ is meant to be an attempt to reach an agreement with life," but he insisted that he intended it to be only "an attempt and not a completed result."[80] Guido does admit in one version of his final speech: "The truth is that I do not know. I seek. I have not yet found." That is not complacent. Similarly, Guido admits in the other version of his speech that he still lives in "endless confusion," as he acknowledges that there is much that "I'm still looking for. . . ." Neither is that complacent. How to say and show, both in thought and feeling, both the acceptance *and* the continuation? The dining car sequence didn't really do it. It was dull. It was unclear. It remained too much an intellectual statement. Fellini still wasn't able to see sufficient images for what he wanted to say. It all still seemed too much like a final pat destination rather than an imaged further step along the road.

The Circle

The right ending, the sufficient images, began to appear before Fellini as he was planning a "coming attractions" trailer for the film: "Before the picture was finished I wanted to shoot a trailer. So I asked the producer if it was possible to call back all the actors and all the extras who worked on the picture. . . . Just to shoot an extravagant trailer. So, they came—two hundred people—and I asked for seven cameras."[81]

Deena Boyer was confused as she watched these preparations. On Monday, September 17, 1962, she wrote in her diary: "Something is going on at the side of the tower, in front of the stairway. Half a circus arena has been marked out facing the stairway and surrounded by the customary ring."[82] Earlier that month, on September 3, Boyer had noted that someone on the set told her that "Fellini has made up his mind to reveal himself completely. Guido's recollections will include a circus, the one that was in *La Strada*. . . ."[83] And in that predicted circus setting Fellini found the images which were not, finally, a trailer at all, but which became the perfectly visualized ending of the film itself. It became an ending, Fellini decided, which was "more honest, more in keeping with the tone of the film," than was the rejected ending in the dining car.[84] "The meaning was always the same as in the ending with the train. . . . But that was expressed in an intellectual way. . . . When I saw this house of people, of harmony, I felt that it was the real ending of the picture."[85] The final images became ones of harmony.

To complete this most personal of films, Fellini pictures a return of the circus, his refuge when he was a little boy, and his persistent and personal symbol of the bittersweet vision of his adult life. The circus is the place of happy confusion, of everything at once finally blending into spontaneous harmony. Guido had wanted to include "everything." Fellini does. At the moment when Luisa expresses her willingness to try to accept Guido as he is, a little circus band, quite like the one in *La Strada*, with clowns dressed in horizontal stripes, walks into the picture, led by little Guido, wearing his childhood cape that comes down to his feet, playing his flute.

Maurice the magician appears again just when he is needed, comes toward the camera, turns and surveys all the waiting people of Guido's life and shouts happily to them, "Welcome Back!" The little band plays its circus music. The adult Guido is now in the center of the circus ring. After his fantasy suicide, and after having abandoned his film and its creative search, Guido is now back in control. When Guido is integrated as a person, so can be the parts of his film. With his film director's megaphone in hand, Guido is ordering and directing the young Guido, the band, the circus, his fantasies, his film, his life, and Fellini's greatest work of art.

Little Guido is directed by big Guido to a white curtain hiding the stairway to the launching tower of Guido's film. The entire screen becomes the pure white of the curtain, the pure white of the comforting sheets from Guido's childhood. Little Guido magically parts the curtain, and what was once the trailer, and is now the ending, begins. Down—from the tower to the earth—walks the cast of the film, which is the cast of Guido's life. They chatter happily and communally, the extras and the walk-ons all intermixing with the principals who had appeared earlier in the field. "When the music, the band, started to play and all the people came down," Fellini explained, "I was very moved by this scene and this atmosphere."[86] But he had to control the atmosphere a bit longer. Now Guido kneels to kiss the ring of the Cardinal, who walks into a spotlight as he goes to join a large circle of people, forming themselves around the center circus ring. The sea is visible in the background. Guido's father and mother join the circle. Carla, in her down-to-earth simplicity, understands and accepts her role, necessary as she is, as one of many: "I understand. You are trying to say that you can't do without us. Will you call me tomorrow?" "Yes," Guido affirms, "Now go join the others." Guido summons Maurice who runs up, tips his hat, and escorts Carla to the circus ring. Guido shouts directions into his megaphone: "Everybody hold hands. Spread out. Everybody together." Everybody is indeed together; mistress and parents, the Cardinal and Saraghina, all link hands and dance. Guido moves in the opposite direction, directing them all. The people of his life begin to run, laughing, freely, gaily, round and round, holding hands in shared acceptance, led by the magician.

Only Luisa is left standing alone, off to the side, eyes cast down. She seems reluctant to resume a role in one of Guido's imaginative creations, to be used once more. But now Guido seems to promise more. Guido walks to Luisa, takes her hand lovingly, leads her into the circle, and Guido and Luisa enter it together, hand in hand, dancing in a circular procession which is also a festive celebration, a fulfillment of significant Fellini imagery. (i. 36)

We now actually view Guido as part of his own environment, the camera showing *him* in his full context. He is now a *part* of the circle of his own life, moving along with it, in harmony with it. The Nino Rota music plays on and on. The endless circle has replaced both the ascents and descents of this film, and the *La Dolce Vita* terrors of the downward spiral. The parts of the kaleidoscope form themselves into a whole.

Guido's journey has not been a journey from here to there. It has not been a departure from one place so as to arrive at another place. This

i. 36. The harmony of the circle: Guido joins all the others, between Luisa and Rossella.

journey was not one of rejection and acceptance, but, as Guido continually insisted, he wanted to do and to accept *everything*. He managed to arrive without leaving. The film became a journey into guilt and forgiveness, childhood and maturity, past and future, time and transcendence, reality and fantasy, self and the other, the personal and the mythic, intuition and the intellect, spontaneity and art. The circle is the right image. The film has been a journey into unity.

Guido is now in step with all the people of his life, including Fellini, who is now clearly in charge of this wonderfully characteristic and yet climactic Fellini statement. Somewhere off camera, Fellini is directing Guido who, with his megaphone, is directing the others, at the same time as he is a part of them.

Very slowly, darkness falls; but a spotlight, that sign of performance, of art, of creativity, conquers the darkness as it illuminates the little circus band, still led by little Guido, who is little Fellini, now obviously understood and accepted by big Guido, who is big Fellini, who has been able to direct the integration of his former self into the climax of his current art. (i. 37) The camera pulls back and shows the entire circus circle. Life literally becomes a circus as, within a circus ring, in the sight of the sea, Guido is made whole. Fellini had said, "The cinema is very much like the circus."[87] And now he has proven it. Little Guido is left alone in the spotlight, still playing his flute.

Fellini released the film with the only possible title. "*8½*" tells us that this is a film in a series. This ultimately personal film had as its purpose not only the harmonizing of the ideas, myths, images, forms of previous Fellini films, but the integration of the very act of filmmaking into the life of the creator. "*8½*," decorated in the style of the 1930s, the period of Fellini's own youth, fills the screen. But Fellini has one more assertion, one more possibility to affirm, a few more words. We read: "Created and directed by Federico Fellini." The possibility of creation is affirmed. During the credits, Nino Rota once more integrates the part into the whole in this act of creation: he reviews the music of the entire film, ending this film of Fellini's maturity with the lullaby from Guido's boyhood.

i. 37. In the center spotlight, little Guido directs the music of the circus.

JULIET OF THE SPIRITS

AFTER *8½*, FEDERICO FELLINI SAID: "For me, working on a film is a journey."[1] We have been watching that metaphor grow. We know that each Fellini film is not only a journey in itself, but is also a movement along the road in Fellini's longer personal and artistic journey: "My work can't be anything other than a testimony of what I am looking for. It is a mirror of my searching."[2] We also know that each new Fellini journey is undertaken in fear: "When I start to make each new picture, I start with the same fear every time of what it is I have to do." The source of the fear is, of course, Fellini's recognition that the only material he has to work with, as he tries to create the mirror that reflects his searching, is his self as he finds it now: "What I am able to do in a picture all has to come from inside me."[3] After *8½*, which Fellini himself called "a shameless and brazen confession,"[4] the question was whether Fellini had anything unrevealed left inside him. "After *8½*," Tullio Kezich, a friend of Fellini's has written, "one could have presumed that Fellini had reached the end of his repertory, that his whole world was unwound in the beautiful confusion around the first-person hero."[5]

But *8½* was not the end of the road. Fellini had learned something in the making of the film, something that would inform the rest of his

149

work. "What Fellini had learned," in Kezich's view, "is a kind of availability of consciousness."[6] Fellini had found a form which allowed him to probe into his own consciousness and to transform the story of his personal obsessions into a sharable experience. He had long ago discovered that, to him, along with story must come the development of the meaning and form of that story.[7] Now that, in $8\frac{1}{2}$, he had invented a form that could tell the story of "the world inside my mind," perhaps he could develop a *new* form that could show the world inside the mind of someone else.[8]

Fellini now embarked on a journey to make available the consciousness of someone else: the woman with whom he shared his life. Guido, after all, would have to understand not only himself, but his wife Luisa as well, if their holiday life was to be a successful mutual continuation of the search for self. Would that be possible? Guido's consciousness became available to himself; but could Luisa's also somehow be accessible to him? Could indeed a wife's consciousness ever become available to a husband, or any woman's to any man? "To undertake to speak calmly and clearly about a woman is almost impossible for a man," Fellini admitted during the shooting of *Juliet of the Spirits*.[9] But, nevertheless, that undertaking became the journey of the new film. In his continuing probe of the availability of consciousness, Fellini turned from himself to his wife. The Guido/Federico quest in the one film became the Juliet/Giulietta quest in the next.

Juliet of the Spirits was not to be pure biography any more than $8\frac{1}{2}$ was pure autobiography. Fellini wanted, *through* his wife, Giulietta Masina, to use his art to penetrate the hitherto unavailable reality of another consciousness. "I felt," he said while filming *Juliet of the Spirits*, "that my desire to use the cinema as an instrument to penetrate certain areas of reality could find the perfect guide in Giulietta."[10] She was the starting point and guide into Juliet, just as Fellini himself had been the guide into Guido. Giulietta Masina had inspired Fellini before—in *La Strada* and in *Nights of Cabiria*. Like a real-life Claudia, Giulietta led Fellini on toward form: "She leads me by the hand into certain territories, magic gardens, where my imagination can run wild in a very fruitful way."[11] Throughout the filming, Fellini needed Giulietta's active help: "In this film there has been much more collaboration between Giulietta and myself. From my point of view it was easy. A number of times, on the spur of the moment, I just asked Giulietta what she would say, what she would do; and I accepted her solutions without the slightest change."[12] The new film, Fellini summarized, "was born as a film about Giulietta, and for Giulietta," a film in which his own wife "assumes a concrete form" in art.[13]

Since the subject of the new story was an inner consciousness, its form would be developed from *8½*. As in *8½*, reality and art were to be confusingly intertwined. The actors, as usual, were to blend with their roles. Not only did Giulietta herself keep her first name; so did Valentina Cortese, Sylva Koscina, José de Villalonga, Elena Fondra, Elisabetta Gray. The new film, like the previous one, was intended to delve into a consciousness not only on the level of the present, but in dreams, memories, fantasies, and wishes. Fellini said that he wanted "to bring in pieces of the different dreams I have had during my life . . . all the places I have visited during the night."[14] Like other Fellini movies, this one could be "a way of interpreting and remaking reality, through fantasy and imagination."[15] He wanted this film to be a "human commentary," but he wanted it "enriched by a seductive fantasy."[16] He asked that the viewer now look not only into the dream world but also into the viewer's own realities, and to "think what a bale of memories and associations and all we carry about with us. It's like seeing a dozen films simultaneously."[17] All those inner films would become the externalized and concrete *Juliet of the Spirits*.

He would provide the necessary magic: "We need sorcerers in the cinema."[18] To lead him through all of this, through the materialization of her realities and fantasies as well as his own and even ours, he needed someone who was herself a bit of a sorcerer. Giulietta could do it. Giulietta Masina, said Fellini, "is a person of mystery who can embody, in relationship to me, a consuming nostalgia for innocence, for perfection."[19] So the story and theme, as well as both the character and the actress, demanded a film form which made available for wife and husband the nostalgia of the past as well as the mutual questing toward a future perfection.

The viewers' collaboration would be a required part of the whole. The new film needed to be *8½*, plus. In the year of *Juliet of the Spirits*, Fellini said: "Movies have gone past the phase of prose narrative and are coming nearer and nearer to poetry. I am trying to free my work from certain restrictions—a story with a beginning, a development, an ending. It should be more like a poem, with metre and cadence."[20] In form, Fellini is continually in the process of adapting, renewing, and inventing. As he said: "An artist evolves; he goes through changes like any other man."[21]

As soon as the screen lights up at the beginning of *Juliet of the Spirits*, Fellini shows that a major change has taken place in this artist: the playful sorcerer now has a new toy in his bag of tricks. *Juliet of the Spirits* is Fellini's first full-length film in color. The film begins—as it ends—on the bright blue of life, of sea and sky. Under the credits,

Fellini fills the screen with a background of bright blue. After the credits, his camera slowly moves through a fertile green garden. The camera brushes past an expansive willow, then moves slowly toward Juliet's peaceful and pure white house, illuminated against the surrounding night. Although Fellini admitted that he was sometimes frustrated by the fact that carefully controlled greens had a way of mischievously turning into pinks in the laboratory, he was excited by the possibilities of color and soon learned how to use it: "Color adds a new dimension to a film like mine, something that black and white could never have given it." The new dimension is the actual creation, "through colored illuminations," of dreams, of fantasies, reflected into our imaginations. It is color that does much of the creating, for Fellini conceives of fantasies and dreams as color. Therefore, "just as it is in great paintings," color in *Juliet of the Spirits* "participates in the language" of the art. In this film, color is not mere representation: "Color is part of the ideas, the concepts." Finally and simply, "Color is an essential part of the film."[22]

Inside Juliet's house, the peace of harmoniously colored nature gives way to color clashes and to nervous preparations for Juliet's wedding anniversary dinner for her husband Giorgio. Juliet bustles about amid splashes of red. She can't decide how to costume herself for the coming celebration. After a series of variously colored wigs, she rejects a final red one: "It looks horrible." She chooses her natural hair instead. She casts aside dresses. She gives them to her maids. What fits her? What suits her? Who is she? The theme is established already. The camera acts as insecure as Juliet, never knowing where to focus or when to be still. We get no sure and substantial view of Juliet. For the first several minutes, we see only glimpses of Juliet's back, or an arm, or pieces of her reflection in a mirror. We can't tell when we are seeing parts of Juliet, or of her maids, or when we are seeing Juliet, or a reflected image of Juliet. We don't see her face. We have as hard a time finding her as, we come to learn, she will have finding herself.

And yet Juliet wants to control the situation, wants to be in charge. She tries to avoid the advice of her maid. "Teresina," Juliet insists, "I know what I should wear." But she doesn't. And she herself wants to be the light-bringer, forbidding anyone else to light the candles. Finally, those candles light her, as her husband walks in, and thus we see Giulietta's face for the first time, her smile filling the screen precisely as it had in the final frame of *The Nights of Cabiria*. But this is a beginning rather than an ending. And it is not for Juliet a promising beginning. It is only when her husband appears that we see Juliet's face. She seems to acquire her person from him, not from her self. Quickly her face changes from a happy smile in anticipation of pleasing Giorgio to a grimace of disappointment when she realizes that Giorgio has forgotten their anniversary. As the smile disappears, Juliet, dressed in an unobtrusive black chiffon gown, fades into the black background.

In the next shot, Fellini signals that this film will not remain fixed in realism. We begin to see things as Juliet sees them. When Juliet realizes that her intimate party is about to be crashed by a group of Giorgio's friends, she looks out the window and sees them all frozen on the front lawn, as if they are an invasion force poised to strike. They do. The whole group swarms noisily into the house, turning the planned quiet private anniversary dinner into public bedlam. The overwrought camera can't even locate all of the invaders; nor can it find time or patience to listen to an entire sentence or to sort out the source of one or another meaningless comment. This is the first of many invasions into Juliet's private world.

Now intimations of something beyond the merely real are added to the jumbled conversations as well as to the cinematic technique. Valentina has brought a gift of wind bells, "to ward off the spirits." Genius is introduced as "the greatest seer in the world," and he begins to chatter about astrology, and then about dream interpretation. The sculptor Elena, the worshipper of muscular flesh, brings up the subject of a séance. In Juliet's bathroom, amid more mirror imagery, Genius's pendulum announces that, near Juliet, "there is a strong magnetic force." With billows of incense adding to the heady spiritualistic mood, Valentina, announcing her fear of "restless spirits," prepares the guests for her séance. Spirits were involved in a deathly séance in *La Dolce Vita*. Rossella in *8½* invoked wise spirits who told Guido to choose. Silly artificial Val, who thinks a sprinkler is the dew, is about to invoke her own kind of playful and mischievous spirits. The original screenplay makes clear her intention. Val asks the spirits: "Can you tell us something sweet, which might help us live, help us understand the meaning of our lives?"[23]

The Spirits

The séance sequence introduces us to Juliet's spirits, inner forces that are important enough to share with her the title of the film. "God, how many spirits!" announces Val. "They're all around!" But we discover that two spirits are the important ones. First "Iris" introduces herself. Iris in classical mythology is a messenger goddess who is the personification of the rainbow. Iris announces that she is beautiful; and "love for everyone" is her message. But then Iris's opposite interrupts her, and "Olaf" introduces himself. He is disruptive, and his message is a barrage of dirty language and insults. Together, Juliet's two special spirits bring to her in a public way her own special message: "Who do you think you are?" her spirits ask. And then they answer, for all to hear: "You're no one to anybody. You don't count, you wretched thing." Once more, Fellini proves that he is always making the same film at the same time as he is always making a different film. The spirits speak to Juliet the same sentiment that Gelsomina had spoken to herself. Just before the Fool delivered his parable of the stone, proving that everyone serves some purpose, Gelsomina had told him: "I'm no good to anyone." Both Giulietta Masinas receive messages: stories, tales, and parables of mythic import.

Both before and during the séance, Juliet frequently is shown as quite literally in the dark. We have had to strain to see her through the obscuring shadows. (i. 38) She eagerly cooperated with the séance, as if hoping that it might bring her to the light. But the truth that her spirits tell her brings her only more darkness. Juliet breaks the circle. She stands up, right into the camera, and her black dress blanks out the screen. To escape the truth that she is nothing, she faints dead away. The lights are turned on. Juliet sees all her friends staring at her, enclosing her in an accusing, threatening, mocking circle. She seems to see, beneath appearances, their true attitude toward her. Juliet has received the clear message that she is no one to anybody.

The next morning, Juliet remembers the particular message of Iris, and obviously sees it as a way of becoming someone to somebody. She looks into herself to determine how to become a part of the love-for-everone Iris message. But that easy sharing of love is not how, deep inside, Juliet knows herself to be. Juliet is annoyed when she catches her maid Teresina in an across-the-fence embrace with a visiting plumber. With chagrin, Juliet realizes that even her maid is someone to somebody. At this crucial moment of self-doubt, Juliet walks to her mirror, looks at herself, whispers hopefully the message of Iris. Trying to teach herself, Juliet repeats into the mirror: "Love for everyone."

This self-reflective film works often with mirror imagery, as did the even more directly self-reflective 8½. The mirror is a symbol that comes easily to the self-reflective Fellini. It is featured not only in most of his films, but also in one of his many definitions of the cinema itself: "the art in which man recognizes himself in the most direct way, the

i. 38. Juliet the obscure: "You don't count, you wretched thing."

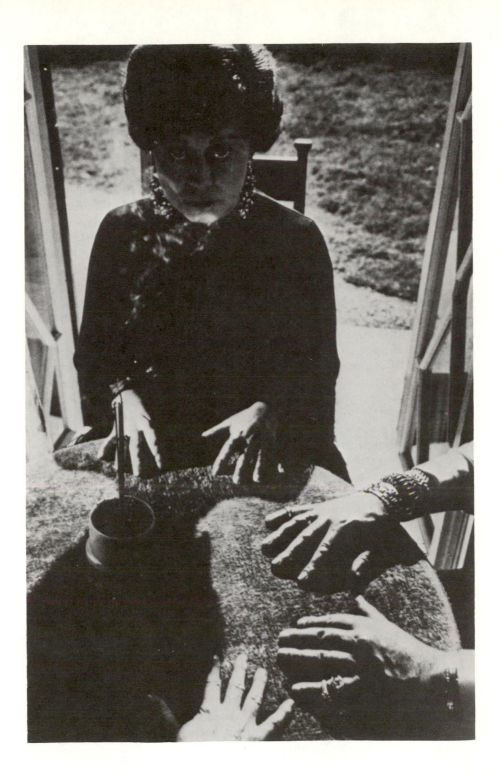

mirror in front of which we must have the courage to discover our souls."[24] That discovery is, of course, Juliet's job, just as much as Guido's or Fellini's. And so reflections and mirrorings go on through the film. We saw the reflection of Juliet before we saw Juliet herself. In her introspection, in her probing inward, Juliet often catches, and studies, her image in a mirror. Thanks to Ballantine Books, which has published an English version of both Fellini's original screenplay and a transcript of the final film, we know that the idea of using mirrors as a major motif in this film was with Fellini from the beginning. But Fellini interestingly refined his artistic use of mirrors between script and screen. In the unshot script, Valentina explicitly articulates Juliet's mirror obsession: "You've always had a complex about mirrors." Valentina goes on to explain to a psychologist who is interested in Juliet's psyche: "She was always looking at mirrors, poor thing. Even when she was a little girl."[25] On the screen Fellini cut out all the *language* about mirrors. He simply shows us, again and again, Juliet seeking after her reflected image.

When Elisabetta, the sweet and innocent one of Juliet's two contrasting maids, sets up the séance table as a breakfast table in the garden, Juliet approaches it with eagerness as well as with fear. Ominous winds blow. Valentina's wind bells chime above the table. Juliet lightly touches the tabletop, and Iris immediately taps out a response, indicating that she is still there with Juliet. Juliet smiles. She caresses the tabletop, recognizing, she hopes, a strong ally in her quest to find love.

Juliet knows the message of Iris. But will Iris be an ally? Iris herself will appear in the next sequence. And so will many of the other spirits who are vying to show Juliet the way. It is time for Fellini to try another approach. In his deepening desire to probe the individual consciousness, he decides to go further into non-realism, further than ever before into the inner world of the fantastic and the bizarre. Color will help. And so will the new freedom that the cinema had earned by 1965. Fellini will initiate with this sequence in *Juliet of the Spirits* a break from traditional cinematic imaginative restraints, and that initiative will become more and more, in his late work, a kind of Fellini trademark. He knew that this was an important step along his road. "I have been impelled by a psychological point of view," he explained simply, so that this new film had to "contain the most unrestrained fantasy."[26] He is perfecting a formal equivalent to his long-held fascination with the irrational, the extraordinary, the baroque. He is about to jump ahead in his gradual movement from neo-realism to surrealism. He had always filmed things in such a way as to show what they looked like; more and more he will be filming things in such a way as to show what they feel like. More and more, Fellini gets inside.

Juliet, her two little nieces, their nurse, Juliet's doctor and his wife are all sitting in a white and orange tent on the beach near Juliet's home. The doctor is trying to soothe Juliet with a scientific explanation of last night's spiritualist occurrences: "These are only electrical forces, whims of unknown substances. . . ." Juliet by day is even less colorful than she was by night. She is without makeup, pale in the cheeks. She is dressed all in white, topped by a huge white sunhat that obscures her face from view. She is sitting in a white beach chair. Every time Fellini shoots Juliet in this beach scene, he is careful to shoot her against the stark white part of the tent. And he overexposes his film, so that even the beach and the sky surrounding Juliet are bleached into white. When Fellini shoots the suntanned, fleshy, worldly doctor, the representative of the physical, whose prescription for Juliet is to indulge in sex more often, he is careful to shoot him against the bright orange portion of the tent.

Juliet's fantasy life, her inner self, she tells the doctor, had once been colorful, unlike her own view of her colorless outer self. When she was young, hers was a fantasy life filled with bright "castles, piazzas, life at night, forests, tiny faces that would stare at me with huge, shining eyes." We remember that inside her rational house is a colorful mural of a bizarre fantasy castle. On the beach, as Juliet closes her eyes in happy memory of her inner riches, Fellini flashes onto the screen the first of the many apparitions which will, throughout the course of the film, interrupt Juliet's current banal life in an attempt to call her to something else. A beautiful, full-bodied, confidently sexy circus ballerina appears on a flower-bedecked trapeze, open and free, suspended between the vast sky and the blue sea. That vision incorporates most of Fellini's favorite life-affirming symbols, all of which we have seen many times by now, and all of which are here condensed, not only into one film, but into one tempting image. Juliet knows that this vision is an incarnation of Iris. (i. 39)

Juliet of the Spirits takes on a new dimension: we no longer see and hear only the current and real, plus Juliet's vision of how such real things *seem* to be, plus spiritualistic messages which are reflections of Juliet's inner desires. We now also experience Juliet's apparitions, which are an unrestrained combination of Juliet's subjective memory of how the past was, plus both fearful and hopeful fantasies of how the future might be.

Immediately after the vision of Iris, Juliet's neighbor Susy appears, as a "real" version of Iris, the spirit of tempting feminine sexuality. Again and again, society will tempt Juliet with the message of Iris, a message which seems to Juliet to be contrary to the self which she intuits but has not yet found. The doctor had given Juliet the same

i. 39. The first spirit: Iris appears on Fanny's circus swing.

advice as Iris did: "There is no better remedy than making love." Susy's message will be the same again. As Juliet sits on the beach, she suddenly looks puzzled. We see what Juliet sees. At the doctor's mere mention of making love, a vision appears which seems at least as unreal as the vision of Iris had been:

> A canopied raft, pulled by a small flat-bottomed boat, approaches the beach. The raft and the boat are filled with an amazing variety of exotic characters—colorful, beautiful, fascinating. A lovely young Eurasian woman stands at the prow of the boat. Susy reclines on pillows on the barge. As the boat runs ashore, two Oriental boys jump out and begin rolling two huge, thin-spoked wooden wheels up the beach.[27]

As Susy arrives from the water, a sultry female voice is heard intoning a chantlike but decidedly earthy song. The doctor stands up amazed, goggle-eyed and appreciative, and exclaims, "This is a real apparition!" Only then do we understand that this exotic spectacle is not wholly Juliet's imagination. However much Juliet's imagination may contribute to the exaggeration of what we are seeing, Juliet's neighbor Susy does obviously exist on some level more "real" than Iris. And yet, to a viewer who can recognize actress Sandra Milo in both parts, it is also obvious that Iris and Susy are strangely and closely related. They surely *look* the same.

As usual, Fellini understands very well his own symbols. In his original screenplay, he established the symbolic function of Susy. In that early version, Susy was to drop from the sky in a helicopter. Messengers from the sky are not new to Fellini. This first appearance of Susy was to be "like an apparition of a superb feminine divinity."[28] Fellini later explained that he pondered for a long time whether that helicopter would, after all, be the best way to introduce Susy. He finally changed his mind, choosing, instead, the only really appropriate entrance: "It seemed to me right for her to arrive from the water. . . . Susy couldn't arrive from the sky; ideas come from the sky; she had to come from the water, which is the world of Venus."[29]

After Susy and her entourage set themselves up in a portable Oriental pavilion, surrounded by colorful baskets of food and fruit, the camera compares Susy's group with Juliet's group, and Susy with Juliet. The camera sees Susy's outlandish golden veil, fringed in red. The veil, which obscures nothing, comes directly out of her hat and cascades down her body. The camera sees her yellow hat, her golden bikini, her tanned and voluptuous body, which she exhibits in silhouette against a sun which even seems to be outshone. (i. 40) Susy

i. 40. The "real" apparition: Susy on the beach.

is as opulent and naked as Juliet is restrained and covered. Juliet looks at herself in her mirror. The camera looks at Juliet's dowdy little whiteness. Indeed, the inconsequential Juliet even disappears from our view as she falls asleep, for her white broad hat dips down and fills the entire screen.

Even more than in *8½*, we seldom know in *Juliet of the Spirits* precisely where we are in the interconnected realms of reality, dream, fantasy, and memory. Juliet's own imagination is so obviously able to distort the image of reality, and her own sensitivity to spiritual forces is so strong, that various levels of apparition continually interrupt and form the images on our screen. The complexity that results stuns us with its likeness to the deeper reality which we all know. Fellini has explained what he found to be the central artistic problem concerning his use of Juliet's apparitions:

> The problem was to make them clear on a symbolic level, but of not having them fall into an overwhelming symbolism. I didn't want them to be shown on a neurotic, psychological, scientific level, and I didn't want them to be looked at like the drawings of the insane. . . . It's fine that something of all that did remain, but in an allusive manner and in the context of an image from a collective unconscious.[30]

The next apparition is the most obviously Jungian in its springing up from that well of the collective unconscious. Now that Juliet and we have heard from the spirit Iris, have seen Iris, and have seen her embodiment in the neighbor Susy, it is time for the shadow side of Iris/Susy to appear. During the séance, Iris had been introduced as the beautiful and exuberant and enticingly light aspect of human sexuality. She was obviously attractive to the repressed Juliet. But Olaf had been introduced as Iris's other side, as the disruptive, violent, and dangerously dark side of human sexuality. He was obviously frightening to the repressed Juliet. Now, still on the beach, as Juliet looks at herself in her mirror, the doctor speaks a sentence which prepares the viewer for another apparition, as it gives us some guidance in all this confusion of levels: "Our lovely Juliet always sees obscure, magical things, everywhere." Then we see her dream apparition of Olaf, not as a single beautiful woman as was Iris, but as a series of seaborne dark and indistinctly threatening brutal sexual forces. The natural blue of the sea turns a stale and ugly green. In some Fellini moods, the sea can be more the birthplace of frightening fantasies rather than visions of the natural and the loving: "I find the sea so fascinating, as an element I have never conquered: the place from which come our monsters and ghosts."[31] Prominent among the new Juliet monsters is a vague ghostly Oriental pavilion, a darker version of Susy's pavilion on the beach. Here is how the published transcript of the final film describes part of the Olaf apparitions:

> The sea and sky—dark green, ominous. Silence. At the left edge of the screen, slowly, the black silhouette of a ship's prow appears. From behind it, slowly, a raft floats into view. Two emaciated, exhausted horses, ribs showing, stand with their heads hanging to the raft's floor. Another horse lies on its back, motionless. Its legs, bent at the knees, stick up into the air; its neck arches upward; its head twists painfully off to the side, like a figure from Guernica.[32]

As early as the time of the original screenplay, Fellini had been as certain of the symbolic function of the Olaf apparition as he had been of the symbolic function of the Susy apparition. Fellini's first description of the Olaf raft abounds with words like "ferocious," "savage," "barbaric," "skull and crossbones," "monsters," "dragons." And the original screenplay, unlike the final film, explicitly identified the apparition: the word "OLAF" was to be scrawled on the side of the raft in big crude letters.[33]

After this preliminary vision of violence, horror, starvation, and death, the Olaf image turns explicitly sexual. It becomes as Freudian as it is Jungian. The published transcript describes the continuation of the Olaf apparition:

Like a landing barge, the large ship drops its prow onto the beach. Inside the barge an eerie light reveals a bizarre, motionless tableau—naked or nearly naked men. . . . The nudity is disgusting. . . . One man holds a sword. . . . The emaciated man . . . holds a sword over his head as if he had drawn it upward before delivering a blow, or as if it were bearing a flag. . . . A strong man . . . holds a club threateningly.[34]

In a universal dream symbol, we then see Juliet trying to escape from this dark side of human sexuality, but she is running in sand, sinking back as she desperately tries to run forward. Fellini is well carrying-out his early description of the film: "It is the story of the struggle taken up by a woman against certain monsters in herself."[35]

Just before Juliet awakens, Fellini shows us an image which reminds us of one we had seen previously. Thus this entire sequence, in true dreamlike fashion, ties up with a previous triggering image. Before Juliet had gone to the beach, she had watched her gardener, Gasperino, fat. and covered with tangled weeds, frighteningly emerge from a clogged green pond outside her window. Modestly, she had pulled her white dressing gown more protectively around herself. Now the apparition dream ends when, similarly, "out of the sea between the raft and the beach, the huge, bald head of a strong man appears," emerging from the green sea, and approaching a now vulnerable Juliet.[36]

Always the careful craftsman, in spite of the appearance of free spontaneity within his art, Fellini not only ended the Olaf apparition with a connection to a previous image, he also began the Olaf apparition with a connection to a subsequent image. Before the dark Olaf ship appeared, Juliet had seen another old man rising from the sea, this one pulling a rope that seemed to have a heavy burden behind it. The man whispered for Juliet's help, insisting that "this really is your concern." Juliet reluctantly took the rope, and began to pull something out of the depths. As she labored, she was once more blocked from our view by her obscuring hat. We did not know yet who that old man was, or what hidden thing was to be revealed by the cooperation between him and Juliet. But we will soon learn that the man with the rope is Lynx Eyes, the detective who divulges some secrets which will only increase Juliet's feelings of obscurity and unimportance.

Juliet is delivered from the primitive threats of Olaf when she is awakened by the modern noise of a jet. She receives a basket of fruit from Susy, and watches her neighbor drop her veil on the shore, and, stretching languidly, exhibit her voluptuous and nearly naked body. Then Venus returns to the sea.

Home and Family

Juliet looks content, free of her spirits, in her element, as she follows her nieces and their nurse toward home, through the lovely woods which lie between Juliet's house and the sea. As they were in the first shot of the film, the color and the imagery are once again positive, with green, healthy tree branches which brush against the camera as it follows the freely moving Juliet. Fellini was careful to choose a location where all of this nature imagery could comfort his Juliet. He built her white house "in a heavily wooded area, with many tall pines," in Fregene, just a few minutes from Fellini's own country house where he lives with his Giulietta.[37] In the pine forest, Juliet's mood of natural happiness lasts until she hears someone or something, some alien kind of unnatural voice which has invaded the peace of her forest. That voice seems to call Juliet's name. It is as if Fellini has marked these woods for some special later purpose.

Juliet's private composure is further disturbed by three human invaders who come into her forest to meet her. Juliet greets her remarkably pregnant sister Adele and her vision-lovely television actress sister Sylva. Juliet is overshadowed by both sisters, by both the feminine figure of maternity and the feminine figure of sexuality. Juliet is neither sexy nor a mother. Adele is aggressive, as Juliet is submissive. Sylva is frivolous, as Juliet is serious. The dominant sisters lead Juliet to the most dominating figure of all, to her extravagantly gorgeous mother. Caterina Boratto moves—still queenlike—from 8½ to *Juliet of the Spirits*, but she is now no longer the Queen of Heaven but rather the icily quintessentially beautiful Evil Queen from scary childhood fairy tales. When Juliet sees her mother, she instinctively puts her head down, in a kind of humble bow; and once more she hides herself completely beneath her own hat. The camera squashes the tiny Juliet among these three overpowering women. As they all walk along, parts of the colorful and exuberant costumes on the sisters flick in front of little Juliet, who hardly comes up to their shoulders. The bright pieces of cloth again and again hide plain Juliet from our view. (i. 41)

Our common sense tells us that Adele, Sylva, and Mother cannot in any real world be so gorgeously garbed and hatted as they are here in the sprite-filled forest. We see it all, but we don't quite believe in it. We recognize here again a kind of fairy tale view of reality. We realize that even the extremely fertile forest looks as artificial as do Juliet's relatives. Perhaps seeing is not believing? Or perhaps we are seeing in a special way. The most troubling ambiguity in the film is created by scenes like this, and like Susy's appearance at the beach, where the

i. 41. Contrasts: Juliet walks through her magic forest between sister and mother.

supposedly real characters take on a look, a color, a quality as strange as that of any of the apparitions in the film. "The apparitions in the film have the same substance as the real characters, and vice versa," Fellini has admitted.[38] No part of *8½* is quite so ambiguous or difficult as these scenes in *Juliet of the Spirits* where we don't seem to be wholly and entirely on any single level of reality, memory, *or* fantasy. We seem to be watching reality colored by a particularly personal view where memory and fantasy both play a part. We eventually realize that we are seeing everything, even Juliet, as everything must seem internally to her. Of course, Fellini does not make use of the traditional clarifying "subjective camera" convention for these shots. Instead, Fellini is after something else. He explains: "Sometimes more than one character is presented suddenly with a completely unreal look, so much so that a stimulating ambiguity between fantasy and reality is created. The ambiguity is intentional, and is one of the keys to the film."[39]

The scene in the forest gives us an astonishing example of how, between script and screen, Fellini worked out portions of that key ambiguity. In the original screenplay, he planned to explain Juliet's inferiority feelings in words. Valentina baldly would explain to a psychologist exactly how Juliet feels: "Poor darling, always something about her mother, her sisters. She always saw herself as the smallest. . . . She has this complex . . . the mother . . . the sisters."[40] In the actual film, Fellini cuts out the verbal explanation; his "stimulating ambiguity" comes from *our* seeing as Juliet's complexes cause her to see, and feel, without nice distinctions between reality and various kinds of illusions.

As the scene continues, Fellini does give us some language, but just barely enough to help us clarify Juliet's self-deprecating mental state. As the camera compares Juliet with her sisters and mother, Juliet nervously chatters on about the wishful possibility of her escaping with Giorgio on a vacation to some faraway spot. Mother interrupts her. As Juliet reaches out toward her mother, the queenlike beauty turns to Juliet with an aloof and disdainful air and says: "Please. You are all sweaty." And then she adds, "Why don't you put on a little makeup and lipstick?" Mother concludes, "You must take better care of yourself." They all leave. No one has touched another, even when kissing goodbye. The kisses fall on veils and air.

In the next scene, when Giorgio arrives home, he does nothing to make Juliet feel better about herself. As they sit watching TV, Juliet props herself up against Giorgio. He discourages conversation. He gets up abruptly. Juliet falls over. To transform subtle pictures into obvious words: Juliet collapses when she doesn't have a man to lean against. Giorgio goes to bed, and, with the aid of earplugs and eyeshades, blocks out Juliet's world and his involvement with it. Like a middle-class Zampano, Giorgio lies in bed, isolated. Juliet lies next to him, entirely separated, as Giorgio, in his dreams, mumbles the name of someone he has not blocked out. As Juliet listens, Giorgio softly whispers, "Gabriella!" Giorgio hugs the empty air.

The next two scenes confirm both Giorgio's infidelity and Juliet's consequent insecurity. We begin to understand Juliet's *need* to try to disprove the message which had told her so truthfully that she was no one to anybody. At breakfast, Giorgio clumsily lies his way through Juliet's questions about the identity of "Gabriella." After Giorgio leaves, Juliet sits staring, with no companion but a ringing telephone and a voice on a TV set. Elisabetta enters and turns toward Juliet with a look of withering compassion. Later that day, in the garden, Juliet doesn't hear the chattering voices of her servants as they talk about unfaithful and untruthful men. Juliet's conversation is reduced to an internal monologue, as she remembers that Giorgio had promised never to lie to her. The situation is now set. Exposition is finished. It is time for Juliet's search to begin.

The Secret of Sex

Valentina bounces into the scene and, as a messenger, moves the film toward its first explicit search episode. Val tells Juliet about Bhisma, "an extraordinary seer, an oracle, the man who holds in himself the secret of both sexes." Val adds: "Who can say that he hasn't come just for you?"

The Bhisma episode begins with a good visual counterpart of Juliet's interior darkness and fear. The lobby of the Plaza Hotel, where the oracle and his entourage are holding court, is in deep darkness when Juliet and Valentina arrive. As a boy with a flashlight is about to lead Juliet on her ascent up the stairs to the heights of Bhisma, Juliet, in her uncertainty about the wisdom of beginning the search, cowers behind a large potted plant. "Let's go back, Valentina," Juliet suggests. As a lightning crash shakes the old hotel, the very gods of the heavens seem to be conspiring to introduce Bhisma dramatically and fearfully.

Much of Juliet's fear, and much of her hope, is of a sexual nature. Valentina had first spoken of Bhisma as a hermaphroditic kind of creature. Juliet's spirits have been luring her, contradictorily, to both the light and dark sides of her sexual nature. Much of the talk surrounding Juliet has concerned whoredom. Even now Valentina remarks that long ago this fancy meeting place "was a hotel for kept women." Much healthy flesh has been displayed so far in the film. After the lights go on, we see that Dolores, the sculptress whose very god is a god of virile male sexuality, appears in Bhisma's suite with a half-naked beautiful man, with darkly tanned and shimmering skin. Dolores had appeared in the séance scene with a muscular, hairy-chested lover, whom we had watched her kiss deeply and hungrily. There seems to be no reason in the realm of reality for Dolores's second lover to be displaying his torso here in Bhisma's suite. We must wonder if all the sexuality, both female and male, which has been both talked about and exhibited, might not be another external sign of Juliet's internal feelings. Everyone except Juliet seems to accept and glory in sexuality. More and more Juliet is led to understand that open acceptance of sexuality is society's best advice. As she goes to see Bhisma, Juliet's blue-green suit is accented, in lining, blouse, trim, scarf, and gloves, with Susy's sexual red.

However strongly the Iris/Susy message is impressing Juliet, she still places her sexuality within her traditional ideal of married life and love. On her way down the hotel corridor to Bhisma, Juliet stops and looks in on a marriage party. Now alone, Juliet gazes in at the communal feast, with a white-clad bride at its center, much as the isolated Gelsomina had smiled wistfully at the festive bride in *La Strada*. Juliet listens to the priest intone the message of love which still holds Juliet's favor: "He who cherishes his wife, brings himself honor." She then hears, both from the priest in front of her and in her own memory, the words of her own wedding service: "Love each other for better or for worse, for richer or for poorer, in health or in sickness." Juliet's resultant smile is one of appreciation and acceptance, with a bit of rueful recognition that Giorgio's love for her has not matched that ideal. Ideal the picture is: the visual tableau of the traditional wedding party around a long festive table is as harmonized, as frozen in ordered time, as a mural by Leonardo.

i. 42. Fellini faces: silent commentary from Bhisma's votaries.

Fellini moves from a traditional and solemn ritual to a modern and obviously silly one. His camera, picking up haggard old faces and overly made-up young ones, mocks the tape-recorded cant of the cult session on Bhisma's terrace. (i. 42) Juliet doesn't enter into the service. Her fear increases.

By the time that Juliet is admitted alone to Bhisma's private suite, her psychic and sexual excitement are so pronounced that we see her as a tiny figure almost overwhelmed by a blood-red sofa and a huge expanse of bright red wall. A large fan tries unsuccessfully to cool the atmosphere. Just a little spot of Juliet blue-green holds out against all that red heat. When Bhisma goes into his trance, he is filmed behind a white curtain which drains all appearance of life from him and which distances him from the all-too-real concerns and worries of Juliet as she sits in the midst of blazing reds. Bhisma's words, as Juliet might have known, confirms all the worldly advice that she has heard so far. If she is to be a self-confident and fulfilled woman, she must become a full and satisfying sex object. The role of woman is to fulfill the function of whore. She is to study and perfect the bites and sounds of sex. Sex must become for her the new religion. "Your husband is your God," Bhisma insists. And Juliet's role is to serve that God, as "the priestess of the cult." Juliet is asked if she has any questions. In a confessional scene transformed by the modern temper, Juliet admits: "I seem to be nothing at all." And for her to gain absolution, her penance is simple: "Please your husband. . . ." Bhisma tells Juliet to practice her womanly "trade."

Juliet's anger at being told to be a whore throws Bhisma into a fit of repulsive sexuality, violent and sick. He becomes male; he becomes female; he becomes both at once. Against the violence of Bhisma's sexual explosion, Juliet sees Iris, while the ugly Bhisma, now becoming Iris, says: "You must become beautiful like me, beautiful like me, like me, like me!" Juliet then sees a series of apparitions which connect Bhisma not only with Iris, but, one after another, with a circus trapeze artist, and with Susy—as Bhisma looks around the room and calls out the name of Olaf. All of these familiar spirit forces besiege Juliet at once. She brushes her clothes frantically, and swats at the air, as if trying to rid herself of a plague of insects. She calls out a loud, "No!" She gets up, shouting, "I want to go out! I want to go out!" What began as search ends as flight.

Juliet runs from Bhisma's room. Her spirits and her associates have all given her the same message, a message from which she flees. As Juliet hurries down the hotel corridor, Bhisma's female assistant calls out one more message, this one strangely romantic: "Something new is going to happen tonight—something new and beautiful." The voice of Bhisma mysteriously adds: "Sangrilla quenches all thirst for anyone who drinks it . . . even that thirst which is never acknowledged." An unknown male voice with a soothing and beautiful Spanish accent adds: "They call it the drink of oblivion." Perhaps this will become— for Juliet—a more acceptable message.

The Circus

While Juliet drives home, she reminisces to her lady friends about her youth; and, as she does so, many of the mysteries of the film begin to clear up. Juliet wonders out loud whether Iris may be Fanny, the trapeze artist who ran away with her grandfather when Juliet was a little girl. At that, the scene flashes back to Juliet as a little girl at the circus, and we come to understand that many of the apparitions which have appeared so far in the film have roots deep in Juliet's psyche and memory. The pieces begin to fall into place. To Grandfather, the circus is obviously the same happy, free, spontaneous place that the circus is to Fellini. As Juliet watches the circus, we see a beautiful trapeze ballerina, dressed as Iris was when she appeared on the beach and in Bhisma's suite. As we look at Grandfather's Fanny we remember Iris and Susy, and we recognize that Sandra Milo is playing three roles, not two, and that all three are blended in Juliet's psyche as the spirit of lighthearted and abundantly free sexuality. That same Sandra Milo was the similarly sexual Carla in *8½*.

Fanny, Iris, and Susy are not the only sexual forces in Juliet's psyche. Seated next to Juliet, eternally youthful Mother, exactly as she was when she met Juliet in the forest, watches the circus show, and admires a handsome gilded muscleman. In this film of the female psyche, Fellini is managing to show as many beautiful men as, in *8½*, the film of the male psyche, he pictured beautiful women.

Juliet and Grandfather meet Fanny, and Grandfather establishes in his compliment to Fanny the connection in Juliet's mind between religion and sex. "A beautiful woman," Grandfather asserts piously, as Fanny does a Carla-like Sandra Milo dip, "makes me feel more religious."

Juliet watches—and runs from—a frenzied dance by barbaric, nearly naked savages, as the Olaf side of sexuality in Juliet's psyche finds its source.

An antique biplane appears on the screen, and we hear a memory of the circus music from *8½*. "I always thought," muses Juliet to her friends in the car, "that Grandfather and the dancer ran off in that circus plane." We watch an escape in the biplane that shows us clearly what Juliet herself would now love to do. And it is surely not surprising that the fantasy escape scene is placed by Fellini into the setting of a circus. We know that he has made a personal myth out of the childhood incident which he calls "my escape with the circus."[41] To gay circus music, Grandfather and Fanny fly away, high above the shocked and protesting figure of Mother, high above a raging, bearded authority figure who insists: "Professor De Filippi, in the name of God, stop! I command you to come down! I am your headmaster, and you will have to give me an explanation of your abominable conduct!" Juliet explains to the women in her car that Grandfather did escape with his Fanny, but that her mother would never again accept him.

And then Mother again appears, looking stern and disapproving, another restrictive authority figure. Juliet remembers: "One night I got up and met her in the corridor. She looked like a Queen. Perhaps she was going to a dance with Father. . . ." We see more clearly than ever the icy Evil Queen from fairy tales, staring threateningly at Juliet and at us. (i. 43)

The memory sequence ends with Grandfather's cheerful face winking at Juliet, as if to encourage her to escape as he did from those who are threatening and restricting her.

i. 43. Another face of Caterina Boratto: from elusive Madonna, to disapproving Mother, to Evil Queen of fairy tales.

Romance

In the next episode, Juliet finds an ideal romantic figure of masculine love. As if in reaction to Bhisma's view of woman as whore who participates in alternately flamboyant and savage sexuality, Juliet encounters a handsome gentleman of charm, grace, and gentleness, who treats her with deference, with respect, with an ever soft, consoling, and protective sexual regard. Giorgio has invited a friend from Valencia to enjoy the peace of the villa near the sea. As Juliet approaches her yard, she sees José as if he were another apparition, almost hovering, seeming to float in the mist of her garden. We see him, as Juliet does, through the trees; he speaks the name of a rose; he stops to listen to the birds.

Fellini's original screenplay describes the romantic perfection of José's magical appearance before Juliet: "In the middle of the flowering tree stands a man—tall, elegant, extremely handsome, with an air of nobility and vaguely melancholy. He is looking at a rose bush with detachment, but also with a certain very sad grace."[42]

The entire José scene is photographed in a style which is romantic and quiet. The rhythms are slow. The compositions are harmonious. Most of the takes are long and smooth, with little cutting. The gentle atmosphere is in marked contrast to the probing, nervous style of the rest of the film.

As if he had known her always, and known her to the heart, and understood her needs, José brings to the insecure Juliet the confident message of her own strong capacity for real love. José sees her love in her flowers: "If you can give so much love every day, your heart must be filled with love." In true fantasy-fashion, José can see truths about Juliet which, in Giorgio's awful reality, the mere husband misses. José prepares elaborately for a ritual cup, requiring a special kind of holy vessel. José officiates, as Fellini's original screenplay describes his actions, "with the grace of a priest handling a chalice."[43] As José presents the mystic cup of Sangrilla to Juliet for her to drink, he intones: "They say it quenches all thirst of anyone who drinks it, even the thirst which is never acknowledged. They call it the drink of oblivion." The voice is the same soft and assured voice that Juliet had heard speaking that last sentence outside of Bhisma's suite. And the words suggest that Juliet has a thirst for romantic love, a thirst that, in her repression, she had never acknowledged. But the words might also suggest, with sad inevitability, that the libation which is offered by this romantic ritual exists only in a state of oblivion, does *not* thus exist— that José is not a real possibility for Juliet. But the mysterious words of José have other possible interpretations. Perhaps this offered cup is a dangerous drink of oblivion because if Juliet accepts fully this romantic dream, if she allows herself to be satisfied with an apparition of a perfect man—gentle, knowledgeable, sophisticated, protective, loving—then she will have given up the search for *her* true self. And surely that, we know from other Fellini films, would be to consign herself forever to oblivion. Just how much of José is, in fact, "real" neither we nor Juliet will ever know. "Afraid of making a mistake," instructs the screenplay, "uncertain whether this man is an apparition or a real presence, Juliet looks around as if for help."[44] But only José is there, and for the moment he is to Juliet real, present, attractive, and obtainable. He is obviously the promised "something new and beautiful."

Like Steiner, José becomes the earthly ideal: he is the brave bullfighter, he is "like a priest," or he is like "a dancer," as he himself explains the qualities which are important. José sees the significance of, and is himself connected with, religion and art, with bravery and spontaneity. José describes for Juliet a perfected world where ritual prevents even death from becoming real death: "Look, the bull dies in his mystery. It is not the sword which kills him—it is the magic with which he is guided. I kill him with illusory blows, and the wretched bull goes into the void." José and his friends in religion and art are those who, like Claudia, can put off destruction and bring harmony and order and peace: "Poetry is never dangerous. My best friends are bullfighters. They compose music, they write poetry. . . . They have an abhorrence for blood. The Cordoba way of fighting, for example, has an unsurpassed harmony." José recognizes in Juliet that same capacity for creating the same kind of harmony: "Now I am here, and I am very happy. What would be left in this world if we took away the harmony of an evening like this one? I'm in debt to you for this moment of real happiness."

Like the Fool, José is a messenger from another world. And he now speaks words which will come to Juliet again from yet another messenger. José advises "a spontaneity which springs from a pure heart." That is, of course, opposite advice to the calculated whoredom advised so far by the spirits, by Bhisma, and by the world. José expresses the wish that he could be a part of Juliet's sought-for pure and spontaneous happiness, and he mystically predicts what will, indeed, be discovered by Juliet at the end of the film: "A little can be everything. Yes. A quick decision, meeting an old friend by the sea, lost calm found again—everything becomes clear and plausible."

But not yet. As José kisses Juliet's hand, and as she gazes at him with wonder and warmth, Giorgio calls out, and Juliet returns from romance to reality, from a wished-for harmony to a current disorder. Giorgio sets up a telescope, a gift from José, and Giorgio leers at the well-displayed body of Susy in the next-door window. José, on Juliet's side, disapproves.

The contrast between Giorgio and José develops throughout the scene. The camera compares the face of the dissipated Giorgio with the face of the noble José. One seems weak, the other firm. In a mock bullfight, Giorgio is suddenly animalistic, a Zampano, savage and frightening; José is gentle and protective. In the final scene of the episode, Giorgio lies next to Juliet in bed, but separated from her, cut off once more by plugged ears and sheltered eyes. Juliet's eyes are open, a beam of light is shining on them, and they seem to look up through the ceiling to the intense yet placid José, contemplative, pacing his room, slowly circling. We see a José who is out of reach, a story above Juliet.

Juliet awakens to discover that she is alone in her bed. Giorgio is speaking affectionately on the phone, obviously talking to Gabriella. Juliet gets up out of bed and listens. As before, when Juliet confronts him, Giorgio lies. In his relationship with his wife, Giorgio mixes up truth and falsehood as easily as did Guido. Giorgio goes back to bed and leaves Juliet standing alone, isolated by the camera in the loneliness of the quiet house. This short interlude provides the thrust that leads Juliet into the next search episode of the film: Lynx Eyes and his detective agency.

Detection

The Lynx Eyes episode opens on a cold reflection-filled modern corridor, with Adele, alone in the picture, urging a reluctant Juliet to move on, to catch up with her, to enter the frame, to set up a pursuit of Giorgio. Juliet is dressed in frigid white; she is hooded, enclosed, encased. Adele is expansive, maternity gown flowing, huge hat flying free. Juliet is even more hesitant than she was when she was about to consult Bhisma. All life seems drained from her. The cold corridor gives way to an elevator that looks as if it were made of refrigeration coils. Juliet says, "Adele, let's come back another day—or you go alone."

Adele's response is to move the imagery into a Felliniesque sacrament-parody. Adele urges faith in Lynx Eyes: "Think of him like a confessor." And when Juliet and Adele leave the elevator, they do indeed find Lynx Eyes dressed as a priest. In his office, he speaks the commonplaces of the clerical marriage counsellor as he slowly removes his clerical garb. Juliet's subsequent confession brings no absolution, and surely no sense of forgiveness and peace. Instead, Juliet's confession becomes simply an occasion for an invasion of her privacy by detectives with a business mentality and a religious zeal. By the time Lynx Eyes' Roman collar is off, he is speaking the jargon of the private

eye. The Headmaster, the figure of righteous authority who had declared vengeance against Grandfather, now appears before Juliet in
Lynx Eyes' office, to demand vengeance against Juliet herself if she
dare refuse to seek the punishment of Giorgio: "Woe to those who
tolerate sin, because thus they become accomplices of the sinner, and
therefore must burn with him in the eternal fires. Claim your vengeance before the Lord!"

The appearance here of the Headmaster demanding vengeance
shows an important Fellini improvement between script and screen. In
the original screenplay, Fellini had placed the vengeance speech in the
mouth of an anonymous hermit, who appeared to Juliet much later in
the film. That hermit had no clear connection with Juliet's youth, and
the speech played no role at all in Juliet's decision not to tolerate
Giorgio's sin.[45] By placing the speech in Lynx Eyes' office, and by
giving the speech to the Headmaster, whom we already know to be a
figure of punishment from Juliet's sin-and-suffering-centered Catholic
girlhood, Fellini efficiently established another connection between
past and present, and enriched the heated religious atmosphere of this
significant scene. In a renewal of the righteousness of her religious
youth, Juliet demands that the detectives spy on Giorgio.

i. 44. Juliet in Dolores's studio: modern gods of flesh and stone.

Lynx Eyes had promised: "We will present you with a husband you never knew before." Juliet decides that that is just what she wants, to probe into the inner self of Giorgio. She decides, "I want to know everything, everything, everything!" She had told Lynx Eyes: "I no longer know who I am." To find out who Giorgio is will perhaps tell her who she is.

New Gods

The scene cuts to Juliet walking along the picket fence outside her home. The camera, shooting through the picket fence, creates a strobe-light effect, as if Juliet were jerking uncontrollably through time and space. We see her huddled inside her cloak and hood, much like one of the anonymous nuns whom we are about to see. Juliet turns away from a romantic image of José, who is sitting in her yard with his guitar, because, right now, the reality of her past and present are too much with her.

The scene shifts to a picturization of one of the many religions which are all around the adult Juliet. Silly scatterbrained Val has her cults. Intense single-minded Dolores has hers. Val worships the exotic and the occult. Dolores worships the physical potency of the male, that harsh, hard sexuality which Juliet fears. Juliet is in Dolores's sculpture studio, gazing at an almost naked male model and a buxom female model, both of whom seem to be bursting through their tanned and oiled skins. Dolores, surrounded by her massive naked statues, pronounces her belief in and worship of the new god of the sexual body. (i. 44) In response, Juliet, looking especially small amid the stony statues, remarks, "When I was a child I imagined that God was hidden in the nuns' theatre . . . " and the scene flashes back to another memory sequence, and at the same time to more revelations concerning the current psyche of Juliet.

Suffer!

We have already noted that during the filming of *Juliet of the Spirits* Fellini praised his wife, Giulietta Masina, as an actress who was able to convey "a consuming nostalgia for innocence, for perfection."[46] That consuming nostalgia is the dominant note of the next evocative childhood memory sequence. Indeed, it is one of Fellini's obsessions, shown in many of his films: "I want to give back to man a virginal availability, his innocence as he had it in childhood. . . . *8½, Giulietta degli Spiriti,* and even *La Dolce Vita* tried to propose this backward walk."[47] Juliet's trip back to her virginal state shows the childhood source of Juliet's adult willingness to suffer at the hands of Giorgio, to accept her own martyrdom. In a school play, innocent little Juliet re-enacts in her own person the death of a martyr, accepting pain and suffering as the road to perfection.

The scene is monochromatic, shot in soft light, with everything reflecting the slight rosy hue of memory. A nun appears, so enrobed as to hide any sign of her own person or individuality, let alone the sexuality displayed and worshipped in Dolores's studio. The nun gazes with little Juliet at a picture of a martyred saint roasting on a grill. The face of the saint shows what innocence means to Juliet: It is the face of her sweet and unworldly maid, Elisabetta, the one whose smile had expressed compassion for Juliet's own pain and suffering. And it is a face that shows what innocence means to Fellini, for it is a face mysteriously like that of Paola, whose smile was the symbol of innocence in *La Dolce Vita*. Young Juliet and her little friend Laura both understand this dramatic questing for perfection, this sacrificial roasting on a grill, as an attempt to see God. To fly up to heaven, they need to accept the wings which the nuns are eager to attach to them. Juliet, both child and adult, accepts martyrdom as the price and the reward of the quest. When asked by the little boy playing the role of the Emperor if she is willing to accept martyrdom, little Juliet opens her mouth in response, but it is the voice of big Juliet which replies, formally and meaningfully, "Yes, I accept it." Little Juliet allows herself to be tied to the grill. But we then see big Juliet suffering on the grill, whose fiery red paper streamers are the only harsh color in this muted yet vivid memory. (i. 45)

Juliet, on her grill, winds up and up, higher and higher, as she approaches the trapdoor in the nuns' theatre, where she expects to see God. Juliet becomes still another Fellini figure symbolically suspended between earth and sky, but Grandfather, always the rebel and the earthly spokesman for the unrepressed free life, does not accept Juliet's heavenly ambitions. Grandfather stops the play, and denounces the proceedings: "It's disgusting! Give me back my granddaughter!" He unwinds the grill, bringing it back down to earth. The Headmaster, the voice of authority who had tried to stop Grandfather's escape during the circus scene and who had urged Juliet to seek vengeance against Giorgio, speaks lines which we have heard before, echoing in Juliet's memory: "Professor De Filippi, enough! Come to your senses! Stop this abominable behavior!" Juliet's mother, the other repressive authority figure who has been haunting Juliet's adult life, shows her displeasure at Grandfather's liberating conduct by collapsing in a faint.

i.45. Ascension: the adult Juliet rises up toward God on the martyr's grill of her youth.

In his original screenplay, Fellini ended this childhood memory sequence with a description indicating Juliet's disappointment not to have found the God she sought:

> Crying silently, crushed, Juliet lets herself be led away by her grandfather, but as she walks, she twists her face, and she looks upward at the closed shutters, which now are distant, with regret and disillusion. They are like a fading planet and become, beyond the bands of white light, darker and emptier.[48]

But these moving words are, obviously, more a literary explanation of a mood than a series of images for a film. In the final film, Fellini created a mood similar to that described in the screenplay, but without the planet imagery. The published transcript of what we actually see on the screen describes a film, and not literature, and gives us a wonderful image of narrow enclosure:

> Grandfather leads the young Juliet away from the camera, back down the long corridor, holding her by the hand and talking to her. We don't hear his words, only the sound of a child crying. As they walk, nuns file down the sides of the corridor, forming two rows of blackness through which Juliet

and her grandfather walk. The camera rolls backward between
the rows of nuns so that they frame the sides of the shot.[49]

Back in the current world of reality, we fade into the innocent face of
Elisabetta, not now on a grill but in the garden with Juliet. The adult
Juliet is in a sense still on a grill, still trying to find a hidden God, or at
least some hidden something which will allow her to understand
herself. We are watching Juliet's own version of Guido's search for
"anima." Her childhood memory tells her to be a martyr, to sacrifice
herself, to choose Gelsomina's route. Her spirits voice the current
message that the God to whom she must sacrifice herself is her husband Giorgio, that she must become a whore for him. Susy is about to
reinforce the worldly message that it is the role of woman to become a
whore, not just for her husband but for everyone, as Iris had recom-
mended in the first message that Juliet received from her spirits.

Enjoy!

The search becomes more active; the messages become more frequent. The messenger does not now come to Juliet; Juliet goes to visit
Susy. But, as if to summon Juliet, an extravagantly beautiful, heavily
furred cat, wearing a bright red bow and a name tag that says "Susy,"
appears at Juliet's home. To return the cat, Juliet approaches the realm
of the fabulous villa next door. Iron bars of a high gate seem to block the
way, but a female voice calls out, laughing gaily, "The gates are open!"
This world of Susy is easy to enter. The elaborately crowned head of a
regal white peacock introduces the apparitionlike world inhabited by
Susy. Her wildly disordered garden and home are the opposite of
Juliet's manicured lawns and domestic neatness. Huge white flowers
at the end of leafless stems suggest flowers in a fairy tale or dream. The
leaf-strewn yard surrounds a cracked and towering mansion guarded
by huge statues of fierce hawklike birds with enormous naked female
breasts. It is the realm of both Olaf and Iris.

Susy's house is decorated like an elaborate exotic whorehouse, all
glass and reflections, brilliant reds and deep purples, but messy,
disordered, unfinished, chaotic. The set is a perfect example of how
Fellini communicates through visual values. "You write pages and
pages of dialogue," Fellini has said, "then you talk a little bit with the
set designer and put together a room that says everything."[50] Like so
many other scenes in *Juliet of the Spirits*, the effect depends largely on
Fellini's new mastery of color. Fellini explains: "Color produces an
extraordinary result in many scenes in this picture. I am thinking

i. 46. Another ascension: Susy leads Juliet on a tour of her temple of sex.

particularly of the scene in Susy's house. The glass doors, the gauze, the shining nylon, the side walks covered with glass that sends forth lights—it's much more effective than it could ever have been in black and white.[51]

In that colorful house Juliet finds Susy, lying on her bed—her throne, or perhaps her altar. Susy is wrapped in heavy fur, just like her cat. But much of Susy's white flesh is carefully exhibited. As she lies on her bed, Susy speaks softly on the telephone—about love. In attendance is a friar, whose prayer for Susy is, "May God make you even more beautiful for His glory." Lola, the former whore who is also in attendance on Susy, wants the friar to perform his usual religious function in this household, to tell dirty convent stories. The friar assures Susy that she is "an angel," and promises to return tomorrow for another service. Also in attendance are several acolytes: a foot fetishist in love with Susy; Senya, Susy's exotic Eurasian masseuse; a muscular workman, dressed only in a loincloth, who opens a libation of champagne for Susy as she remarks on the beauty of his sweaty body. After greeting her neighbor as a potential new worshipper, Susy leads Juliet on a tour of this temple of sex. During the tour, a bowl of bright purple flowers is carried into Susy's boudoir by the whore Lola. The flowers speak to Juliet in Iris's voice, and explain the purpose of this visit to the holy sanctuary: "Susy will be your teacher. Listen to her." (i. 46)

Susy well knows the contrast between herself and Juliet, between teacher and novice, and it becomes clear that, like Juliet's spirits, Susy is trying to lure Juliet into her religion. Susy tells Juliet of a dream in which Juliet was a nun and Susy was a tart. And then Susy invites Juliet to a party here at her house next Saturday night. As they tour the house, bright colors continue to flash in our eyes: walls, floors, parrots, fixtures. Susy says, "I adore bright colors." Indeed, she is remodeling so as to make the house still brighter. Even outside the house itself, Susy's vines and trees are red and gold and russet, in contrast to the tranquil green of Juliet's peaceful forest and garden.

From Susy's tarty boudoir, the camera looks out onto Juliet's conventlike house: white in the midst of pretty natural green. The house is viewed in a picture-postcard kind of perfection, or perhaps it is more like a stage set. As we look at Juliet's house through Susy's window we realize how much of the film has a stagey quality, as if the film were always asking us what kind of reality lies behind the cardboard walls, the painted flats, the props of art.

The camera turns to Susy lying on her huge round bed, as she summons her novice: "Come here, Juliet." Susy looks up at the mirror on the ceiling over the bed and inquires slyly, "Do you have a mirror like this, too? . . . It's like having four in bed." It is as if somehow Susy knew about the introspective Juliet's fascination with mirrors. Embarrassed, Juliet looks away. Once more Juliet hears Susy's voice calling her name, this time as Susy slides toward a pool at the bottom of a long chute. Susy is swimming, nude, as once more she summons Juliet to follow her: "Join me, Juliet—the water's warm. This is another one of my ideas. After we make love, my boyfriend and I slide down. It's wonderful. Come on, Juliet. Take off your clothes." Juliet sees that the entrance to the chute is in the shape of a giant scallop's shell. Venus has returned once more to the water whence she came. (i. 47)

During the tour of Susy's love temple, Juliet meets a victim of love. They visit Arlette, who is staring and vacant, obviously mad. She has tried suicide many times. Susy's explanation: "She is very unlucky in love." The same power that can create the bountiful Susy can, if it turns its shadow side, destroy. Arlette is as thin and plain and sullen and lifeless as Susy is fleshy and flamboyant and vivacious. Arlette reminds Juliet of another victim of the dark side of love. She thinks of her friend Laura, the one who had as a child, like Juliet, sought God. But instead of the God of her childhood, Laura had turned, as Juliet is

i. 47. Susy at home: Venus returns to the water of her birth.

being tempted to do, to new gods. At the age of fifteen, Juliet explains, Laura "committed suicide for love." As Juliet looks at Arlette and thinks of Laura, she obviously feels closer to them than to Susy. Juliet still thinks of herself as victim, as sufferer, as isolated outsider. As Gelsomina had recognized herself in Oswaldo, so Juliet's staring face suggests that she recognizes herself in Arlette. Perhaps Juliet, too, is somehow killing herself for "love" in her total dependence upon Giorgio.

The Susy sequence continues in a new setting. Now that Juliet has visited the world of Susy, it is time for Susy to visit the world of Juliet. The scene fades from the water of Susy's pool to the path of Juliet's forest. The camera catches Susy and Juliet riding bicycles together past the lovely green pines. This scene is a fascinating improvement over Fellini's original idea. Fellini had planned to show Susy's increasing dominance over Juliet by picturing them shopping together at Susy's sybaritic fancy shops.[52] Instead, Fellini shows not Juliet on Susy's ground, but Susy's perverted misuse of Juliet's own special ground. The temptation of Susy is more dangerous to Juliet when it takes place on what Juliet assumes is safe territory. It is precisely because Susy is "the image of a neglected and repressed aspect of Juliet," Fellini has said, that Susy is able to acquire her "greater strength," to administer "more poison" to Juliet.[53]

Susy has invaded the forest. As always, Susy is almost naked, dressed in a tiny bra and bikini which are visible through a thin veil hanging down from a huge hat. Now that Juliet is Susy's willing pupil, Juliet wears more of Susy's red: a vivid red sweater is pulled down long over Juliet's white slacks. The force of Susy is so dominant that her spirit is the only one now felt in the forest. This time the camera does not gently brush past hanging branches. It moves with quick bursts of speed in an effort to follow the awkward little bikes. The camera lingers on no lovely scenery. Susy and Juliet ride their bikes through a downpour, but we see that the water is not rain but some sort of huge artificial sprinkler. The natural has no role in the scene. The sprinkler is the kind used in movies to simulate rain. Fellini lets us see how false it all is. Susy seems to be conquering Juliet.

The towering trees become themselves an extension of Susy's temple of sex. Susy shows Juliet her sunbathing platform high in a tree. This goddess of love, in her several manifestations, is always in the heights, above the earth—on a trapeze, in a biplane, now in a basket ascending to the treetops. "In Greece," says Susy, "there is a monastery on a mountain, and the monks get up just like this." As Susy sits in her ascending basket, her veil billows out, and she looks for all the world like a witch in a cauldron floating up into a haunted sky. Up in the holy treetops, Susy admits that this is a fine vantage point for voyeuristically watching sex activities down below. She suggests to her pupil: "Sit down—let's drink. Let's sunbathe naked." The contrast between Susy and Juliet is pictured once more: Susy sunbathes, Juliet remains covered. They talk seriously, each presenting her philosophy. Susy's is one of acceptance of all life as it is centered on herself: "I deny myself nothing." Juliet's is one of acceptance of only that which is centered on Giorgio: "He became my whole world—my husband, my lover, my father, my friend, my house. I didn't need anything else."

Two young men in a red sports car drive up, with the Charleston, the sound of the Roaring Twenties, playing on their car radio. They hop out of their car, gaily seeking their flappers. Susy takes a mirror, turns it not reflectively on herself, but turns it to the boys, making signals with the sun. The boys come up; Juliet goes down. As she is about to leave the forest for home, Juliet turns to look up to the treetops. She sees the obscene image of the two boys moving slowly up the strong thick straight trunk of the tree, toward the gaping opening at the top, with Susy standing, a grotesquerie, legs spread wide apart, leering, waiting, ready for both young men to enter. Juliet, small among the trees, walks away.

Fellini has summarized in an interview the function of Susy. "She is shown," he said, "as an exaggerated, inflated figure—all sex. She's a kind of enchantress of love, a mistress of eroticism. . . . She's a kind of idealization of a pagan divinity, similar to Anitona [*i.e.*, Anita Ekberg] in *La Dolce Vita*." Susy as a goddess of sex is thus one extreme calling to Juliet. Susy is, according to Fellini, "the other face of the saint on the grating."[54] The saints of the present tell Juliet: "Enjoy!" The saints of her childhood tell Juliet: "Suffer!" But no voice has yet told her to be herself.

Exposure

Juliet is about to pull the rope out of the depths and to discover her heaviest burden. Perhaps out of these depths will also emerge some true Juliet. We remember that Guido had to suffer a death before he could experience the rebirth of himself.

A telephone call interrupts a typical afternoon at home. Juliet, herself in a maze, has been telling her nieces the story of the labyrinth. "The more one wanders around," Juliet explains, "the worse it gets." Lynx Eyes says on the phone that the detectives are ready to report what they have discovered about Giorgio's hidden life. Juliet goes to their office, and watches, as we do, a stunning and vulgar multimedia exhibition of privacy made public. As Juliet's world is turned inside out, Lynx Eyes, not realizing a possible profundity in his words, chatters on about the paradox involved in outer and inner truth: "Since we are confined to facts, our information of course is completely objective, and is therefore perhaps limited. The reality of the situation could be something quite different. . . . Of course, the interpretation of all this must be left up to you." In sound and in pictures, on film, on tape, on slides, the outside facts about Giorgio's infidelity are flashed before Juliet. Modern technology tells Juliet more truth about Giorgio than sleeping next to him for years had ever told her. At the end of the show, Juliet stands up between the film projector and the screen, and some little shred of her own innate dignity manages to block out the image of Giorgio's car, carrying Giorgio and Gabriella, together, along a busy highway. But that dignity is fragile. Now completely vulnerable, Juliet seems to be only a shadow, and that shadow is reflected on a screen in the middle of the threatening traffic.

Saturday Night

As in *La Dolce Vita*, after the despair comes the orgy. Another Fellini party is in full swing. Juliet will now know what kind of festive communal rites go on behind Susy's walls. Juliet's imagination is obviously ready to paint this scene in especially gaudy colors. Throughout the party, the color of the background behind Juliet is almost always a flaming red. For the first time, Juliet is dressed entirely in red. She is drinking a red liquor, the same as Susy. The costumes of the guests match the decor of Susy's house. This is a bordello, and they are the whores. Sounding much like Iris, Susy announces: "I want to embrace everybody!" Their major game is imitating whores, and they are instructed by Lola the expert. Juliet turns to a feathered girl whose performance was judged by Lola to be "perfect." Juliet asks her whether she is a model, whether she knows Gabriella, and whether Gabriella is very beautiful. When all the answers are affirmative, Juliet adds, "She's also a little bit of a slut, too, isn't she?" Apparently learning how to meet the competition, Juliet walks down the stairs as if she, too, were a slut. Susy is delighted with her pupil: "Isn't she perfect!" Susy exclaims.

The whoredom imagery of the film has reached its climax. Susy approves of the new role that Juliet, her pupil, is learning to perform.

Susy literally leads Juliet by the hand. Throughout the film, the "be a whore" advice has been continual. The original screenplay included a Juliet speech which shows us Juliet's impatience with the advice which all women receive: "Make yourself beautiful, be more of a whore—hair this way, make-up that way, move your rear when you walk, look straight at men, laugh, clear your throat—just be a little more of a whore. . . . Have your nose fixed, lose weight, gain weight." Juliet adds her own comment: "What the hell!"[55]

We watch a series of rituals of the sex religion, as practiced in Susy's temple. A woman announces, "I am the Goddess of Vice." A man performs an Egyptian fertility rite. He later insists to an anonymous woman, "Your name is Sex," and then changes it to "Your name is Womb," and then changes it to "Your name is that of the goddess." A tall slinky black girl fills the room with the sound of a throaty ritual chanting, an echo of the sound that we had heard when Susy first emerged from the water and into the film. Susy's handsome young godson, himself garbed in a priestlike flowing white robe, processes solemnly into the room, announced by the sound of the chanting. Slowly, the other guests go off, now that their time of pretending is over, to be whores in actuality. In a striking and suddenly static shot, Susy is shown sitting, straight and attentive, as if officiating at a most solemn ceremony. Her brightly lighted face is cut right down the middle by a stabbing shaft of darkness: Susy is light and dark. She is both Iris and Olaf, together at last, as Juliet is about to be led off to taste the depths of love as whore.

Susy had been Hostess, Priestess, Goddess. And now, as Novice-mistress, Susy introduces her godson to Juliet. We hear Juliet's teacher, whispering her invitation for Juliet to follow in her path. "Juliet," whispers Susy, "Come on. I'm up here. . . ." Susy's costume suddenly makes her look like a winged insect, as she lures her victim toward her. Susy leads Juliet up the steps, past quick flashes of lovemaking, with dominating women looking like vampires, past sounds of gasps and sighs and hoarse laughter. Susy continues to lead. "He's waiting," whispers Susy. "He wants you."

Together, teacher and pupil enter the boudoir/novitiate. Attendants, with incense and chalices of champagne, prepare for the service. Juliet looks into a Susy mirror and sees a new kind of Juliet: flushed, red-clad, ready. Susy withdraws. The voice of Iris comes from the scallop shell, reassuring, still tempting: "Juliet! Susy is your teacher. Listen to her; learn from her." But as Susy's godson approaches, Juliet hears someone else calling her in desperate fear: "Juliet! What are you doing?" It is not Iris; it is Elisabetta, it is young Laura, it is young Juliet.

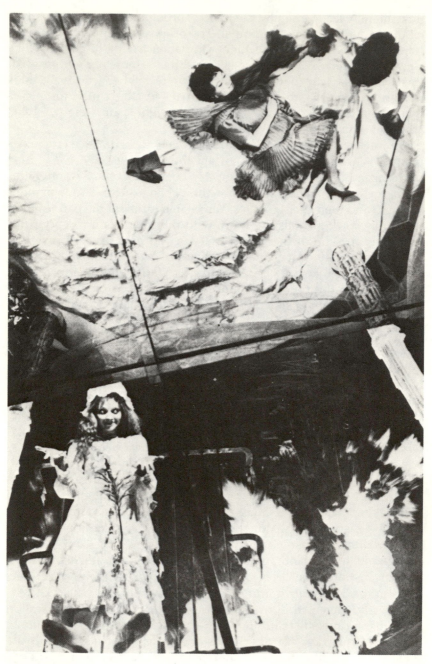

i. 48. The battle for Juliet's soul: as Susy's godson makes his move, the saint on the grill calls her back.

Juliet sees, in the mirror above Susy's bed, the saint on the grill. (i. 48) Juliet flees from the room, as the voices of Susy and the attendants call after her. As Juliet escapes, the camera lingers on the monstrous statues of the devouring birds with the bare female breasts that guard the entrance to Susy's temple. Juliet has fled from the world of Susy; she has temporarily escaped Olaf and Iris.

Psychodrama

All but one of the final scenes of *Juliet of the Spirits* take place at Juliet's own house. These final scenes show that, as she has fled, Juliet is pursued. After Susy's house, Juliet's own home seems for a time to be a citadel of purity and natural order. The scene shifts from a Susy party to a Juliet party. We are no longer in a lush red indoors but in a serene green outdoors. Juliet and Giorgio are giving a lawn party for their friends. Juliet's blond and pretty nieces, dressed in pure white, dance on the bright green carpet of the well-mowed lawn. Even Valentina arrives dressed all in white, as if she were ready to receive her first communion. The table is bountiful with beautiful and dew-covered fruits and foods of nature. At this party the main game is not the Susy obsession: how to be a good whore. At this party the main game is a Juliet obsession: how to discover the deep and true self. An American woman psychologist, Dr. Miller, says to the wife of Juliet's doctor, as she begins to play psychodrama with her: "Now begin to concentrate. Try to remember what's deep within you." The purpose of psychodrama, she explains, is the discovery of truth. The psychologist who leads the game looks and sounds serene. Her face is strong, self-assured; her voice is modulated, penetrating. Fellini's genius for casting assures us at once that this will be a positive figure, one to listen to, and to learn from. Dr. Miller has all the aura of soundness and health that Bhisma lacked. The character of Dr. Miller is another important change from the original screenplay. In the earlier version, the psychologist was an entirely negative figure, an ugly male full of tics who spoke in Bhisma-like cant and who never gave Juliet any help at all.[56]

Dr. Miller is present in this film to help Juliet. She explains that any self-discovery depends upon "an atmosphere of total, absolute truth." Much of the film has been about the search for truth, which has been Juliet's role, and about the avoidance of truth, which has been Giorgio's role. So Dr. Miller's game is signalled to us as significant. Juliet will be anxious to play it. Giorgio mocks it. Giorgio and Mother, as if afraid of truth, sound the first disruptive note in this positive garden setting. Their comments about Dr. Miller's game indicate that they consider it an opportunity for flirtatious and sexually suggestive jokes.

Dolores, at the party with still another muscular lover, adds the second disruptive note. She tells Genius, the medium in the séance scene, that she is "only interested in what happens to me here, today, now." Suddenly Dolores's words about her interest in the present are interrupted with a picture from the past. Elisabetta stands burning on Juliet's grill, between two bowls of fruit on the table. Nobody seems to see her.

Juliet is inside her house, surveying the party which is taking place outside. Juliet's house represents her as accurately as Susy's house represents her. The exterior of Juliet's house is neat, ordered, suburban, controlled; but inside it is secretly seething. We now see Juliet in her own ordered and harmonious bedroom. She is dressed in white, here in her home seemingly secure from the forces represented by Susy. But temptations have disturbed her conscience. "Forgive me!" she prays. The compassionate, and apparently real, face of Elisabetta appears outside the window, as if the saint on the grill is answering Juliet's prayer for forgiveness.

But now the pursuit actively begins again: the suppressed interior explodes. Juliet goes to a closet, colored a neutral gray. She opens the door, and suddenly the screen fills with an apparition of golden hair. Inside the closet, a woman tosses her head; the lush hair flicks aside, revealing a full, rounded, naked female breast, against a bright red background. The color progression suggests Juliet's growing frenzy. Juliet opens another closet door, and this time the apparition sounds the opposite call: not sex but suffering. Flames shoot out from the closet toward Juliet. She recoils. Juliet pleads: "Enough! Leave me in peace! Leave me in peace!" But, instead of peace, a series of conflicting apparitions vie for her attention and for her acquiescence. In the bathroom Juliet sees Elisabetta burning on the grill. Outside Juliet's bathroom window the foliage turns blood red; and Susy's face peeks through. Juliet hears a voice, moaning, calling her name. She sees a white-clad figure slumped against a wall. The figure seems to be Elisabetta, freed from her grill. But the figure suddenly turns into Susy, breasts bulging from beneath a virginal white gown, red tongue lasciviously flapping. Frantically, Juliet tries once more, in her search for truth, to reject Susy: "You shameless liar! I won't believe a word you ever say to me—never! Go away! Go away!" What seems to be reality then intervenes, and Juliet sees her maid Teresina dismissing a male caller with those same words: "Go away." Did Juliet actually speak, or was it Teresina we heard? Outside, Juliet sees the spirit of Iris as a nearly naked, sexy Eve-like figure hiding behind a tree. And, of course, she then sees the spirit of Olaf, this time as a cluster of the ferocious savages who danced in the circus ring of Juliet's childhood.

By now the contrasts which have clashed within Juliet throughout the film have finally come clear. The polarity was first reflected by her two maids, the innocent and the experienced. The innocent is Elisabetta, the saint, the martyr, one side of herself. The experienced is Teresina, and the contrasting sexual messages of Iris and Olaf, another side of herself. The message of Iris/Fanny/Susy is the adult view: a modern secular message of the attraction of free and unlimited love. The message of Olaf is the childhood view: an old-fashioned Christian message of the fear of dangerous and barbarous sex.

In her effort to restore order, to end this war within her, Juliet, now dressed in a lovely patterned gold kimono, leaves the house, enters the garden, and joins the party. Juliet tries to small talk with her guests. Mother coolly remarks that Juliet's eyes are red from crying. Both Valentina and Sylva encourage Juliet to play the psychodrama game. They use exactly the right words, keeping up the imagery of the film. Valentina says, "You'll feel liberated." Sylva says, "It's like seeing yourself in a mirror." When Dr. Miller begins to give Juliet psychodrama instructions, Juliet looks into the understanding eyes of the doctor and quietly delivers her desperate plea: "Will you please help me?"

Before Dr. Miller can answer Juliet, the siege of opposing apparitions begins again. First from her childhood: Elisabetta burns on her grill. Then from Olaf: A nearly naked man hides behind a wild bush. Then from her childhood again: A procession of black-robed nuns, as sexless as the priests in $8\frac{1}{2}$, sneaks along behind her. Then from Susy: In front of the nuns—and framed into the same shot with them— stands a nude Venus in a scallop shell. The Headmaster who had admonished Grandfather appears as a sort of avenging angel of righteousness, with huge batlike wings. Eve, naked, wrapped in her serpent, appears in her eternal role of temptress. Juliet's mind rehearses, in tune with the conflicting images, the conflicting advice she has been given. She listens to the call to be a martyr, and murmurs, "Life is all sacrifice." She listens to the call to be a whore, and murmurs, "Be more feminine." Suddenly a close-up camera watches Juliet dismiss both the message of her past and the message of the current age. She looks directly into the camera and shouts aloud: "Get out! All of you! Go away!" The apparitions vanish, and Juliet sees that the garden party is progressing peacefully. The psychodrama of Dr. Miller, out here on the green natural lawn, seems—for a time—to have brought Juliet one step closer to freedom.

José is deep in conversation with Juliet. He presents her with an offering of pure water. It seems as if he has been talking with her for the last several minutes, perhaps during the time when she dismissed her disputatious spirits. Perhaps it was somehow José who gave her the strength to dismiss them. José and Juliet dance, that important Fellini ritual, and he continues to talk with her, continues to give her strength. (i. 49) José's advice is the kind that Juliet needs, the kind that José had begun to deliver in his first appearance. In a proverb, José advises Juliet to be herself: "In my country, we have a proverb that says: 'I am my own roof, my own window, my own hearth. My words are my food, my thoughts are my drink. Thus am I happy.' " Of the people Juliet has known, only Grandfather has been as self-sufficient as José's proverb advises. José makes his words, and Grandfather's actions, all the more significant to Juliet by connecting self-sufficiency with truth and with freedom, specific goals that have been dangling out of reach throughout Juliet's long search. "Don't be afraid of the truth," counsels José. He adds, "Truth makes us free." Juliet's response is, "Are you real?" She poses a question that the viewer, too, would like answered. But José does not answer that perhaps unanswerable question. Juliet also asks for explicit advice: "What should I do?" José responds with another key message, a familiar one in the life-affirming films of Fellini: "I advise that you live completely."

i. 49. In front of the orderly little white house in Fregene, José comforts the embattled Juliet.

But where will Juliet find her completeness? She still thinks that all of life must be found in Giorgio. She has in the past hesitated to leave her house lest she miss a phone call from Giorgio. She now turns away from José and asks, frightened, "Where's Giorgio?" Elisabetta tells her that Giorgio has already left the party. Another possible path toward completeness now presents itself. Perhaps she could do what Giorgio does. "Listen to me," pleads Juliet's lawyer, who has discreetly pursued her throughout the film. He asks, "Is there hope for me?" Juliet looks exhausted by the turmoil of conflicting calls and questions and advice, from both spirits and people. Calmly, Dr. Miller walks toward Juliet, as if to rescue her.

The psychologist finds words to describe what we have witnessed. She says to Juliet: "I would like to explore the turmoil haunting you." And the site of this exploration could easily have been guessed. "Would you like to go for a little walk in the forest with me?" asks Dr. Miller. As the two women walk side by side beneath the huge, noble, independent, protective trees, Dr. Miller uses nature, as Fellini has always done, as her basic symbol: "These trees. . . . They're deeply rooted in the earth, yet their branches reach out in every direction. Their growth is completely spontaneous. This is the greatest secret of all. . . . To be liberated. Be spontaneous. Be yourself." Dr. Miller has repeated the advice of José, but her words are not spoken with the aura of doubtful romance about them, nor are they obscured in a proverb; they are spoken in the clear natural light of the real forest. As if very much at home in this setting, Dr. Miller lies down on the forest ground, the foliage all around her green and flourishing. She repeats more of José's advice. "Don't be afraid," says Dr. Miller, gazing into Juliet's face. Under Juliet, the forest grass is sere. Dr. Miller adds, "Look at the sun, through the trees. Everything is peaceful, serene."

Before Dr. Miller completes her session with Juliet, she prepares Juliet, and the viewer, for the next two scenes. Dr. Miller startles Juliet by insisting that deep in her real self, Juliet wants Giorgio to leave her, because he is the cause of her suffering, because her dependence on him is preventing her from finding herself. "Without Giorgio," predicts Dr. Miller, "you'd be able to breathe again. You'd be able to live." And she adds the climactic sentence which has been the theme of all Fellini: "You'd find yourself."

The Other Woman

Fellini now shows us three scenes in which Dr. Miller's prediction begins to come true. In the first of these, Juliet visits the apartment of Gabriella, and discovers that, in the furnishings, in the pictures, in the whole atmosphere, Giorgio already resides there in Gabriella's home rather than in Juliet's home. Juliet has become so unimportant in the Giorgio-Gabriella relationship that she has no real role at all. Juliet is merely a visitor. Gabriella doesn't even choose to meet her. Gabriella has already won. Over the phone, Gabriella explains the facts to Juliet: "I don't enjoy someone else's defeat. . . . I don't think we have anything to talk about." The battle is not between Juliet and Gabriella; the battle is within Juliet. This is a wonderfully subtle and understated scene. Juliet sits in the dark on Gabriella's sofa, which creates a burning orange background similar to the blaze of the red sofa in Bhisma's suite. Then Juliet waited in expectation. Now Juliet waits for no purpose. She is already abandoned. The rejected version of this scene in the original screenplay was an inefficient and rather vulgar confrontation between Gabriella and Juliet in which Gabriella, in a long discussion, falsely convinced Juliet that nothing really serious existed between Gabriella and Giorgio. It would have retarded the quickening pace of the film.[57]

Departure

Dr. Miller's prediction moves still closer to fulfillment in the next scene, back in Juliet and Giorgio's home. We see by the style of the filming that Giorgio is less present here than he was in Gabriella's apartment. The entire scene of Giorgio's actual physical departure from Juliet's life is a masterpiece of the stark, the empty, the isolating. Fellini is justly pround of his success with this extraordinary scene. He has cited it as an example of the triumph of the visual over the verbal. The original screenplay, as written by Fellini with Tullio Pinelli and Brunello Rondi, had, in this scene, boasted Fellini, "excellent dialogue, really very well written, just right." Nevertheless, "I ended up shooting the scene," Fellini went on, not quite accurately, "so that neither of the characters said a word."[58] As a matter of fact, in the final film both Juliet and Giorgio do speak, although not as fully as they did in the original screenplay. In the final film, their language is clipped and self-conscious, and extraordinarily weary, as if all the vitality were drained from both of them.

In his interview with Kezich, Fellini briefly described the action of the departure scene: "She finds him while he is packing his suitcase, she gives him something to eat, and they stand together in silence. At the end he says 'Ciao,' and he leaves her in an unadorned, empty room, from which I had all the furniture removed."[59]

A little more activity than that does take place in this stunning scene, and it is so effective and so typical of Fellini that it is worth recounting in detail. The scene begins with a remembrance of the first shot of the film. Once gain it is night, and once again the camera moves up Juliet's front walk toward her house. But this time the camera brushes past no hopefully green and fertile tree branches; instead, the camera, in a deadly slow pace, moves past clipped, boxed trees, wrapped in plastic coverings. The camera enters the house. Inside, the setting is mono-chromatic. Throughout the scene, the camera is carefully placed so that the background is often a blank white wall. The house has always before been filled with flowers; now no sudden splashes of color interrupt the somber mood. Giorgio, isolated by the frame of the bedroom doorway, is seen packing, alone. Juliet, apparently just com-ing from Gabriella's apartment, senses the mood of separation. In contrast to the reality in this house, two fictional lovers kiss on the television, and their words speak of happiness and love. Giorgio's words tell Juliet that he is going to Milan on business. He carries his suitcase from his bedroom. Juliet helps Teresina fix a small supper for Giorgio. Each character does his own job, alone, separated from all others. Juliet remarks that this is the first time that Giorgio has packed his own clothes. Many of the shots are of their backs. The composition is excessively formal, planned, constrained and self-conscious. The TV set is placed in the exact center of a shot; clowns and dancers entertain, as circus music ironically fills the sound track. The real characters show less life. Juliet is framed into an enclosing service window between the kitchen and dining room.

The camera begins to focus more on the furniture than on the people. As Giorgio tells Juliet that he will be gone for a few days, a shot of the back of the TV set takes up most of the screen, with Juliet shoved off into a tiny corner of the frame. Juliet turns to stare absently at the TV. A clown, so close to the soul of Fellini's bittersweet questing characters, looks out at Juliet from the TV screen, and smiles toward her, sad and compassionate. The clown seems to understand, as had the innocent Elisabetta. Giorgio eats without appetite. Giorgio tells Juliet that he may be away for several days. The room seems to get smaller. Teresina closes curtains and shutters, blocking out the rest of the world. The phone rings. All action stops. Giorgio and his table are frozen into the formal center of the frame, as Juliet still sees him as the center of her life. That centrality is threatened by Gabriella, the unacknowledged ring on the telephone. No one answers it. A few shots later Giorgio is pictured formally from the side: exactly half of the screen shows Gior-gio at his table; the other half shows the mural of a ruined castle. As

i. 50. Separation and silence: Giorgio's departure.

small talk continues, we see alternately the back of Giorgio's head and the back of Juliet's head. Giorgio says, "Frankly, I need to be alone for a while."

Juliet looks out the window, and we see a memory scene of Juliet happily introducing Giorgio to her family. Giorgio continues: "It is true that between that person and myself there has been a friendship, a deep friendship. . . . The truth is that I'm going through a period of uncertainty, of confusion. I want to be alone." We watch the shutters close over the windows, blacking out Juliet's happy memory. The shutters form a lattice pattern, like a chain-link fence. Juliet sits on the window seat, off in the lower corner of the screen, almost out of the picture. Much of the screen is occupied with the dark and blocked windows. (i. 50) We see a memory scene of Giorgio and Juliet asleep in bed, close together, hands clasped, Giorgio without eyeshades. Juliet is still sitting on her dark window seat. She is partially obscured by the curtains. A shot shows Giorgio sitting in a chair on the far side of the room. Shadows form around him, isolating him. Only emptiness is between them. Giorgio says goodbye to Juliet. We see a fantasy scene of Giorgio and Gabriella embracing in a convertible sports car, with dark dead leaves of autumn swirling about them. Giorgio stands up, almost obscuring Juliet from sight. As he bends over to kiss her good-bye, he totally obliterates her from the frame. He walks to the door. The entire doorway is filled with the huge, departing shadow of Giorgio. He says that he will call, maybe tomorrow; he asks her to put aside the mail; he says goodbye one final time. As he speaks, the camera moves away from Juliet, showing her smaller and smaller, isolated on the window seat, as she responds with an empty affirmation, as if in a trance, to each of Giorgio's final sentences. Giorgio closes the door behind him. We see, one after another, shots of the empty living room, the empty staircase, the empty place at the table, then the isolated and covered trees lining the empty path to the house. Juliet sits alone on the window seat.

Both José and Dr. Miller had told Juliet not to be afraid. And they had both told her to be herself. But apparently fear must be endured before the discovery can occur. Zampano and Guido had to go through great fear and anguish; they both had to die, in a way, before they could find themselves. Marcello only suffered the fear and death; he did not experience the rebirth. Now Fellini puts Juliet through her final trial, her time of fear, anguish, death. We don't know yet whether Juliet will end like Marcello or like Guido.

Invasion

The abandoned Juliet remains seated on the window seat. Now, at her low point, she is most susceptible. She is alone. The great final battle for her soul begins. Juliet sits, waiting for the invaders. The first invasion comes from a black canvas pavilion, billowing in heavy wind, fearsomely threatening. This black pavilion is clearly a carrier of death, and Juliet sees that its captains are Lynx Eyes and his assistant. Will the message that they have already brought to her be the sentence of her death? Will Juliet, as she obviously fears, wither and die without Giorgio? Juliet tries to avoid the invasion. She walks quickly across the room to watch TV. But she hears a voice calling her: "Juliet, do you remember me?" It is another messenger of death; the call is from her childhood friend Laura, who had died of love. From the bottom of a shadowy pool of shallow water, Laura calls temptingly: "Do what I did. Here, everything is gray stillness and silence. . . . Come with me—a long sleep, with no more pain." Just then Juliet sees the robe of a nun protruding from behind the sofa. This is a contrary temptation, not to easeful death but to embrace her own sufferings as a martyrdom.

The quiet invasion turns into an active pursuit. Throughout the film, everyone has called Juliet's name. Now the calls echo and overlap like hollow memories. As Juliet sits before the TV, Gabriella's maid examines Juliet's curtains, as if to suggest that she is preparing this house for Juliet's eviction by Gabriella. Juliet sees a row of nuns, José, Genius. Juliet had seen the sexual barbarism of Olaf; now another kind of barbarism flashes before her eyes. Two German officers in Nazi SS uniforms march past outside the living room window. The original screenplay had been filled with Fascist memories, mostly connected with Juliet's father, who was originally conceived as a staunch supporter of Il Duce. In that early version, Juliet viewed Il Duce, all Fascists, the Nazi invaders, and her father as one intermixed repressive authority figure.[60] In the final film, Fellini eliminated Juliet's father altogether, and eliminated the Fascist references, probably to keep the film more internal than external, more psychological than political. The authoritarian repression figures now are Giorgio, the Headmaster, and Mother. They become embodied in the Nazi invaders outside Juliet's window. Then Susy's godson beckons to Juliet, as the temptation to whoredom is renewed. But a row of nuns interferes with that apparition, as it also interferes with the romantic apparition of José, who next appears and disappears. Juliet, frantic, shouts: "It's not real. You don't exist! Go away!" All sounds stop. All the apparitions disappear, as if in sudden obedience to Juliet's command.

But they don't stay away. Lola the whore peeks over the back of the sofa. So do Juliet's maids. And more nuns. Susy descends into the living room in her witch basket; but when we look closely we see that it is not Susy at all, but a woman much like the one at Susy's party who had known Gabriella. What does it matter? The sexy women are all alike to Juliet. Lynx Eyes and his assistants sit on the steps. Death imagery reappears in the form of a horse-drawn hearse. Arlette, who tried to die for love, identifies the hearse of Laura, who did die for love. Juliet's friends—Elena, Valentina, the doctor, Dolores, another muscular lover—look in the windows as if to discover whether Juliet will follow the path of Laura by accepting the temptation now voiced by Arlette: "And now she's at peace—no pain for evermore." The lawyer presents himself to Juliet as an alternative to suicide. Dr. Miller appears and reminds Juliet that Giorgio's departure might not mean death, but, just the contrary, it might be Juliet's chance to live: "Without Giorgio," Dr. Miller predicts once more, "you'll begin to breathe, to become yourself, to become yourself."

More Nazis, more friends, more strangers, appear, leer, and leave. Grandfather flies by in his biplane, now out of Juliet's reach. He accuses her, and pleads with her: "I can't come down, I can't land! It's your fault, Juliet—it all depends on you!" The Headmaster in all his authority appears, growing in threatening stature as he gets closer to

Grandfather, his old antagonist. The Headmaster is now two stories tall, his head high above the balcony over the living room. Laura's voice once more promises Juliet "a long sleep." Susy smiles; forces of Iris and Olaf appear.

Juliet, in an attempt to escape, goes into the bathroom, she goes into the bedroom, she tries to read. Mother appears, in the guise once more of the Evil Queen of fairy tales. Juliet pleads: "Mother! Help me! *You* help me!" Mother stares disapprovingly at Juliet. Mother makes no reply. Juliet hears someone calling her, but Mother sharply commands: "Don't move! Obey your mother!" Juliet sees a small door in the bedroom wall, with a light shining behind it. She is drawn toward the door, as Mother repeats her imperious command: "Don't move!" Juliet's face registers both fear and determination as she performs her first rebellious act. She turns, faces her mother, and says, firmly and bravely: "You don't frighten me any more." As in other Fellini films, choice and freedom are connected. At the moment of Juliet's choice, the little door snaps open, as Juliet has begun to free herself from the domination of others.

But Juliet is still enslaved to her own past, with its repressions, and to her present, with its fears and its conflicting temptations. We watch Juliet begin to free herself from the bonds of her past. She walks down an endless corridor to little Juliet who lies burning on her grill. The

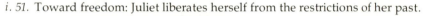

i. 51. Toward freedom: Juliet liberates herself from the restrictions of her past.

apparitions in the living room look frightened and threatened. Big
Juliet looks lovingly and acceptingly at little Juliet, and she begins to
loose her bonds. We see the apparitions in the living room fade away,
dissolving into another dimension. Grandfather had scolded little
Juliet as he freed her from her grill: "Don't you rebel?" And now she
does, for the second time. After freeing herself from her mother, she
frees herself from other aspects of her past. (i. 51) Big Juliet frees little
Juliet from the grill, as Grandfather had freed her once before. She
does not then dismiss her liberated young self; she embraces her.

When Juliet is freed from the negations of her own past, she is finally
freed from her obsessive images of repressive outside authority.
Mother, suddenly aged, turns to leave. Perhaps for the first time, Juliet
is seeing clearly and objectively. To Juliet, Mother has been an almost
archetypal distant motherly admiration/fear figure. She was, at the
same time, a kind of beautiful queen and evil witch. Now, as Juliet frees
herself, Mother is just a little old lady.

Now Grandfather can appear. Juliet has prepared the way for her
integration of him into her present life. She can now accept the freedom that he has always represented to her. Grandfather stands beside
his biplane. He is another Fellini messenger-from-the-sky. Fellini
clearly recognized Grandfather's antecedents: "Isn't he a little bit like
the Fool in *La Strada*?" he asked a friend.[61] Grandfather calls out an
affectionate greeting to Juliet, laughing happily all the while: "My little
Beefsteak! How are you? Where'd you leave your grill?" Little Juliet
runs to him, he takes her hand, and he calls out gaily: "Let's say
good-bye to these boors! You see them! Look!" As happy circus music,
reminiscent of the music in the final scene of *8½*, begins to play, all of
Juliet's apparitions of past and present are packed onto a cumbersome
wagon and onto a vehicle with a canopy of the kind that had brought
Susy to the beach, that had held Olaf's invaders, that had been Laura's
hearse. They all ride by and fade away.

The adult Juliet stands at the door of her house, smiling, as the
invasion vehicles retreat. Grandfather tells her that it is time for him to
go too, and he climbs aboard his plane. Juliet, still uncertain whether
she is ready to seek her *own* way, hesitantly asks, "Take me with you,
Grandpa?" But he answers: "Where? This is an old plane; it doesn't go
anywhere. It only had to come this far." From the plane, a laughing
Fanny joins Grandfather in loving good-byes to Juliet. Grandfather's
parting words continue Juliet's process of liberation, indicating that
she is now free even from himself: "Good-bye. Don't hold on to
me—you don't need me any longer." Grandfather dissolves out of
sight, but we hear him speak from the skies the explicit words of
Juliet's rebirth: ". . . .but *you* are full of life!"

Little Juliet walks across the lawn, but she too dissolves out of sight as Grandfather says to her a final affectionate dismissal: "Good-bye, little Beefsteak." Juliet is liberated from all her spirits, past and present, real and imagined and mixed, from outside and inside her self. Susy is as absent as the saint on the grill. Juliet is called to be neither saint nor whore, but woman.

Choice

As always in Fellini, the solution has been a simple one. "How simple it is," Guido had discovered. "A little can be everything . . . everything becomes clear and plausible," José had told Juliet. The solution in *Juliet of the Spirits* is as simple as it was in *8½*. Juliet, like Guido, simply chooses. The simple choice that turns out to be everything does not follow any single dramatic plot event. The choice follows no rational process, no deliberation. The sacramental imagery of Fellini films has been leading to this memory from Fellini's, and Juliet's, Catholic childhood: A sacrament is an external sign; it is accompanied by grace. The external sign of Juliet's choice is her subsequent freedom of movement. Juliet's choice, like Guido's, is a gift of grace. She is free.

At the end of her film, Juliet is outside in her garden. Like *La Strada*, *Juliet of the Spirits* will end as it began. The circle will be completed. *La Strada* began and ended at the sea. *Juliet of the Spirits* begins and ends on the green promise of growth. But *Juliet of the Spirits* is more than a circle; it is a progression. The film has moved from night to day. In lovely shining sunlight, Juliet walks toward a picket gate that had been closing her in. She opens the gate easily, looks out into the open field, then walks, with a free and happy gait, onto the wide green carpet of grass that leads all the way to the forest. Juliet breathes deeply. She smiles, a Paola smile, like the one that ended *La Dolce Vita*, like her own Masina smile that had ended *Nights of Cabiria*. High in the air, urgent voices begin to call: "Juliet . . . Juliet . . . Juliet!" Juliet is still in tune with her spirits, still possesses an inner life, still can hear them when they call her. Quietly and calmly, Juliet asks: "Who are you?" The spirit voices respond: "True friends." They add: "Now, if you want us to, we can stay." Juliet is in charge. She can take them or leave them. In pleading tones, the spirits beg: "Listen to us, listen closely!" But Juliet walks away from the voices, not listening, as she looks directly into the camera and asserts, simply and confidently, without moving her lips: "I don't need you any more." She is obviously talking about Giorgio, about the modern people around her, about her own personal demons. Perhaps even about Fellini. An independent Juliet is born.

Freedom

The last time that we see the newly free and independent Juliet, now having chosen, now knowing herself, now in calm self-possession of her inner and her outer life, of the material and of the spiritual, Fellini places her into context: He shows us a distant ordered shot of Juliet's neat little home, white and shining. Juliet walks past it, to the right, toward the forest. Juliet is shown as a small part of immense and ordered nature. She is not lost within it; she is not overwhelmed by it; rather, she is a harmonious part of it. As Juliet continues to walk steadily toward the forest, the camera views her from the side, the camera itself moving at the same speed along with Juliet, from left to right, in harmony with the dominant camera motion throughout the film. Therefore, the virtually limitless space in front of Juliet never shrinks. Juliet is in the lower left corner of the screen, so that behind her there is no distance whatever. All space, all freedom, the endless road, lies in front of Juliet.

Happy music fills the sound track as Fellini's camera shows the solid trunks of the trees of the forest, and their wide-spreading branches. The credits begin. Susy's sexy music plays on the sound track, while we watch a blazing red screen. But the Susy music gives way to Juliet music, the same basic Nino Rota tune, now turned quiet and confident, as the screen of Susy red gives way to Juliet blue. As the credits continue, Juliet's and Susy's music and colors continue to alternate, not in a clash but harmoniously.

Fellini has always contended that for him an original screenplay is intended to be just a sketch for his final film. "As is my habit," he wrote about the screenplay for *Juliet of the Spirits*, "I retained the right to revise, to specify changes and substitute scenes and characters, to enrich situations, to set the pace of the film as well as the dialogue and atmosphere."[62] The ending of *Juliet of the Spirits* was particularly enriched in its revisions and changes. Originally, Fellini had planned to end the film with Juliet on a swing:

> Juliet is quiet, almost serene, as she lightly swings. She looks around her at a world that more and more takes on—in ways so simple, so stable—both the real and the unreal pulse of everyday magic. . . . Everything in her is anchored in peaceful harmony, beyond the mystifying ghosts that have until now besieged her: she is concerned with the daily miracle of simple reality. Juliet smiles, liberated, at peace.[63]

Although in his actual film Fellini kept the same mood and meaning as in the original screenplay, he creatively improved the imagery.

Instead of the swing, which surely would have suggested Fanny and Iris, he used once more the symbols of progression and of nature that have always meant so much to him.

Fellini's friend Tullio Kezich expressed to Fellini his understanding of *Juliet of the Spirits*: "Your film might be the story of her progressive liberation." Yes, affirmed Fellini, "This is a fundamental theme for me."[64] Fellini explained still more about the liberating ending of this film:

> Juliet alone, at the end of the film, should mean the discovery of an individuality. The thing she feared the most, the departure of her husband, is revealed as a gift of providence. Juliet will no longer depend on the paternal figure of Giorgio, who has, nonetheless, enriched her life. To him, too, as to everyone and everything, Juliet feels grateful because they all—even those who seem the most fearful enemies—helped in the process of her liberation.[65]

How far the distance between 1954 and 1965, the distance between *La Strada* and *Juliet of the Spirits*. How far the distance between the Gelsomina played by Giulietta Masina and the Juliet later played by Giulietta Masina. Fellini *is* right when he identifies the "motif that returns incessantly in my films." That constant motif is, as he once phrased it, "the attempt to create an emancipation." Fellini is right when he says that that theme of freedom "is the idea that is found in all my films, from *The White Sheik* to the film I am making at the moment: *Juliet of the Spirits*." But Gelsomina and Juliet find their liberation, their emancipation, their true selves, in very different ways. Gelsomina finds herself through self-sacrifice; a more contemporary Juliet finds herself through self-discovery. But both of these Masina heroines confirm the basic Fellini doctrine that discovery of self only follows discovery of one's relationship with others. Gelsomina discovered that Zampano needed her in order to find himself. And so she finds herself by giving up her self to him. Juliet discovered that Giorgio did not need her, that he was bored by her sacrifice, that he was seeking something more exciting and modern and external from Gabriella. Juliet discovered that in giving herself completely to her husband, her self had not been discovered; it had been crushed, just as it had in childhood. What was a birth to Gelsomina was a death to Juliet. She locates her self not through submission but through liberation. "In the end," Fellini says, "Juliet's real life begins when she comes out of the shadow of Giorgio." In telling this "story of a woman's slow progress toward her freedom, her independence," Fellini speaks with a raised consciousness: "The independence of woman is the theme of the future." This film, as it looks forward, is for and about Giulietta as woman: "I do not see why a woman must wait for everything to come from a man, or from the convention of the relationship between man and women. . . . It seems to me that freedom, especially a woman's freedom, is a conquest to be made, not a gift to be received. It isn't granted. It must be taken." Juliet takes that freedom, and, in so doing, discovers "her own reality, a different one." In freedom one finds "a bigger means of knowing oneself."[66]

Juliet's discovery is also different from Guido's. Guido had needed to free himself from dependence upon only himself, so that he could try to find himself in and through and in relation to others. He had needed interdependence. But Juliet had to go back further than that. She needed first to free herself from dependence upon others and from a false self-conception before she could find her true self, so that she could then begin to find others. She needed independence.

At the end of *Juliet of the Spirits*, Juliet is shown walking toward the forest. She may be liberated and independent, but the search for "anima" for "knowing oneself," does not end. Nor does Fellini. He made films after *Juliet of the Spirits*, as he made them before *La Strada*. And he makes them still. And they continue to be films of search. He ends *La Strada* with a shot of sea and sky. He ends *La Dolce Vita* with a smile. He ends *8½* with a spotlight and a flute. And he ends *Juliet of the Spirits* with a forest. But always, in each of those settings—of nature, of humanity, or of art—his endings are always continuations. It is the spirit to continue the journey that gives dignity to humankind. "The intention of the film," Fellini said while working on *Juliet of the Spirits*, is to give to Juliet, and to Giulietta, "her true independence, her indisputable and inalienable dignity."[67] At the end of *Juliet of the Spirits*, Juliet—with dignity—is still walking.

Zampano will continue to live, a life more human than the one before. Marcello will continue to live, a life less human than the one before. Guido's story is even more of a continuation, and even less of a conclusion. Guido's triumph lies in his simple choice to continue. When we stop looking at Guido, he is directing his self, his own inner life. The entire cast of Fellini's film enters Guido's movie (i.e., his life), is integrated into Guido himself, and is finally able to leave. Little boy Guido, accepted, is the last to leave. Juliet's triumph, too, lies in her simple choice to continue. When we stop looking at Juliet, she has learned to control her self, her own inner life. The entire cast of Fellini's film enters Juliet's house (i.e., her life), is integrated into Juliet herself, and is finally able to leave. Little girl Juliet, accepted, is the last to leave. Both of these continuations are the opposite of "endings." That is

Fellini's point. "My pictures never end," he said. To end a film would be to suggest that the search is over. Therefore, "I think it is immoral (in the true sense of the word) to tell a story that has a conclusion. Because you cut out your audience the moment you present a solution on the screen. Because there are no 'solutions' in their lives."[68]

And as the individual Fellini picture never ends, neither does the larger Fellini journey. Guido's picture refused to end just when Guido discovered that his film was becoming more personal, more peopled with figures from his own life. The same thing happened to Fellini after *Juliet of the Spirits*. After this film about his own wife's inner consciousness, Fellini gave us film essays, in new and ever more personal documentary/autobiographical forms, about his own filmmaking notebooks, about his own memories of the circus, about his own Rome, about his own Rimini. He imposed his own strong personality and attitudes upon the works of others, in dealing with Poe, with Petronius, and with Casanova. He continued his personal obsession with creativity, as he focussed his camera on an orchestra conductor. He continued his personal obsession with women, as he focussed his camera on a whole city of them. Fellini's career has been a continuing journey from the "other" of neo-realism toward the "self" of his personal films. From fact and reportage toward fantasy and dreams and memories. From objective reality toward subjective reality. From mere reality toward the higher reality of imagination.

Fellini's search may be slowing, but it isn't over. As there are yet no solutions, we believe Fellini when he says that there can be no conclusions. The characters continue. The stories and forms continue. The images and myths continue. Fellini continues. Because there are no solutions in our own lives, we too continue, along our own roads. Fellini's whole point is that our roads do not end.

Notes

Introduction

1. Lillian Ross, "Profiles: 10 ½," *The New Yorker*, 30 Oct. 1965, p. 76.
2. Federico Fellini, "Entretiens avec Federico Fellini," *Les Cahiers R.T.B. Série Télécinéma*, 1962, excerpted in Suzanne Budgen, *Fellini* (London: The British Film Institute Education Department, 1966), p. 91.
3. Federico Fellini, "Sweet Beginnings," *Atlas*, Feb. 1962, rpt. in *Fellini on Fellini*, ed. Anna Keel and Christian Strich (New York: Dell, 1974), p. 46.
4. Pierre Kast, "Interview with Federico Fellini," *Cahiers du Cinema in English* 5 (1966), rpt. in *Interviews with Film Directors*, ed. Andrew Sarris (New York: Avon, 1967), pp. 182, 183.
5. André Bazin, "*Cabiria*: The Voyage to the End of Neo-realism," *Cahiers du Cinema*, Nov. 1957, rpt. in *What is Cinema*? vol. II, ed. Hugh Gray (Berkeley: Univ. of California Press, 1971), pp. 86, 87.
6. Federico Fellini, "Letter to a Jesuit Priest," *Der Filmberater* 15, Sept. 1957, rpt. in Keel and Strich, p. 66.
7. Renzo Peri, "Federico Fellini: An Interview," *Film Quarterly* 15 (Fall 1961), p. 30.
8. Irving Levine, "I Was Born for the Cinema—A Conversation with Federico Fellini," *Film Comment*, Fall 1966, p. 80.

La Strada

1. Gideon Bachmann, "Federico Fellini: An Interview," in *Film: Book One*, ed. Robert Hughes (New York: Grove Press, 1959), p. 102.
2. Angelo Solmi, *Fellini* (London: Merlin Press, 1967), p. 17.
3. André Bazin, "*La Strada*," *Cross Currents* 6 (1956), rpt. in *Federico Fellini: Essays in Criticism*, ed. Peter Bondanella (Oxford: Oxford Univ. Press, 1978), p. 55.
4. Federico Fellini, "Letter to a Marxist Critic," *Il Contemporaneo* 15, 9 April

1955, rpt. in *Fellini on Fellini*, ed. Anna Keel and Christian Strich (New York: Dell, 1974), p. 63.

5. Tullio Kezich and Federico Fellini, "The Long Interview," in *Federico Fellini's Juliet of the Spirits*, ed. Tullio Kezich (New York: Ballantine Books, 1966), p. 30.

6. Lillian Ross, "Profiles: 10½," *The New Yorker*, 30 Oct. 1965, p. 68.

7. Ibid.

8. Genevieve Agel, *Les chemins de Fellini* (Paris: Editions du Cerf, 1956), excerpted in Gilbert Salachas, *Federico Fellini* (New York: Crown Publishers, 1963), pp. 173, 174.

9. Federico Fellini, *L'Arc* 45 (1971), rpt. in Keel and Strich, p. 54.

10. For a particularly good discussion of Zampano's imagery, see Suzanne Budgen, *Fellini* (London: The British Film Institute Education Department, 1966), passim.

11. Kezich and Fellini, p. 22.

12. For Fellini's attitude toward the circus, as quoted here, see Federico Fellini, "Un viaggio nell'ombra," *I Clowns*, ed. Renzo Renzi (Bologna: Capelli, 1970), rpt. in Keel and Strich, pp. 121, 123; Renato Barneschi, *Oggi Illustrato*, Feb. 12, 1972, rpt. in Keel and Strich, pp. 144, 146; Edward Murray, *Fellini the Artist* (New York: Frederick Ungar Publishing Co., 1976), p. 191; Ross, p. 76; Solmi, p. 64; Federico Fellini, "Fellini's Formula," *Esquire*, Aug. 1970, p. 18; Federico Fellini, "Entretiens avec Federico Fellini," *Les Cahiers R.T.B. Série Télécinéma*, 1962, rpt. in Keel and Strich, p. 98.

13. Solmi, p. 54.

14. Budgen, p. 10.

15. Federico Fellini, "My Experiences as a Director," *International Film Annual*, No. 3, ed. William Whitebait (London: John Calder, 1959), rpt. in Bondanella, p. 9.

16. Solmi, p. 111.

17. Salachas, p. 108.

18. Fellini, *L'Arc*, rpt. in Keel and Strich, p. 57.

19. Solmi, p. 111.

20. Federico Fellini, "Letter to a Jesuit Priest," *Der Filmberater* 15 (Sept. 1957), rpt. in Keel and Strich, p. 66.

21. Federico Fellini, "Il mio paese," *La Mia Rimini*, ed. Renzo Renzi (Bologna: Capelli, 1967), rpt. in Keel and Strich, p. 28.

22. Bachmann, p. 97.

23. Salachas, p. 115.

24. Bazin, "La Strada," in Bondanella, p. 58.

25. Murray, p. 23.

26. Stuart Rosenthal describes this characteristic of Gelsomina: "Gelsomina has a mystical correspondence to nature which reveals her total innocence. The weather always anticipates her moods. And while she is happy in the summer and becomes withdrawn and near death in the winter, the context of the film makes it seem as though the seasons are changing in sympathy with her condition, rather than the other way around. This communication with the

elements tells of her purity, metaphorically describes her mood, manipulates the film's atmosphere and facilitates and intensifies our sharing of her feelings." See *The Cinema of Federico Fellini* (South Brunswick, N.J.: A. S. Barnes, 1976), p. 42.

27. Bazin, "La Strada," in Bondanella, p. 58.

28. For a discussion of the disconnection between Gelsomina and the family of man, see Rosenthal, p. 111.

29. Ibid., p. 46.

30. Budgen, p. 11.

31. Murray, p. 82.

32. Solmi, p. 113.

33. Kezich and Fellini, p. 61.

34. Fellini, "Letter to a Jesuit Priest," in Keel and Strich, p. 66.

La Dolce Vita

1. Angelo Solmi, *Fellini* (London: Merlin Press, 1967), p. 116.

2. Renzo Peri, "Federico Fellini: An Interview," *Film Quarterly* 15 (Fall 1961), p. 32.

3. Andrew Sarris, "Federico Fellini," in *Interviews with Film Directors*, ed. Andrew Sarris (New York: Avon, 1967), p. 175.

4. Solmi, p. 138.

5. Gilbert Salachas recounts the story of Fellini's intended use of the Mario Tupino novel, first told by Lo Duca in *Cahiers du Cinema* in 1957. See Gilbert Salachas, *Federico Fellini* (New York: Crown Publishers, 1963), p. 169.

6. Federico Fellini, "My Experiences as a Director," *International Film Annual*, No. 3, ed. William Whitebait (London: John Calder, 1959), rpt. in *Federico Fellini: Essays in Criticism*, ed. Peter Bondanella (Oxford: Oxford Univ. Press, 1978), p. 10.

7. Solmi, p. 139.

8. Federico Fellini, "Su La Dolce Vita la parola a Fellini," *Bianco e Nero*, No. 9–10, Sept.–Oct. 1954, excerpted in Suzanne Budgen, *Fellini* (London: The British Film Institute Education Department, 1966), p. 101.

9. Salachas, p. 113.

10. John Russell Taylor, *Cinema Eye, Cinema Ear* (New York: Hill and Wang, 1964), p. 43.

11. Genevieve Agel, quoted in Solmi, p. 34.

12. Pierre Kast's interview with Fellini first appeared in *Cahiers du Cinema*, No. 164, in March of 1965, and then later in *Cahiers'* English edition, No. 5, in 1966, in an English translation by Rose Kaplin. Fellini's attitude toward the "baroque" in his work is quoted from Kast's mixture of paraphrase and direct quotation, from Sarris, pp. 178, 191.

13. Peri, p. 31.

14. Federico Fellini, *La Dolce Vita* (New York: Ballantine Books, 1961), back cover.

15. Federico Fellini, *L'Arc* 45 (1971), rpt. in *Fellini on Fellini*, ed. Anna Keel and Christian Strich (New York: Dell, 1974), p. 53.

16. Eugene Walter, "Federico Fellini: Wizard of Film," *The Atlantic Monthly*, Dec. 1965, p. 67.

17. James R. Silke, *Dialogue on Film: Federico Fellini* (Beverly Hills: American Film Institute, 1972), p. 11.

18. Gideon Bachmann, "Federico Fellini: An Interview," in *Film: Book One*, ed. Robert Hughes (New York: Grove Press, 1959), p. 100.

19. Federico Fellini, *Etudes Cinématographiques*, No. 32-35 (1964), rpt. in Keel and Strich, p. 152.

20. Fellini, *L'Arc*, rpt. in Keel and Strich, p. 52.

21. Federico Fellini, *Der Regisseur Federico Fellini*, No. 5, ed. Rudolph S. Joseph (Munich: Photo- und Filmmuseum im Münchner Stadtmuseum, n.d.), rpt. in Keel and Strich, p. 152.

22. All quoted descriptions of the film are from the 1961 Ballantine Books screenplay, translation by Oscar DeLiso and Bernard Shir-Cliff.

23. Salachas, p. 59.

24. Eric Rhode, "Federico Fellini," *Tower of Babel: Speculations on the Cinema* (London: Widenfeld and Nicholson, 1966), p. 128.

25. Edward Murray, *Fellini the Artist* (New York: Frederick Ungar, 1976), p. 128.

26. The published Ballantine screenplay is wrong when it says that "Sylvia takes off her glasses and turns to Marcello." In the actual film, Sylvia takes off Marcello's sunglasses, the better to discover him.

27. Federico Fellini, "Via Veneto: dolce vita," *L'Europeo* 27 (1962), rpt. in Keel and Strich, p. 69.

28. Murray, p. 227.

29. Budgen, p. 38.

30. Fellini, "Su La Dolce Vita. . . ," in Budgen, p. 99.

31. Marsha Kinder and Beverly Houston, "Three Films from Fellini's Mythology," *Close-Up* (New York: Harcourt Brace Jovanovich, 1972), p. 322.

32. Fellini, "Via Veneto: dolce vita," in Keel and Strich, p. 69.

33. Solmi, p. 61.

34. For more about the projected "Moraldo in Citta" see Taylor, p. 38.

35. Rhode, p. 127.

36. Fellini, "My Experiences as a Director," in Bondanella, p. 10.

37. Fellini, "Via Veneto: dolce vita," in Keel and Strich, p. 79.

38. Solmi, p. 118.

39. Murray, p. 126.

40. Federico Fellini, "A Conversation with Enzo Siciliano," *Il Mondo*, 13 Sept. 1973, rpt. in Keel and Strich, p. 159.

41. Bachmann, p. 134.

42. Salachas, p. 74.

43. Peri, p. 31.

44. For a fuller discussion of communication in *La Dolce Vita*, see Stuart

Rosenthal, *The Cinema of Federico Fellini* (South Brunswick, N.J.: A. S. Barnes, 1976), p. 136.

45. Peri, p. 32.

8½

1. Angelo Solmi, *Fellini* (London: Merlin Press, 1967), p. 16.

2. Tullio Kezich and Federico Fellini, "The Long Interview," in *Federico Fellini's Juliet of the Spirits*, ed. Tullio Kezich (New York: Ballantine Books, 1966), p. 53.

3. Federico Fellini, "Entretiens avec Federico Fellini," *Les Cahiers R.T.B. Série Télécinéma*, 1962, excerpted in Suzanne Budgen, *Fellini* (London: The British Film Institute Education Department, 1966), p. 95.

4. Renzo Peri, "Federico Fellini: An Interview," *Film Quarterly* 15 (Fall 1961), p. 33.

5. Solmi, p. 168.

6. Ibid., p. 164.

7. Federico Fellini, "Via Veneto: dolce vita," *L'Europeo* 27 (1962), rpt. in *Fellini on Fellini*, ed. Anna Keel and Christian Strich (New York: Dell, 1974), p. 83.

8. Deena Boyer, *The Two Hundred Days of 8½* (New York: Macmillan, 1964), pp. 10, 11.

9. Kezich and Fellini, p. 17.

10. Federico Fellini, "The Bitter Life—of Money," *Films and Filming*, Jan. 1961, rpt. in *Film Makers on Film Making*, ed. Harry M. Geduld (Bloomington: Indiana Univ. Press, 1967), p. 192.

11. Boyer, p. 10.

12. Solmi, p. 166.

13. Boyer, p. 12.

14. Federico Fellini, *L'Arc* 45 (1971), rpt. in Keel and Strich, p. 53.

15. Solmi, p. 165.

16. Boyer, p. 10.

17. Kezich and Fellini, p. 48.

18. Gilbert Salachas, *Federico Fellini* (New York: Crown Publishers, 1963), p. 93.

19. Peri, p. 32.

20. Ibid.

21. Salachas, p. 116.

22. Federico Fellini, "Su La Dolce Vita la parola a Fellini," *Bianco e Nero*, No. 9–10, Sept.–Oct. 1954, excerpted in Budgen, p. 101.

23. Ted Perry, *Filmguide to 8½* (Bloomington: Indiana University Press, 1975), p. 59.

24. Solmi, p. 166.

25. Jungian critics, as one might suspect, have asserted that "anima" sug-

gests more than Guido's search for soul. Albert Edward Benderson, for example, connects Guido's search for Asa Nisi Masa with his attempt to integrate projections, such as the "anima," in the unification of the self which Jung calls "individuation." Benderson quotes from "Two Essays on Analytical Psychology" by C. G. Jung: "We could therefore translate individuation as a 'coming to selfhood' or 'self-realization,' " quite obviously the Guido and the Fellini goal. See Albert Edward Benderson, *Critical Approaches to Federico Fellini's 8½* (New York: Arno Press, 1974), p. 101 and passim. See also Carolyn Geduld, "*Juliet of the Spirits*: Fellini and Jung," in *Federico Fellini: Essays in Criticism*, ed. Peter Bondanella (Oxford: Oxford Univ. Press, 1978), pp. 137–151.

26. Boyer, passim.

27. Ibid., p. 43.

28. Solmi, p. 23.

29. Ibid., p. 168.

30. Boyer, p. 181.

31. Timothy Hyman, "8½ as An Anatomy of Melancholy," *Sight and Sound* 43 (1974), rpt. in Bondanella, p. 123. Hyman also argues: "The syntax of the film becomes the embodiment of Fellini's doctrine: that our experience is cyclic, that pleasure comes out of pain, true out of false, comedy out of tragedy."

32. Edward Murray, *Fellini the Artist* (New York: Frederick Ungar, 1976), p. 232.

33. Kezich and Fellini, pp. 31, 32.

34. John Russell Taylor, *Cinema Eye, Cinema Ear* (New York: Hill and Wang, 1964), p. 50.

35. In Barbara K. Lewalski's "Federico Fellini's Purgatorio," *The Massachusetts Review* 5 (1964), pp. 567–573, the film is read as a confession parody, leading to a purgatory of renewal.

36. Boyer, p. 21.

37. Ibid., pp. 57, 59, 204, and passim.

38. In his *Filmguide to 8½*, Ted Perry discusses several of these fascinating relationships between the technique and the theme of this film. In the midst of many fine insights, he writes: "For Guido, the distinction between what his imagination creates and the rest of experience is often meaningless. Indeed, for him, everything is imagined, in the sense that his imagination is the constitutive power that creates his world," p. 57.

39. Boyer, p. 47.

40. Ibid., p. 14.

41. Solmi, p. 165.

42. Boyer, p. 16.

43. Ibid., p. 52.

44. Federico Fellini, from a manuscript in his own possession, quoted in Keel and Strich, p. 154.

45. Kezich and Fellini, p. 24.

46. Fellini, *L'Arc*, rpt. in Keel and Strich, p. 104.

47. Benderson, p. 56.

48. Federico Fellini, "Un viaggio nell'ombra," *I Clowns*, ed. Renzo Renzi (Bologna: Capelli, 1970), rpt. in Keel and Strich, p. 119.

49. For more suggestions from Jungian psychology—and Jung is Fellini's favorite psychologist—see especially Benderson, chapter 3: "8½: An Archetypal Analysis," pp. 97–148.

50. The bond between Maurice and Guido reminds us that Fellini has always recognized a bond between the maker of magic and the maker of films. He acknowledged, for example, that Bergman's film *The Magician* is "very close to my own temperament." Fellini said of Bergman: "He is a conjurer." Kezich and Fellini, p. 23.

51. Solmi, p. 169.

52. Boyer, p. 96.

53. Salachas, p. 24.

54. Ibid., p. 27.

55. Boyer, p. 174.

56. Federico Fellini, "Il mio paese," *La Mia Rimini*, ed. Renzo Renzi (Bologna : Capelli, 1967), rpt. in Keel and Strich, p. 13.

57. Fellini, "Entretiens avec Federico Fellini," excerpted in Budgen, p. 86.

58. Solmi, p. 62.

59. Salachas, p. 22.

60. Boyer, p. 94.

61. Ibid., p. 174.

62. Kezich and Fellini, p. 53.

63. Fellini, *Films and Filming*, rpt. in Harry Geduld, p. 193.

64. Boyer, p. 186.

65. Solmi, p. 165.

66. Kezich and Fellini, p. 32.

67. Sigmund Freud, *Character and Culture* (New York: Collier Books, 1963), p. 38. In his discussion of: "8½: An Archetypal Analysis," Benderson discusses Freud as well as Jung.

68. Kezich and Fellini, p. 24.

69. Boyer, p. 159.

70. Ibid., pp. 162, 163.

71. Some of these dizzying mirrorings are discussed brilliantly by Christian Metz in his essay entitled "Mirror Construction in Fellini's 8½," *Film Language: A Semiotics of the Cinema* (Oxford: Oxford Univ. Press, 1974), pp. 228–234.

72. Boyer, pp. 17, 18.

73. Ibid., p. 6.

74. Budgen, p. 63.

75. Boyer, p. 45.

76. Gideon Bachmann, "Interview with Federico Fellini," *Cinema 65* 99 (1965), p. 85.

77. Kezich and Fellini, p. 26.

78. Boyer, p. 29.

79. Ibid., pp. 199, 200.
80. Kezich and Fellini, p. 30.
81. James R. Silke, *Dialogue on Film: Federico Fellini* (Beverly Hills: American Film Institute, 1972), p. 6.
82. Boyer, p. 183.
83. Ibid., p. 171.
84. Kezich and Fellini, p. 26.
85. Silke, p. 7.
86. Ibid.
87. Salachas, p. 93.

Juliet of the Spirits

1. Tullio Kezich and Federico Fellini, "The Long Interview," in *Federico Fellini's Juliet of the Spirits*, ed. Tullio Kezich (New York: Ballantine Books, 1966), p. 41.
2. Eileen Lanouette Hughes, *On the Set of Fellini Satyricon: A Behind-The-Scenes Diary* (New York: William Morrow, 1971), p. 246.
3. Lillian Ross, "Profiles: 10½" *The New Yorker*, 30 Oct. 1965, p. 107.
4. Angelo Solmi, *Fellini* (London: Merlin Press, 1967), p. 171.
5. Kezich and Fellini, p. xiv.
6. Ibid., p. x.
7. Speaking about *Juliet of the Spirits*, Fellini described his process of making art: "I don't think I have ever set out with the decision to choose a certain form of story. It has always been the subject that has determined the proper solution for me." See ibid., p. 48. At another time, speaking about *La Dolce Vita*, he said something similar about the close relationship between theme and form in his art: "It seems to me that the style of this film is its very substance, and the substance of the film consists in the very style in which it is made." Federico Fellini, "Su La Dolce Vita la parola a Fellini," *Bianco e Nero*, No. 9–10, Sept.–Oct. 1954, excerpted in Suzanne Budgen, *Fellini* (London: The British Film Institute Education Department, 1966), p. 102.
8. *8½* taught Fellini that a certain film form could make consciousness available, so that he was able to continue for years working that form. In 1971, while making *I Clowns*, Fellini told Doris Hamblin about the form of that new film: "I am doing the world inside my mind." See Doris Hamblin, "Which Face is Fellini?" *Life*, July 30, 1971, pp. 58–60.
9. Kezich and Fellini, p. 54.
10. Ibid., p. 57.
11. Federico Fellini, "Entretiens avec Federico Fellini," *Les Cahiers R.T.B. Série Télécinéma*, 1962, excerpted in Budgen, p. 95.
12. Kezich and Fellini, pp. 56, 57.
13. Ibid., pp. 57, 56.
14. Ross, p. 64.

15. Federico Fellini, from a manuscript in his own possession, quoted in *Fellini on Fellini*, ed. Anna Keel and Christian Strich (New York: Dell, 1974), p. 111.

16. Kezich and Fellini, p. 46.

17. Eugene Walter, "Federico Fellini: Wizard of Film," *The Atlantic Monthly*, Dec. 1965, p. 64.

18. Kezich and Fellini, p. 40.

19. Ibid., p. 55.

20. Ross, p. 66.

21. Edward Murray, *Fellini the Artist* (New York: Frederick Ungar Publishing Co., 1976), p. 37.

22. For Fellini on color, and its relationship to dreams and fantasies, see Kezich and Fellini, pp. 35, 37; and see Pierre Kast, "Interview with Federico Fellini," *Cahiers du Cinema in English* 5 (1966), rpt. in *Interviews with Film Directors*, ed. Andrew Sarris (New York: Avon, 1967), p. 180.

23. Kezich and Fellini, p. 75.

24. Solmi, p. 18.

25. Kezich and Fellini, p. 152.

26. Ibid., p. 58.

27. Ibid., p. 200.

28. Ibid., p. 80.

29. Ibid., p. 45.

30. Ibid. *Juliet of the Spirits* is at least as Jungian in its implications as is *8½*. Surely Fellini's use here of the classic Jungian term is no accident. Continually the pictures of Fellini illustrate the theories of Jung. An interesting example is Juliet's visual relationship to her dominating mother. In his "Psychological Aspects of the Mother Archetype," in *Collected Works*, 9.1 (New York: Pantheon Books, 1959), p. 74, Jung writes of mothers who appear to their daughters as "a sort of superwoman (admired involuntarily by the daughter)" so that "the daughter leads a shadow existence, often visibly sucked dry by her mother." See Carolyn Geduld, "*Juliet of the Spirits*: Fellini and Jung," *Federico Fellini: Essays in Criticism*, ed. Peter Bondanella (Oxford: Oxford University Press, 1978), pp. 137–151.

31. Federico Fellini, "Il mio paese," *La Mia Rimini*, ed. Renzo Renzi (Bologna: Capelli, 1967), rpt. in Keel and Strich, p. 16.

32. Kezich and Fellini, p. 203.

33. Ibid., p. 80.

34. Ibid., pp. 203–205.

35. Kast, p. 182.

36. Kezich and Fellini, p. 205.

37. Ross, pp. 64, 65.

38. Kezich and Fellini, p. 58.

39. Ibid.

40. Ibid., p. 151.

41. Ibid., p. 33.

42. Ibid., p. 98.

43. Ibid., p. 100.

44. Ibid., p. 99.

45. Ibid., p. 152.

46. Ibid., p. 55.

47. Irving Levine, "I Was Born for the Cinema—A Conversation with Federico Fellini," *Film Comment*, Fall 1966, p. 81.

48. Kezich and Fellini, p. 119.

49. Ibid., p. 257.

50. Ibid., p. 43.

51. Ibid., p. 38.

52. Ibid., pp. 124–127.

53. Ibid., p. 45.

54. Ibid.

55. Ibid., p. 166.

56. Ibid., pp. 145–154.

57. Ibid., pp. 154–159.

58. Ibid., p. 43.

59. Ibid., pp. 43, 44.

60. Ibid., p. 97.

61. Ibid., p. 44.

62. Ibid., p. 166.

63. Ibid., pp. 173, 174.

64. Ibid., p. 29.

65. Ibid., pp. 63, 64.

66. For Fellini on the final meaning of *Juliet of the Spirits*, see Kast, pp. 178, 179; Levine, p. 80; Kezich and Fellini, pp. 62, 64; Kast, pp. 190, 191; Kezich and Fellini, p. 63.

67. Kezich and Fellini, p. 62.

68. Gideon Bachmann, "Federico Fellini: An Interview," rpt. in *Film: Book One*, ed. Robert Hughes (New York: Grove Press, 1959), p. 101.